MURDER IN
ROOM 1406

WENSLEY CLARKSON

Published by Blake Publishing Ltd,
3 Bramber Court, 2 Bramber Road, London W14 9PB, England

First published in paperback in Great Britain 2002

ISBN 1 85782 560 8

British Library Cataloguing-in-Publication Data:
A catalogue record for this book is available from
the British Library.

Typeset by Jon Davies

Printed and bound in Great Britain by
Bookmarque Ltd, Croydon, Surrey

1 3 5 7 9 10 8 6 4 2

'A Tribute to Jonathan' reproduced by kind permission of
Defence Helicopter World.

This book is dedicated to Jonathan Moyle
and his parents Tony and Diana.
May Jonathan's spirit rest in peace
and his courage continue to provide
them with the fuel for life.

Val+kyr•ie (væl'kɪ rɪ)

Norse myth   any of the beautiful
maidens who serve Odin and ride
over the battlefields to claim the
dead heroes chosen by him and take
them to Valhalla.

Preface

This book began as an entirely different work. It was to have been a crime reporter's chronicling of the inexplicable death of a young ex-RAF helicopter pilot in mysterious circumstances. It was an intriguing scenario. However, by its very nature, the book was to have been detached, the result of extensive research. Instead, it has evolved into my route along death's bloody trail, the story of a true patriot's murder that has somehow transcended all the claims produced in countless newspaper, television and radio investigations into Jonathan Moyle's death. As the years passed, I gradually unravelled the truth at the centre of a fast-fading enquiry by investigators and lawyers that seemed destined to disappear into oblivion. Moyle's parents had tried without real success for almost eight years to find out what really happened to their beloved only child. There were many clues but nothing really concrete.

The Moyles' desperate search for the truth was highly infectious; my instincts as an investigative reporter were fuelled and I became convinced that with enough time and effort the truth could be uncovered. Justice had to prevail, eventually.

To write a book about an unsolved crime is one thing. To write such a book and find yourself solving the crime in the process is quite another — although that is exactly what happened. My contract to write this book was signed long before I discovered the identity of Jonathan Moyle's killer. My book would not be about a faceless name in a newspaper, a little-known former serviceman who met a sad and tragic death; it would be about the experiences of an enthusiastic young adventurer who paid the ultimate price for his unquestionable patriotism. And it would finally solve the mystery of one of the most outrageous crimes committed during this trouble-torn decade.

Wensley Clarkson
London, August 2002

Author's Note

The world in which Jonathan Moyle lived and died has been reconstructed in this book not only from the memories of his family and friends but also from the recollections of scores of people who now reside in more than a dozen countries across the globe. All the names, places and dates are real. Every incident described in this book has been re-created with the help of at least two people interviewed independently of each other. Interviews were recorded — secretly in the case of unco-operative witnesses — and translated where necessary. The transcribed interviews and the documents I collected — including journals, letters, military reports, photographs and maps — fill a wall of files in my home.

Some of those interviewed possess a remarkable memory and were able to describe in precise detail not only incidents but also how the people involved were dressed, moved and spoke. In other instances, however, I was given only the rudiments of a conversation and, following the example of Thucydides, 'I put into the mouth of each speaker the sentiments proper to the occasion, expressed as I thought he would be likely to express them.'

To bring characters in the book to life, I have sometimes described their thoughts and feelings as well as their actions. Most of the thoughts of Jonathan Moyle and others who are dead were deduced from conversations they had with surviving relatives and friends, who then passed them on to me. In a few instances when no information was available — such as the last images Moyle saw before his death — I went to the actual sites and tried to imagine myself in his place.

All the skills learned and sharpened during my two decades as an investigative reporter were put to use in this most difficult and important investigation. From the testimony of servicemen, relatives, friends, colleagues and enemies — culled from the seemingly endless, double-spaced transcripts of interviews and the yellowing documents stored in my files — I have gained, to my own satisfaction, a true vision of the person who was Jonathan Moyle and of the world that created his life and death.

Glossary

AOC	Air Officer Commanding
Bunny suit	Flying suit
Carabiñeros	Chilean paramilitary force
CIA	Central Intelligence Agency
DEA	Drug Enforcement Agency
DHW	*Defence Helicopter World* magazine
FAA	Federal Air Authority
FBI	Federal Bureau of Investigations
FCO	Foreign and Commonwealth Office
FIDAE	Feria International del Aire y del Espacio (Chilean International Air and Space Fair)
Helios	Weapons guidance system
Interpol	European police authority
Investigaciones	Chilean detectives
Kit	Modern weapons
MoD	Ministry of Defence
MI5	Military Intelligence (UK)
MI6	Military Intelligence (worldwide)
MLU	Mid-Life update
MSc	Master of Sciences Degree
Mukhabarat	Iraqi Secret Police
Negative G	A feeling of weightlessness
OS7	Chilean secret police
Penguin	Missile guidance system
Provost	Jet fighter trainer
QFI	Qualified Flying Instructor
Retrofitting	Rebuilding
SB	Special Branch (British)
SIB	Special Investigations Branch (RAF)
Spooks	RAF police, including Special Investigators
Turn-key	Arms factory set-up
Zero G	An absence of gravity (e.g. in flight)

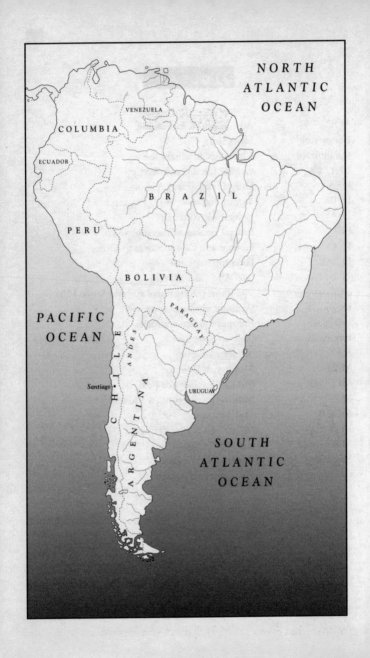

`Prologue`

Santiago, Chile
Saturday, 31 March 1990
7.00am

A crisp, early autumn mist slowly melted toward the stillness of a mild Chilean day. No breeze blew, and the Hotel Carrera set back from the Plaza Constitucion was quiet. A hazy sun glimmered hesitantly between the shabby office blocks of downtown Santiago. The hotel seemed becalmed in the midst of the sprawling city.

Upstairs on the fourteenth floor, a chambermaid scurried from room to room as she began her duties. In room 1406, the morning light cast a pearly-grey shadow throughout. The central air-conditioning was turned off. The air was damp and lifeless. Poking under the door was a carefully folded newspaper. On a desk in the hall area of room 1406 were documents and hand-written notes spread out beneath the pale glow of a table lamp. They included technical data on military hardware. A black leather briefcase stood at the end of the bureau next to a silver-coloured wallet. Both lay open.

On the floor, dozens of green and pink five and ten thousand Chilean peso notes were scattered amongst clothes strewn across the carpet. An empty suitcase lay upturned in the corner by the television. A pair of badly creased trousers was draped over the back of a chair. A pillow without its case sat crumpled on the bed. The top sheet had been twisted up tightly like a length of rope. On the lower half of the bottom sheet near the end of the bed was a small blood stain. A laundry bag, also twisted up like a rope, was half hidden under the bed. It was damp and empty. On the floor under the other corner of the bed lay a torn photograph of a military helicopter.

On the bedside table was a recently emptied syringe. The red numbers of the digital clock-radio next to it glowed 7.00am.

In the bathroom, damp, twisted towels were sprawled across the white-tiled floor. Another suitcase blocked the entrance to the bathroom, clothes spilling out of it.

Just inside room 1406 was a walk-in closet — its door was slightly ajar. The light that should have come on automatically was off. There was something inside it.

Slumped in that closet, his neck hooked to the clothes rail by a shirt, his legs bent slightly behind him, was the corpse of a man. His head was hooded by a pillow case and he was naked from the waist up. White long johns covered a bulky, nappy-like garment. Underpants hung around his ankles as if had been desperately trying to kick them off.

So began the riddle of room 1406: the bizarre death of an adventurous Englishman, Jonathan Moyle, 28, military expert, an ex-serviceman on a dangerous assignment in South America.

To begin to unravel the full story of Jonathan Moyle's death, and also of his life, one has to go back to the day he was born ...

Part 1
The Door Opens

'Patriotism is not a short and
frenzied outburst of emotion
but the tranquil and steady
dedication of a lifetime.'

*Adlai Stevenson, in an address
to the American Legion Convention,
30 August 1952*

1

Weybridge, Surrey

'For children are innocent and love justice,
while most of us are wicked
and naturally prefer mercy.'

G K Chesterton

At ten to three on a windy spring day in 1961, a brilliant afternoon that had fulfilled its earlier promise of great heat, Diana Moyle, a pretty young secretary at the Brook Street Employment Bureau, hurried out with her husband Tony from Fairways, their three-bedroom bungalow on the Ham Court housing estate, heading for their car.

Diana was worried. The pains in her stomach indicated the imminent arrival of her baby. Soon, the gleaming, British-racing-green Riley Pathfinder was dashing through the quiet commuter-belt streets of Weybridge, Surrey.

The Riley, with its distinctive sloping rear, continued with obvious urgency, its suspension squeaking as it hit a row of pot-holes. Two miles down the road, it turned sharply into an entrance-way signposted 'The Rodney House Nursing Home'. The car shuddered to a halt, Tony and Diana got out and hurried through the double doors of the entrance.

Inside, the matron swiftly examined Diana and announced it to be a false alarm, and promptly sent her home. Tony Moyle reluctantly accepted the prognosis, despite his wife's protestations, and escorted her back to the Riley. Diana was furious. 'My waters have already broken. I *know* I'm about to give birth but they're treating me like some silly little girl.'

Five minutes later, as the couple drove back towards Weybridge, Diana let out an ear-piercing, agonised scream.

'TONY! DO SOMETHING!' Tony immediately swung the cumbersome Riley round and headed back to the nursing home. He arrived with only minutes to spare. Their child was born virtually the moment Diana arrived in the delivery room on 12 May 1961.

Jonathan Nicholas Moyle weighed eight pounds at birth and he was a pleasant, round-faced baby. No brothers or sisters followed Jonathan because of an illness suffered by Diana. So the little boy with the tuft of dark hair and a chubby smile for everyone became the epicentre of his parents' life. From an early age, Jonathan was read stories by Diana every night until he fell asleep. By 18 months he was walking and talking. At the age of two, he could hold conversations with his parents. He was building toy models from the age of four.

Diana and Tony Moyle heaped loving care and attention on their son, but they never spoiled him because they were always struggling to make ends meet.

Tony Moyle, with his distinctive handlebar moustache, looked every inch the RAF Wing Commander, but was actually a moderately-paid accountant.

His own father, Bill, had faced the full horror of the Great War during the Battle of the Somme when he was buried alive for 36 hours in a trench which collapsed after a direct hit by a German shell. When the auxiliaries finally dug down to him, they found him trapped under the body of a dead soldier, who had lain across his chest throughout. Fifteen other corpses were removed before Bill Moyle could be rescued.

Tony Moyle was raised between the wars in quiet, suburban Heston, Middlesex. The family then moved to nearby Molesey and he developed an interest in rowing while attending Tiffins Boys School, in neighbouring Kingston.

During the Second World War, Tony Moyle served as a cadet with the Air Training Corps before joining the RAF in 1946 for his National Service. Moyle trained on Tiger Moth biplanes. The highlight of his service career came when he was attached to a Canadian Royal Air Force night-time crew on a Dakota and the pilot promptly went to play cards with his pals at the rear of the aircraft, leaving young airman Tony Moyle at the controls. For two hours he flew the Dakota out over the Irish Sea and then helped to navigate it back to base by using guiding beacons dotted throughout the Welsh and English countryside. He cherished the memory of that flight and later enthralled his son Jonathan by recollecting it in vivid detail.

But Tony Moyle's National Service wasn't a happy time. He resented taking orders from 'idiots who spent their time shouting at you' and couldn't wait to get back to civvy street and earn a decent living.

After being demobbed in 1950, Tony moved with his family to Kingston, Surrey, just up the Thames from their previous home at Molesey. He continued rowing and life carried on where he'd left it before joining the RAF. The house they lived in was a four-bedroom Victorian property, which is still occupied by Tony's sister Pat to this day.

On 12 August 1952, Moyle met Diana Copeland Groves, an attractive, petite 23-year-old blonde girl at the Kingston Skiff Club. It wasn't the most romantic of settings but the couple began dating and were soon being introduced to each other's parents.

On 19 June 1954, Tony and Diana married at Kingston Register Office. Both felt it would be hypocritical to marry in church as neither of them were particularly religious.

From an early age, Diana Moyle had a determined streak running through her. She had become well used to the ups and downs of life because her father was an obsessive gambler. One day they'd live like royalty and the next like paupers. Never a year went by without some financial drama or other.

Diana's marriage to solid, reliable Tony Moyle, and the subsequent birth of Jonathan, provided much appreciated security.

By the time their only child had turned four, his reading and writing abilities were developing rapidly. He adored *Winnie the Pooh* and *The Wind in the Willows*. One day, Diana bought him a model car and was still trying to read the instructions when her young son grabbed it from her and assembled the entire vehicle in minutes.

What particularly impressed the Moyles was their son's determination to complete the construction *and* painting of these toys. Usually, children would casually stick them together, tear the transfers and make a mess of the painting. Not Jonathan. He would proudly announce the completion of yet another model by 'flying' it around the sitting-room of the family home, accompanied by sound-effects.

Jonathan's favourites were a Second World War Bleinheim Bomber and a Hurricane. He'd spend hours dive-bombing imaginary Germans on the rug in front of their open fireplace. Jonathan's patriotism knew no boundaries, even at that young age. And he had already earned a reputation within the family of being someone who never started anything he didn't finish ... ever.

2
Surrey and Dorset

'He Who Thinks He Can, Can.'

Foster's Boys School motto

Jonathan Moyle's teacher at the Oakhurst Grange Prep School was so impressed with the six-year-old that she made a point one afternoon of telling Diana, 'You have a very balanced son. He's a remarkable boy.'

Diana was flattered. At the age of five, Jonathan was given a complete set of Ladybird Early Learning books for his birthday and devoured every word of them. He had an insatiable appetite for learning. He loved answering questions in class and he latched on to most subjects with ease.

Although he was quite short for his age, Jonathan had developed into a stocky, energetic figure with a definite air of confidence. He was rarely bullied but would not hesitate to hit back if any of his classmates tried to intimidate him. Jonathan seemed to possess a real sense of right and wrong. His parents insist he was born with it.

At the age of 11, Jonathan was sent to a small, élite grammar school called Foster's Boys School, in Sherborne, Dorset. His parents had recently moved from Surrey to the west of England and were delighted to get their son into such a well-run establishment. The move had been precipitated by Tony's change of career with a new job as a maths teacher at the Buckler's Mead School in nearby Yeovil.

Foster's — founded in 1640 — was an extremely traditional school. Unlike a public school, there were no fees, but it was even more élite in many ways with less than 200 dayboys and boarders, all of whom were expected to wear the school's distinctive dark-blue uniform at all times. The aim of Foster's was to prepare boys for university life or service as soldiers, diplomats and administrators, or to ready them for work in specific professions.

Jonathan passed his Eleven Plus and another more difficult test to gain entrance. Local families were literally falling over themselves to get their sons into this exclusive establishment.

Eleven-year-old Jonathan particularly impressed teachers when he scored 145-plus in an IQ test.

Games at Foster's were almost as important as work, though neither was as crucial to the school's philosophy as the idea of 'independence'. The school's aim was to turn a boy into a man, even if the evidence suggested he was still a child.

When Jonathan was not excelling at his favourite sports like rugby and badminton, he made a memorable impression in other ways. During a school inter-house high-diving competition, he volunteered to take the place of a sick competitor, even though he was barely capable of diving off the side of the school pool. Tony and Diana attended the event and were horrified when Jonathan proudly announced his intention to dive from the top board.

'You must be crazy,' Tony told his son, who just smiled and began climbing the ladder. Somehow, he managed a competent dive. His classmates and parents watched in bewilderment.

By this time, the family lived in the spacious gatehouse of a nearby stately home which they were leasing for a peppercorn rent from a local country squire. It had stone floors, lots of rugs and a plentiful supply of classic English furniture.

During this period in Jonathan's childhood, he became clearly obsessed with flying. Jonathan even told his father that he couldn't wait to get behind the controls of an aircraft.

The schoolboy's open enthusiasm for flying also earned him the nickname 'Biggles' at Foster's, after the fictional hero.

Jonathan had a particularly insatiable appetite for the Second World War and loved playing the board game Colditz about the adventures of British prisoners of war in Germany. He also had an intricately painted mural on one bedroom wall featuring hundreds of aircraft, as well as war scenarios, battle scenes, and even a Lancaster bomber being refuelled. Everything was re-created with pinpoint accuracy. There were also hundreds of perfectly painted soldiers and airmen permanently scattered all over the room.

About the only thing Jonathan Moyle lacked was holidays abroad. By this time, his father was enjoying a second career as a maths teacher in Yeovil and the family simply couldn't afford expensive holidays. Instead, the threesome would drive further into the West Country and drop in at friends' homes for a night or two.

By the age of 12, Jonathan had won a junior public speaking prize and numerous school awards followed. In athletics he somehow came second in the 800 and 1500 metres despite being dubbed 'The Rubber Man', because he was so unco-ordinated he'd nearly always collide with his fellow runners at some point during the races.

Around this time, Jonathan's aunt, Pat Moyle, took him to London to see the film *Star Wars*, followed by a trip around the Tower of London. On the way home, the pair were walking over Westminster Bridge when the young boy began regaling his aunt with a blow-by-blow account of the Charge of the Light Brigade, another of his childhood obsessions. This was followed by a joint recital of Wordsworth's *Composed on Westminster Bridge*. Jonathan also developed a healthy interest in Greek mythology.

But his chief obsession at the time was longbows. He started making his own from an early age and even built one for his beloved Auntie Pat. At weekends at home, he would pin a target to a tree in the back garden and practise for hours with lethal-looking home-made arrows.

Jonathan's loving, warm-hearted parents were undoubtedly prepared to make many sacrifices for their only child. He was brought up on Second World War stories, country houses and traditional values more befitting the 1950s than the 1970s. Jonathan shied away from reading comics and rarely set foot in big cities although he did go abroad on school trips a number of times. His bravado was unquestionable, but his awareness of a world filled with drugs, sex, murder and mayhem remained minimal.

*   *   *

At Foster's School, Jonathan Moyle first met 23-year-old Ian Maun, the newly appointed head of languages. Maun soon mentioned that his own father had been a Spitfire pilot in the RAF, and the two were bound for life. They also shared a mutual interest in war-games and were both avid collectors of battleships.

Within weeks, Maun was a regular guest at the Moyle home at Milburn Court on Saturday afternoons where he and the 15-year-old Jonathan would lay out 12 cast-iron warships each and go to war. They conducted their battles by using dice for scoring. Some of the numbers corresponded to moving the ships while others enabled the player to fire on the enemy.

Maun never forgot how determined Jonathan was to win, and he was also impressed because there was no sneakiness, no gamesmanship. Everything was fair and above board.

But Maun's most vivid memory was of Jonathan's vast bedroom at Milburn Court. Airfix model airplanes hung from virtually every inch of ceiling space and in his cupboard were dozens more brand-new kits awaiting for construction. On one wall were bookshelves handmade by Jonathan and filled with numerous aircraft manuals. His innocent, almost naïve, bravado came to the fore when he casually mentioned he'd caught a bat in the chimney the previous evening and it had bitten him.

Maun noticed that Jonathan found other less well-informed students difficult to get on with. His politics were already clearly conservative and his views were remarkably traditional and rigid for one so young.

At Foster's, Jonathan passed an impressive thirteen 'O'-levels in History (A), Chemistry (A), Mathematics (A), Biology (B), Economics and Public Affairs (B), English Language (B), General Studies (B), Physics (B), English Literature (C), French (C), Geography (C), Additional Mathematics (C) and German (D).

But there were occasions when even Jonathan got up to mischief. One report in the Foster's School magazine about a winter sports trip to Andalo, Italy, perfectly sums up his outlook on life at the time:

> The morning we had free for ourselves, but the afternoons were taken up with skiing lessons with friendly Italian ski instructors who amused us with their

pidgin English. Skiing was a fantastic sensation [one of his favourite words] *although it took three or four days before they were completely in control and even then one or two hadn't quite mastered it. One particular idiot who Mr House swears he would never take again mowed down eleven Italians in the first three days, notching the kills on his boots like a Battle of Britain fighter pilot. This same imbecile wanted a piece of Italian mountain yew, reputedly the best in the world to make a longbow. Having located a suitable tree, a litre of wine secured the loan of an axe from a local woodman. Half an hour later, he was seen travelling down the chair-lift with a piece of wood three inches across and over six feet long. The lunatic even succeeded in taking this lump of tree through Customs and on to the aircraft, despite Mr Shaplin's protestations. But to his utter dismay, flying home our would-be Robin Hood discovered the tree was not yew at all, but larch. The pilot wouldn't let him open the window to throw it out so it had to come the rest of the way home.*

The 'imbecile' in question was, of course, Jonathan, who wrote the article himself and was more than willing to play the court jester when required.

His classmate Mark Brewer vividly recalled Moyle's skiing ability: 'It was erratic. We all started on the nursery slopes but Johnny was flat out all the time. No caution, just completely out of control, flying around colliding with people, skis everywhere.

'One time we all thought we'd lost him because he'd disappeared behind a mountain. Then suddenly he comes screaming and yelling down the mountainside saying he doesn't know how to stop. The next thing you know there's a big pile of skis flying everywhere. That was the way he was.'

But there was a more serious side to Jonathan. He

volunteered for various school committees including the Sherborne Grammar Schools Sixth Form Society, for whom he wrote regular reports. He also represented the school in rotary public speaking competitions and gave talks on subjects such as the Bermuda Triangle.

Jonathan Moyle was a walking contradiction. He was intellectually mature and could easily take on the masters at Foster's. Yet he had an unworldly naïveté when it came to dealing with ordinary people. And his curiosity frequently got him into trouble.

For example, he would often ignore private property signs that were supposed to stop him going into the woods behind his home. He'd jump over a barbed-wire fence and steal newts from the estate near his house and bring them back to his parents' small pond.

Some of his school friends felt he was like a character from Enid Blyton's Famous Five books.

But then Foster's was hardly a hot-bed of radicalism. The most daring event to take place during Jonathan's attendance was when the teachers went on a half-day strike for better pay and the pupils raided a Guinness lorry parked near the school. They ended up getting drunk in a field owned by local landowner Lord Digby.

Corporal punishment was taken for granted at Foster's and consisted of canings on 'the rear end' or the use of a gin slipper. Teachers were even permitted to use a ruler on the hand for class disobedience.

Moyle and his friend Mark Brewer double-dated a few local girls in Sherborne but none of the relationships lasted long.

An evening out with a local girl ended in tears when Jonathan angrily rebuked her for saying that 'the Jews got what they deserved' during the Holocaust. Jonathan's opinions were not always predictable because he had a habit of siding with the oppressed.

Jonathan and Mark were more interested in the big

band sounds of Glen Miller and Syd Lawrence than girls. Tony and Diana even took the boys to a Syd Lawrence concert in Bournemouth one weekend. There was no rock 'n' roll in the Moyle household.

Schoolfriend Mark was particularly impressed by Tony and Diana's attitude towards their son. 'They treated him like an adult,' he recalled, 'and they treated me like an adult and I really liked that.'

And on the rare occasions when Jonathan did go to parties hosted by his contemporaries, he felt distinctly out of place. At one party Jonathan went to the toilet, locked himself in and did not come out. After hours of trying to get a response, other guests, including Mark, broke down the door and found he had escaped through a tiny window, scaled down the drainpipe and disappeared. The next day, Mark confronted Jonathan about his behaviour. Jonathan replied, 'Sorry, I was completely out of it and it just happened.' No further explanation was offered.

At Foster's School, Jonathan — by now a stocky 5ft 7in — proved that he was more than prepared to stand up for himself.

One 6ft rugby player made the mistake of trying to bully Jonathan at the school sports day and the two boys pledged to meet each other for a show-down in the playground the following day. 'Within seconds, Johnny had him in a head-lock and was punching him. The other guy didn't stand a chance,' recalls Mark.

Jonathan was taught business studies at Foster's by Steve Blowers, a so-called left-wing master known as 'Red Steve'. They enjoyed many constructive, yet heated, discussions together and played the board game Diplomacy with fellow master Ian Maun. This particular game involved negotiating deals with 'governments' and signing 'treaties' to invade small countries.

In the sixth form at Foster's, Jonathan earned a reputation for being a studious, almost over-enthusiastic pupil. Teacher Stan McKay remembers, 'He was one of the few sixth-formers I've asked to shut up simply because he could not stop asking questions.'

McKay taught Jonathan and his classmates 16th- and 17th-century European history. Jonathan was particularly interested in the military aspects of that era, especially the switch from bows and arrows to gunpowder that occurred at the end of the 16th century. He was fascinated by bows and arrows because arrows were reusable while shells and bullets were not.

The only fears about Jonathan's academic potential revolved around his handwriting, which was difficult to read because he tended to think faster than he could write.

On one occasion, Jonathan and some of his sixth-form classmates got up to some mischief by tying up one of the other prefects and dumping him outside the teacher's staff room where he was found in a highly distressed state. But it has to be said that this was a rare example of disobedience on Jonathan's part.

The routine at Foster's — complete with mandatory dark-blue uniform, even in the sixth form — was a perfect grounding for life in the military.

Boys turned up before 9.00am for prayers, followed by a roll call. Then there were classes until lunch at 12.45pm, classes recommenced at 2.00pm and school finished at 4.00pm, depending on sporting commitments.

Moyle's 'A'-level results were impressive in two subjects: History (A) and Business Studies and Economics (B), but he only achieved a disappointing E in English.

Jonathan took his Oxbridge entrance exam convinced that he'd pass and be offered a place at Oxford. He chose History as his subject. He travelled back to Dorset from Oxford after taking the exam and confidently telephoned his teacher Miss Austen to tell her he thought he'd clinched it. He was offered a deferred place, but chose Aberystwyth as it had the best strategic studies course.

He also applied for a place at King's College, London, where Jonathan's integrity and determination came fully to the fore. One of the tutors had written a biography of Oliver Cromwell, which Jonathan felt contained some inaccuracies. Despite the obvious fear of disapproval and recrimination, he challenged the tutor and endured an unpleasant row and a certain amount of trouble. His tenacity and willingness to confront unpleasant truths was unquestioned, however.

In August 1980, Jonathan was awarded an RAF cadetship as a pilot after attending a short course in Hendon, north London. The RAF then agreed to pick up the cost of a three-year strategic studies course at the University College of Wales in Aberystwyth.

During the break between school and university, Jonathan worked as a hospital porter in Sherborne. It was hard work and required a good dose of gallows humour.

He told his parents gruesome stories about body parts and described how he was even expected to take away the remains of a woman patient's breast following a mastectomy.

Jonathan reaffirmed his patriotism during a remarkable incident in Germany while he and his parents were visiting some old family friends.

The teenager noticed a union jack hanging upside down on a flagpole in Bonn so he scaled the pole, took the flag down and rehung it correctly. Everyone was impressed and gave him a round of applause when he came down. He bowed in gratitude at their appreciation.

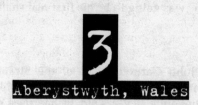

3

Aberystwyth, Wales

'Service life teaches a man to live largely on
little. We belong to a big thing, which will
exist for ever and ever in unnumbered
generations of standard airmen, like ourselves.
Our outward sameness of dress and type reminds
us of that ... As we gain attachment,
so we strip ourselves of personality.'

T E Lawrence

Jonathan Moyle's driving was one of the most hair-raising experiences imaginable. His reflexes were so sharp and his innate trust in his body's responses so strong that he drove the way he led his life — all out, all the time. That meant the winding roads through the hills of mid-Wales en route to Aberystwyth were particularly challenging. He would fly along the tarmac, overtaking just after bends because he could see nothing coming from the opposite direction.

Jonathan, even at 19 years of age, took everything as he saw it. His first day at Aberystwyth in September 1980 brought few fears, just a sense of duty. Being an RAF student did not exactly endear him to his fellows. But he saw their attitude as yet another hurdle to overcome. To be a good student, he had to train all his senses to react instinctively. He was no longer at home with Tony and Diana and their clearly defined set of values. This was going to be his first real challenge.

*   *   *

Professor John Garnett, head of the Strategic Studies Department at the university was a businesslike academic. Although not quite 40 years old, he had risen swiftly to his senior post. He greatly enjoyed his job as it enabled him to teach some of the brightest would-be military strategists in the world. He also had to report on his students' progress as RAF trainees to the Ministry of Defence.

When Jonathan began his studies at Aberystwyth he was a typical military student. His fees and a small salary as a cadet were provided by the MoD, who kept a close eye on all their students.

Jonathan was considered by many fellow students to be an élitist military type with some fairly obvious ideological differences to most others. He also tended to express his opinions very forcefully, something which often upset people.

But as the course progressed, he became noticeably less forthright and seemed more prepared to listen to other opinions, although in the classroom he was just as inquisitive and demanding as ever.

Jonathan's involvement with the RAF was never far from most people's minds. Tutor Professor John Baylis explained, 'There was a feeling amongst us that students like Jonathan had an additional agenda.'

Undoubtedly, the department itself was (and still is) closely aligned to the MoD, especially since it has become renowned as the one of the most highly-rated research departments for strategic studies in the world.

Many tutors are so sensitive about this hidden agenda that they have always refused to comment on the relationship between the department and the MoD.

But according to one tutor, 'Aberystwyth was then

(and still is) a recruitment ground for the security services.'

All the staff insist they have no direct contact with MI5 and MI6 but Professor Baylis did admit that 'security briefing clearance checks' are sometimes carried out on certain students. And another lecturer confirmed that virtually all the senior staff have at one time or another undertaken 'consultancy work' for the MoD. Between 1970 and 1990, the MoD recruited dozens of personnel after they had been 'discovered' at Britain's most highly-acclaimed strategic studies centres Oxbridge, Lancaster and Aberystwyth.

*   *   *

Another body with an interest in the training at Aberystwyth was the Royal Air Force Police, responsible for criminal investigations, counter intelligence and general police matters. Police units had been long established at RAF Stations in the United Kingdom and abroad. Investigations are the responsibility of Headquarters Provost and Security Services (UK) which functionally controls a number of subordinate Units.

During Jonathan's years as an undergraduate at Aberystwyth, he was not only given security clearance by the RAF police but was also closely monitored within the university.

The overall controlling authority for the RAF police is the Ministry of Defence (Air) Directorate-General of Security (RAF) based in Northumberland Avenue, London, and the Commanding Officer normally holds the rank of Air Commodore.

The SIB, as it was originally named, comprises two élite departments within the RAF Police, their respective tasks being criminal investigations and counter-intelligence duties.

All RAF police, including Special Investigators, are graduates of a central training establishment based at RAF Newton, near Nottingham, where the quality of basic and advanced training is such that Air Force Investigators are held in high regard throughout the world. RAF 'spooks' have played an integral part in numerous undercover operations, especially in Northern Ireland in recent years. They have also contributed to the detection and apprehension of a number of foreign agents, both in the United Kingdom and abroad.

'Moyle wasn't recruited at this early stage in his career but he was being carefully observed with a view to using him, depending on how his flight training developed,' explained an MoD source.

Jonathan's only ambition at the time was to become a fast jet pilot. 'The rest of the job is a bit of a bore,' he told his parents on a visit home one weekend.

At Aberystwyth, there were constant rumours of students being approached by the MoD. Jonathan's tutor, Professor Baylis, pointed out, 'I've heard rumours about students going in that direction from this department, but they're not exactly going to call us up afterwards and tell us all about it.'

None of Moyle's tutors rated him as one of the high-fliers in the department, but they were impressed by his ability to be 'well organised, methodical and immensely enthusiastic.'

Professor Baylis added, 'He pursued details that others wouldn't bother with and that made him stand out. Military officers are often better organised and Jonathan had a distinctively logical way of looking at things. He had a very practical knowledge but was not over-critical, which made him seem less of an academic.

'But he had a curiosity. He would not let go. There was a stubbornness about him, but there was also a slight naïveté despite the bravado and "action man" routine.'

Another of the strategic studies tutors admits, 'There was gossip around the department that Moyle was working with the security services virtually from the moment he arrived at the university.'

As part of his studies, Jonathan visited various NATO bases around Europe. Being a student was the perfect background for a host of potential undercover activities.

Other recruits from Aberystwyth have included Richard Gregory Smith, one of the MI5 officers in Northern Ireland who was killed in a Chinook helicopter crash in Scotland in the summer of 1994. Significantly, he was originally recruited by the security services while still at Aberystwyth.

One Aberystwyth lecturer, Colin McInnes, heard that Jonathan was involved with the Special Branch of the local police on a number of undercover operations.

Jonathan actually made contact with local Special Branch officers when he thought he'd stumbled upon a cell of Welsh Nationalists at the university who were planning a series of bomb attacks. They gratefully accepted his help and subsequently raided the homes of three students. But no arrests were ever made because there was no actual evidence of illicit activities.

However, Jonathan's contact with SB did reach the ears of some students and lecturers at Aberystwyth.

'We weren't that surprised because Moyle was such a rigid officer-type,' explained one former student who attended the same course as Moyle.

Jonathan himself mainly socialised with other military students and even hosted occasional drinks parties at his digs. 'They were very grown up affairs, hardly the sort of stuff you expect from university students. But Moyle certainly had friends within that more formal group,' explained one tutor.

A few months after the SB raid on the 'Welsh nationalists', Moyle informed police about a cannabis drug ring inside the university. This time he was entering an even 'greyer' area. Jonathan, like just about every student on the campus, had been offered cannabis. But instead of simply declining it, he decided to find out more about where the drugs were coming from.

For a number of weeks he carried out his own inquiries before handing in a file of information to his contact at SB.

Many students strongly objected to Jonathan taking such a high moral tone about so-called soft drugs. But the young RAF student saw it all in very black and white terms. He had absolutely no interest in taking drugs and couldn't understand why anyone would even want to experiment with them. They were illegal and that meant he had a duty to expose anyone who was involved with them.

Not surprisingly, Jonathan's detective work hardly went unnoticed. 'He dressed a bit smart and his accent and attitude stood out as typical services. He made no attempt to hide the fact, either,' recalled lecturer McInnes.

The police actually made some arrests this time. But the word was out on the campus that Jonathan was a person to avoid.

'In many ways he was damn grown up. University is, for many students, their last opportunity to be young and carefree but Moyle turned his studies into a full-time job, complete with all the normal responsibilities,' explained one lecturer.

Impressed by Jonathan, the local Special Branch actively encouraged him to inform on other students. During meetings in a pub on the outskirts of Aberystwyth, Jonathan and his SB contact would discuss a wide range of subjects.

'SB were delighted to have someone inside the university, which had always been considered a hot-bed of radicalism,' explained one SB source. 'They even briefed

Moyle on what to look out for and bounced some names off him to see if he knew any of the better-known law-breakers inside the university.'

But then Jonathan was hardly unique. Across Britain, dozens of students have been 'recruited' by Special Branch to keep an eye on 'subversive' activities.

Jonathan Moyle considered himself to be a responsible citizen and he couldn't see why he shouldn't do his duty. His deep sense of patriotism obviously extended to being a paragon of law and order, although he certainly had mischievous moments.

But it wasn't just drugs and terrorists that became the focus of Jonathan's attention at Aberystwyth.

Half way through his undergraduate course at the university he became friendly with a girl student and her boyfriend, the son of an African President. The student was being threatened by three men who kept following him everywhere. 'He suspected they were intending to assassinate him because of a plot to overthrow his father back in their homeland,' explained one member of staff at Aberystwyth. 'He was terrified. It seemed quite a dangerous situation.'

Then there was a mysterious 'break-in' at the couple's flat on the outskirts of Aberystwyth while they were out. 'That was a warning to them,' explains the Aberystwyth source. 'In a way, it was their calling card. They wanted him to know they were after him.'

One evening, the couple turned up at Jonathan's digs in Aberystwyth and asked him to let them spend the night. He did not hesitate to help. Says the Aberystwyth contact today: 'Moyle immediately got in touch with his local Special Branch contact and the men who were pursuing his friends were tracked down and then deported. It was one of the most closely-guarded secrets on campus at the time.'

The same Aberystwyth source disclosed that Jonathan

became particularly close with a Sergeant in the Special Branch who eventually began debriefing him at least once a month. Jonathan told his parents that he was even given a false *alias* to use when contacting the SB. His mother was so alarmed by her son's activities that she didn't dare ask him anything more about it. 'I didn't want to know.'

Jonathan's lifestyle at Aberystwyth sounded like something out of a James Bond movie: spying for Special Branch and spending weekends flying with the university air squadron at their base at St Athan. And his academic work continued to go from strength to strength. 'He worked incredibly hard at everything he did. That was the only way he knew,' says his father, Tony, today.

One of the main worries for Tony and Diana was their son's fast driving. The young serviceman rolled his newly-acquired Triumph TR7 sports car while on yet another lightning drive through Wales. He was speeding along a narrow country lane when a lorry pulled out as he was overtaking it. Jonathan walked away from the accident without a scratch and glibly told his mother he was terribly impressed because his stereo tape recorder was still playing with the car upside down on the edge of a ravine.

Afterwards, the owner of the lorry tried to blame Jonathan for the crash. Jonathan insisted on seeing the log book and tachometer record because he suspected the driver to have been at the wheel for more than the legally allowed time. The lorry's insurance company immediately paid Jonathan's claim.

Moyle then replaced the TR7 with a second-hand brown Saab, because he needed something strong and reliable for the journey between Dorset and Aberystwyth.

On another occasion, Jonathan was hairing along the pitch-black roads near the family home when he saw an injured badger illuminated in his headlights. He stopped immediately and jumped out to see if there was anything he could do for the animal. He picked it up, wrapped it in a blanket, put it on the back seat and called a local vet to arrange treatment. 'It was four in the morning and the vet was not amused,' explains his father.

But Jonathan Moyle felt it was his duty to help.

4
West Wales

'Per Ardua ad Astra'
(Through struggles to the stars)

RAF motto

Jonathan Moyle could not remember a time when he did not want to be a pilot. Since he was a small boy, all he ever wanted to do was fly, even before he really knew what flying was about. He had joined the RAF as a cadet with the express intention of achieving a flying scholarship as quickly as possible.

Soon he was zipping around the skies in aircraft like the Cessna 150 in order to get his pilot's licence. He needed at least 40 hours' flying time and as part of his cadetship, the RAF gave him 30 of them — Tony Moyle stumped up for the rest. Jonathan was soon christened 'Genghis' by his colleagues because of his habit of flying planes at all sorts of unusual angles combined with his utter fearlessness. 'He was like a warrior in the skies. Unafraid and willing to try anything,' explains one former colleague.

Jonathan found the freedom of flying a pure joy. He

loved the thrill of skimming over the grey waves of the Irish Sea, and pulling the stick back to raise the nose up 20, 30, 40 degrees, then rolling the aircraft upside-down to see the Welsh countryside laid out above him.

Flying was like a drug to Jonathan. He had no doubt he would remain a pilot for the rest of his life. He could not contemplate a job behind a desk. He even told himself: 'You're either flying in the Air Force or you're out.'

Jonathan knew that in the RAF he would be expected to change squadron regularly, but the unity and loyalty he felt for each squadron was unique.

Inevitably, there were a few close shaves in the airways for 'Genghis' Moyle. His first experience of flying at night almost ended in disaster, even though he was accompanied by an instructor. All went well to begin with as he kept his gaze on the instrument panel. Then, as he lifted his eyes, he realised that the horizon had vanished. This is a sensation all pilots dread. With cloud obscuring the stars, he had no way of knowing where he was or how far he was from the ground. Jonathan was aware simultaneously of the vastness of the space around him and of feeling trapped in a constricting and dangerous little box. He looked down for the flare-path of the runway; he saw nothing, but noticed that he was gaining speed. He jerked back the stick to slow down, but could still see nothing. He half stood up in his seat, craning his neck. Suddenly he saw the lights of the flare-path, there was space between him and earth — he was safe. After a moment of shame, he felt powerful and exhilarated. He experienced a unique feeling of arrogance, of mastery of himself and his destiny, a sensation common to airmen when they regain control of their machines.

*   *   *

Back at Aberystwyth, Jonathan was gaining a reputation as a stickler for detail and his curiosity continued to make him stand out amongst the other students in his department.

'He was particularly adept at understanding the finer details of political and military manoeuvring throughout the world,' said Professor Garnett, the head of the department. That made him a prime candidate for Professor Garnett's special strategic studies retreats.

A large country house had been donated to the university 40 miles from Aberystwyth, where students could be taken out of their normal environment for a couple of days and encouraged to 'role play'.

Professor Garnett explains, 'We devised an international crisis scenario, something which is plausible but not one which has happened. We might look at a crisis in South-East Asia concerning Chinese aggression. We'd look at the roles being played by surrounding countries like Malaysia, Indonesia and other states surrounding mainland China.'

Then a couple of the students would be appointed leaders of certain countries. 'They'd be told "OK, you're in charge of these two places, what are you going to do?"' Over a two-day period, they'd be expected to play out an imaginary scenario in order to get them to understand the difficulties of making diplomatic decisions.

As Professor Garnett explains, 'It's very easy to decide what to do when you don't have to deal with other people. But during these sessions, the students had to take into account who was more powerful than they were. That's when the constraints begin to infringe on you. Basically, it's a wonderful way of teaching people a lesson on how difficult it is to get anything actually done.'

Jonathan adored the role-playing sessions and was particularly keen to play one of the senior leaders. He then 'starred' in live televised news bulletins filmed by a university camera crew. A later *Panorama*-style discussion was also recorded and then edited and played back for everyone to see.

It was quite a high-pressure event because students

were expected to perform in front of real cameras. Some vain students even sat and watched tapes of themselves over and over again to see if they looked acceptable.

Lecturers believed that these types of activities encouraged participation and helped students to think on their feet and appreciate what a complicated place the world is. The key to the exercise was that students could only do everything in real time. This meant that they couldn't suddenly move half their army because that would have been impossible in two days in the real world.

The judges, including Professor Garnett, could inject a few other elements like an earthquake or a tidal wave to confuse the scenario. Eventually the 'crisis' would be halted and the students and their lecturers would hold a debriefing session.

Professor Garnett recalls, 'Students got terribly screwed up about it when they discovered they had been double-crossed and one or two rules were being broken. But Moyle was particularly adept at making secret moves that surprised the opposition and he was very thick-skinned compared to many.'

For Jonathan it was like a dream scenario; a real-life combination of those battleship war games and the Diplomacy board game he played with masters at Foster's School, with a sprinkling of Colditz for good measure.

Back at the university, a stream of VIPs regularly turned up to give lectures. Jonathan's favourite was Lt-Gen Sir Peter de la Billière, later to be hailed as one of the military heroes of the Gulf War.

Jonathan also had the added bonus at Aberystwyth of having the National Library of Wales literally on his doorstep. This was one of Britain's few copyright libraries entitled to have a copy of every published book, ranking alongside the British Library in London and the Bodleian in Oxford. Jonathan spent many hours a week poring over military reference books there.

*   *   *

According to Queen Victoria, when losing one's virginity one must close one's eyes and think of England. Attaching a little more lyricism to the act, the great romantics, from Cervantes to Byron, saw virgins as roses and their deflowering as a poem to passions that would saddle lions.

Jonathan Moyle's first real taste of romance — not necessarily an act of overt passion, but certainly an important point in his romantic development — came when he encountered a German medical student called Annette Kissenbeck.

The couple first met when she visited England as an exchange student and stayed as a guest at the Moyles' family home in Dorset during the summer holidays at the end of his first year at Aberystwyth. Jonathan and Annette fell in love almost instantly, much to Tony and Diana's delight.

The young couple disappeared on a cycling holiday through Devon for a few days. Jonathan, then aged 20, was a breath of fresh air for Annette, a shy, intensely bright 19-year-old academic who found the peace and quiet of the English countryside a delight after being brought up in the bustling city of Bonn.

But the couple drifted apart when Annette decided to travel to India for six months, although they remained in touch by letter. Eventually, Jonathan became so wrapped up in university life and the RAF that he allowed the relationship to wither away.

Annette never forgot how much she enjoyed Britain and decided to study medicine at Aberdeen University and then Durham on her return from India. The couple occasionally met as friends in London and would visit art galleries together, but they were no longer romantically attached. Jonathan had decided it was too early in his life for a serious relationship.

*   *   *

The academic career of RAF cadet Jonathan Moyle seemed to be going perfectly to plan when hepatitis struck him down just a few weeks before he was due to take his finals in International Relations and Strategic Studies.

Professor Garnett and other tutors advised the young airman to consider applying for special dispensation to allow him to take the exams at a later date. Jonathan would hear nothing of it, and went ahead and sat them anyway.

The result when it came astonished everyone who had had anything to do with Jonathan's life at the time. Not only did he pass, but he gained a first-class honours degree.

Jonathan was delighted, but in many ways seemed more concerned by the attitude of the RAF who promptly grounded him for a year until he had completely recovered from the illness.

His senior tutor, Professor Garnett, then suggested that Jonathan do an MSc in strategic studies. It was a perfect opportunity, said the Professor, to use that year to great advantage.

Professor Garnett then made a decision that he has regretted ever since ...

5

Whitehall, London

'It is vain, Sir, to extenuate the matter.
Gentlemen may cry, Peace, Peace! — but there is
no peace. The war is actually begun! The next
gale that sweeps from the North will bring to
our ears the clash of resounding arms! Our
brethren are already in the field! Why stand we
here idle? What is it that Gentlemen wish? What
would they have? Is life so dear, or peace so
sweet, as to be purchased at the price of
chains and slavery? Forbid it, Almighty God! I
know not what course others may take; but as
for me, give me liberty or give me death!'

Patrick Henry, March 1775

Air Vice-Marshall Michael Armitage always took phone calls from old friend and former neighbour Professor John Garnett. The two shared an intense knowledge of strategic studies and Armitage's job as head of a secretive planning unit inside the MoD meant that contacts such as Garnett were very important.

The two men had first met when Garnett worked at the National Defence College in Latimer, Buckinghamshire, almost 20 years earlier. Now Garnett wanted Armitage to use one of his students at Aberystwyth as a researcher.

'Perhaps you could make use of this rather self-confident young man?' Garnett asked his friend. The Professor already had very firm ideas about Jonathan's capabilities and character. 'He's done extremely well to get a First, especially considering the hepatitis,' Garnett told Armitage. 'Moyle has the sort of mind which can assimilate information and synthesise it. He's never going to set the world on fire in the sense of intellectual capabilities but he would be perfect for you.'

When Armitage heard that Jonathan Moyle had gained a first-class degree and was already in the RAF, he immediately took up his old friend's suggestion. *It was the first and only time in MoD history that a student was allowed to work inside such a sensitive department.*

Armitage was, in many ways, a maverick within the cloak-and-dagger world of British military intelligence. He was an intellectual who had climbed the ranks of the RAF. It appealed to him to take on a bright young strategist like Jonathan and try to mould him into a real expert. Professor Garnett's reputation at Aberystwyth was so good that Armitage never had any doubts about accepting the recommendation. As the Professor later conceded, 'It was a highly unusual selection, but then Jonathan Moyle fitted the bill perfectly.'

And Tony Moyle explained, 'Jonathan was tailor-made for the unit because of his knowledge of strategic affairs. He was also damn keen and very bright.'

It seemed that there were very few students with Jonathan's armed forces involvement and qualifications who happened to have a year to kill before rejoining their squadron.

A few days later, Jonathan arrived for an interview at Armitage's office at Astra House in Whitehall. He was immediately encouraged to begin preparing a thesis on a 'Soviet Conventional Air Attack on the United Kingdom'. He would be given access to classified material but none of this could be credited in the thesis otherwise he would be breaking the Official Secrets Act.

So it was that Jonathan Moyle found himself seconded to a secret unit within the MoD, and ordered to prepare a vast document outlining one of the most chilling military scenarios imaginable.

He wasn't the first student to embark on a thesis about the Soviet invasion as this had been a Western preoccupation throughout the previous 30 years. But by being given a free rein inside the strategic studies unit at the MoD, Moyle had an opportunity to carry out some detailed original research. Air Vice-Marshall Michael Armitage's attitude was that a young, fresh mind like Jonathan's might unearth some new strategic information to update any existing battle projections.

Jonathan's recruitment into the unit was also viewed as an unofficial entrance exam into the MoD. He was to be assessed with a view to being offered a position inside this highly select group of military strategists.

While it is true that other students had in the past been offered similar short-term positions within the MoD, they were only ever allowed to work in less sensitive areas. Uniquely, Jonathan found himself actually playing an influential role inside a secretive unit.

*   *   *

As an RAF student, Jonathan's employment at the MoD created some confusion. Professor Garnett explains, 'Moyle was working for the MoD and as a sideline he was producing the thesis for me. It was quite confusing for everyone.'

Jonathan was delighted to have an opportunity to work at the MoD but he soon discovered that it was not nearly as much fun as the thrill of flying with other young trainee pilots. He was working with a small, exclusive, secretive strategic research unit of less than a dozen highly-ranked officers. But he soon began questioning many of their military scenario projections.

'There was no one below the rank of Wing Commander,' says Professor Garnett. 'They didn't suffer fools gladly and certainly didn't take to being told what to do by a 22-year-old. It would have been better if Moyle had been ten years older.'

For a young, brash, confident post-graduate like Jonathan Moyle there were many bitter frustrations. He couldn't resist pointing out that many of the terms of reference being used by the unit were obsolete. Jonathan was amazed that their knowledge of some of the Soviet's most up-to-date weaponry was so limited. 'Jonathan was surprised at how out-of-date some of their data was,' explains one of his RAF friends, Steve Airey.

Michael Armitage was not amused and tensions grew.

By this time, Jonathan was lodging in tatty RAF digs in central London and feeling increasingly isolated. He longed to return to the countryside and drove back to his family's home in Dorset at every opportunity.

There were other more practical problems, such as the fact that the MSc thesis would usually have been in the public domain. In other words, anyone was free to see it. But the MoD insisted on censoring all the sections they deemed to be breaking the Official Secrets Act, leaving little of the original document intact. 'They were literally taking the bones out of the entire thesis, which was very frustrating,' explained one Aberystwyth source.

Jonathan concluded that he would have to produce two versions of his thesis. One would be the MoD highly-classified, top-secret document that outlined in graphic detail the nightmare scenario of a conventional weapons attack by the Soviets. This was the reason why unit chief Michael Armitage agreed to have Jonathan at the MoD in the first place. This document would be kept inside a top-secret file within the unit.

The other thesis would be a sanitised scholar's version with absolutely no sensitive details. Even the acknowledgements section of the 50,000-word thesis was to be censored, because the security services did not want the names of those involved to be revealed to the public.

Jonathan bit his lip admirably and set out to produce two entirely separate theses. His superiors were impressed by the young airman's professionalism, even though they considered him 'a bit of a young upstart'. Eventually, an up-front approach was made by a security services recruitment officer inside the MoD to try and persuade Jonathan to give up his aspirations to be a pilot and join the secret services full-time instead.

Jonathan was puzzled by the job offer because he genuinely had not realised how significant his move to Whitehall had been. He had turned the MoD down because of his aspirations to fly. But then the MoD asked Jonathan if he would consider something else.

Jonathan was introduced to an operational controller/handler inside British intelligence and was asked if he would be prepared to work for them on a freelance basis.

Dozens of counter-intelligence officers run freelancers on a person-to-person basis. Depending on the relationship and nature of the work being carried out by the agent, it is not unusual for the handler to threaten, bribe, or even blackmail their sources. Trickery and coaxing are all part of the handler's methods of operation. For example, he might use some embarrassing detail about a freelancer's personal life to persuade him to supply information. But it was early days and although Jonathan Moyle was against the idea of freelancing, he was actually rather intrigued by it all.

Jonathan was to be gradually 'broken in'. His handler was told to keep in close contact with him but not to encourage him to do anything that might disrupt the research work for his thesis.

It must be noted that the intelligence services were quite prepared to use all sorts of characters to ensure good coverage of a wide range of sensitive subjects even within their own infrastructure. Jonathan may have had a naïve streak about him, but the main concern for both MI5 and MI6 was the ability of people like Jonathan to keep an eye on what was going on.

Around this time, Jonathan bumped into old Foster's schoolmate Steve Weatherly near his parents' home in Dorset and told him that he'd just been offered a job 'in intelligence'. When Weatherly jokingly replied, 'Oh, you mean you're about to become a spy?' Jonathan said, 'Don't be daft!' and the subject was immediately dropped. Jonathan wasn't the first (or last) intelligence operative to let slip his situation. He actually had a deep sense of pride about being recruited because he felt it was an important duty for his country. The intelligence services had no idea just how forthright their new recruit could be.

Jonathan was bursting with pride about his new 'duties' when he met old friend called Christine Whittaker for lunch near the MoD offices in Whitehall, and he mentioned, out of the blue, that he'd been asked to spy by the MoD. Christine Whittaker couldn't quite believe what she was hearing.

'*What* did you say?' she asked.

'I turned them down. I want to fly fast jets,' backtracked Jonathan, who realised he'd once again been incredibly indiscreet. He then dropped the subject. Jonathan's naïveté in mentioning his connections was typical of his character, one which relied upon a black-is-black, white-is-white philosophy.

However, Jonathan's priority at that time was still to fly planes. Those Airfix toy models, the dozens of manuals, and all the stories of friends' and relatives' adventures in the war still resonated. That was what Jonathan Moyle wanted. Spying wasn't nearly as clear-cut as flying jet fighters.

Jonathan rapidly grew bored with the internal clashes and unfriendly atmosphere at Michael Armitage's strategic studies unit inside the MoD. It grew worse after Jonathan was approached to work for the security services because of the fierce rivalry that exists inside the MoD. As one former MoD official explained, 'Moyle's potential had been spotted but that hardly ingratiated him to the others within Armitage's unit.' Jonathan was considered the young upstart and there was virtually no socialising between staff.

Jonathan often worked on the thesis during weekends at his parents' home in Dorset. But he forbade his family from helping to proofread the classified version because it was top-secret. He was encouraged to allow one senior officer inside the Armitage unit to read it, but felt that he needed the input of someone more neutral. In theory, he was not supposed to tell anyone about it, but he knew his parents would be proud and he couldn't help himself. But Jonathan still took his job *very* seriously. He asked close friend and fellow graduate pilot Steve Airey for advice about the most technical aspects of the classified version of the thesis. 'But he was even nervous about allowing me to do that,' recalled Airey.

It had been made very clear to Jonathan by MoD officials that what he was doing was top-secret. But he defied their advice because he wanted a 'real opinion' rather than a sanitised services response.

By November 1984, Jonathan was having so much difficulty finding an acceptable format for the thesis that would gain him an MSc and accommodate the MoD's strict secrecy rules he requested a meeting with Group Captain T Garden, Director of Defence Studies at the RAF Staff College in Bracknell, Berkshire. Garden's job was to co-ordinate all defence studies carried out by RAF students who sometimes ran into problems because of tight secrecy rules.

As Garden conceded in a letter to Jonathan at the time: 'It would be a great shame if you were unable to gain your MSc as a result of the classification problem. I would hope that you could find a suitable form of words to be able to satisfy your examiners.'

The RAF offered little constructive advice. They just told Jonathan to do his best, but that ultimately he would have to do whatever the MoD wanted.

Professor Garnett concedes today, 'I'm not sure I did Jonathan such a good turn by getting him a place on Armitage's unit, because here he was a young man of 22 thrown in with a bunch of pretty senior guys. It wasn't exactly a bed of roses.'

The Professor is reluctant, even today, to be drawn on how the MoD would have used Jonathan's classified version of the thesis but he did say, 'It would be part of a contingency plan.' During the Cold War, detailed research into such scenarios was of vital importance to home defence strategy. Jonathan's MoD version of his thesis could have saved tens of thousands of lives if an attack occurred, because it mentioned specifics about types of weapons, estimated response times and other vital data. It was the first such document to be produced within the MoD for more than two years and featured the most up-to-date information available, much of it provided by spy satellites and through intelligence gathering on the ground.

'This was the time of the Cold War. There was still a lot of paranoia. Most people thought it possible there could be an attack. It was an interesting possibility,' adds Professor Garnett.

As part of his research into the project, Jonathan was allowed to examine highly sensitive documents inside the MoD as well as outlining the effect such an attack would have on things like the nation's transport and communications systems. This meant visiting officials from organisations such as British Rail, British Telecom and many others.

It is very rare for such a thesis to have a classified D notice slapped on it to prevent it being read by virtually anyone outside of the MoD. The MoD felt that if it fell into the hands of the Soviets it could influence them to alter their military tactics in the event of that type of wartime scenario.

Around this time there was a clash between the MoD and Jonathan's immediate superiors at Cranwell's pilot training centre over whom Jonathan was answerable to. His head of department at Aberystwyth, Professor Garnett explains, 'Cranwell were anxious to make the point that he was a university student funded by the RAF. The problem was that he was working for everyone.'

Jonathan Moyle's MSc undoubtedly raised him to a superior intellectual level to most of his trainee pilot colleagues even though he was merely considered a very hard-working, well-organised student at university. It wouldn't have particularly affected the early stages of his career, but once he reached the inevitable desk job he would be able to claim academic superiority.

Towards the end of 1984, just a short time after completing his thesis, Jonathan was promoted to the rank of Flight Lieutenant. His freelance work for the security services was only sporadic around this time, and involved passing on titbits of information that he had gathered during his work for Armitage's MoD unit. Primarily, Jonathan wanted to get on with the business of flying jet fighters.

6

Yorkshire

'The fighter pilot's emotions are those of the
duellist — cool, precise, impersonal. He is
privileged to kill well.
For if one must either kill or be killed, as
now we must, it should, I feel,
be done with dignity. Death should be given the
setting it deserves;
it should never be a pettiness;
and for the fighter pilot it never can be.'

Richard Hillary, The Last Enemy

Flight Lieutenant Jonathan Moyle waddled in his
bunny suit over to the plane in the grey light just
before dawn. He could hear the soft, low purr of the
Provost's jet engines warming up. The ground crew at
Church Fenton RAF base helped him into the tight
cockpit, radio switched on and strapped up tight. The
smell of fuel was overwhelming. On his flying suit was
his nickname 'Genghis'. He wore it with pride.

He went through the final checks consisting of 20
challenges between navigator and pilot, covering every
function of the aircraft, from the emergency power system
to the arming of the ejector seats. The noise of the

Provost's jet rose to a scream as the engine wound up through maximum dry power, the afterburners blasting out flames as the plane bucked and strained against the brakes.

The final checks complete, the brakes were released and throttles rammed forward. With the engines bellowing at full power, the Provost's acceleration pinned Jonathan and his navigator to their seats.

'Forty knots.'

'Sixty knots.'

As the aircraft flashed down the runway, Jonathan called out his speed to his official flight tutor, who was also acting as his navigator. Both of them scanned their instruments and the warning panel for any sign of a problem. Jonathan knew that take-off was a critical time for any aircraft; weighed down with a full load of fuel, a mechanical problem or the loss of an engine could prove fatal.

'Eighty knots.'

They needed almost 100 knots on the clock before they reached the cable-like trip-wire stretched across the runway, which was hooked up to stop a malfunctioning aircraft either on take-off or landing, just as a cable on the flight deck of an aircraft carrier stops a speeding jet in its tracks.

'100 knots. Cable.'

The first hurdle cleared. The runway controller huddled in his battered caravan and gave Jonathan a wave as they passed, reassuring them that nothing was dangling from the aircraft or had fallen off.

'120 knots.'

Despite the weight of the fuel, the Provost was rocketing towards the next crucial speed marker, 135 knots. Beyond that, they could only stop for a catastrophic emergency.

'130 knots.'

Jonathan scanned the warning panel and instruments again — all were clear.

'135 knots.'

The final hurdle. Jonathan 'rotated' — pulled the stick back — and the Provost cleared the perimeter hedge and was up in the air; a long draught of oxygen then chased away the last traces of breakfast.

At 20,000 feet, Jonathan saw the sun shoulder its way up over the horizon. Soon, Jonathan was powering up and down and away to left and right, the G forces pressing his organs against his bones.

The sight of English churches, roads and villages beneath his feet as he straightened up leant a protective edge to his concentration. As he climbed, he saw the occasional cloud below him; it would hang for a moment, then disperse.

After establishing a course, Jonathan held steady ... but not for long. He soon recognised the Dorset countryside below him and took an unplanned swing to his right before dipping the aircraft's nose.

'What's happening?' asked the navigator.

'Just checking something out, sir,' Jonathan replied.

Seconds later, the Provost screamed over the sleepy hamlet of Hardington Moor. The aircraft levelled out at no more than 50 feet as it scorched along the base of the small valley. Then the Provost stood on its toes, climbed straight up into the blue sky and did an impressive loop.

A few thousand feet below, Tony Moyle rushed out of his house and looked up at the tiny speck of grey in the sky and smiled. He knew it was his son, even though he hadn't given them any advance notice of his plans.

In the cockpit of the Provost, Jonathan's training officer was furiously admonishing the young Flight Lieutenant.

They landed at nearby Yeovilton shortly afterwards. As he sauntered confidently to the aerodrome, he watched the aircrew attending to the Provost and smiled. This was the life he had chosen and he adored every minute of it. He wasn't at all bothered by his instructor's anger.

That night, following the training flight, Jonathan and

his instructor made a pre-arranged overnight stopover at his parents' house. After the younger Moyle had retired to bed, his senior officer stayed up for a chat with Tony.

'What Jonathan did today was bloody stupid!' the officer told an embarrassed Tony. 'But there's no real harm in it, I suppose.'

However, Jonathan's swashbuckling attitude was a black mark against him in the eyes of his superiors. While he had rapidly learnt the fighter pilot's art of feeling detached from your actions when you fired a missile, he hadn't yet learned when to draw the line.

*   *   *

At Church Fenton in Yorkshire, Jonathan completed 80 hours of fast-jet flying by the end of 1985, mostly on the Jet Provost Mark V and sometimes a Hunter.

Fellow trainee Steve Airey recalled, 'You had to toe the line at Church Fenton otherwise you'd be out. Johnny was the noisiest guy on the course and was always questioning things.'

But the régime at Church Fenton was fairly relaxed compared with most military establishments. The pilots got up at 7.00am and were expected at their first briefing at 8.15am with or without breakfast.

Then they would be gunned up and ready to go, complete with silk scarfs. That meant flying up to twice a day in the elderly Provost trainer fighters, although frequently they were grounded because of the dense fog that often descended on the area.

Sometimes, the noise of the Provosts screaming across the countryside proved too much for local farmers. Once, Jonathan and some of his comrades spotted a painted sign on the roof of a local farm that said 'PISS OFF, BIGGLES'. It was amusing for Jonathan since that had been his nickname at school.

The young jet fighter pilots all dived down and took turns screaming across the rooftop as a form of protest. The following day the farmer removed his sign.

At night there were drinking sessions in the local pubs and occasional squadron dinners, which traditionally began with a toast to the Queen and ended with 'drink-a-pint-in-one' competitions. Back-slapping in the bar was a popular pastime.

But there was a major drawback to flying for Jonathan, thanks to an unpleasant airsickness problem. There are some crew members in the RAF who are still sick every time they fly. Jonathan suffered badly when he started fast-jet flying. Some mornings he would dread going to work, knowing that in a couple of hours' time, he would have his head in a NATO standard-issue sick-bag, bringing up his breakfast.

One prankster at Church Fenton helpfully cut the bottom out of Moyle's sick bag and restored the bag, neatly folded, to its place, before the Provost took off. Twenty minutes into the flight, Moyle groaned and reached for the bag, only discovering too late that he was vomiting into a hollow tube.

The RAF had an anti-sickness course which the chronic sufferers like Jonathan were encouraged to attend, but it was definitely a case of kill or cure. He was despatched to Farnborough, strapped into a simulator and spun around, turned upside-down and inside out. It made Jonathan so sick that from then on, the most extreme motions of a fast jet would never bother him again.

Jonathan and his close friend, Steve Airey, were considered 'oldies' by this stage because they were still flight training in their mid-20s alongside pilots two or three years younger. Eventually both men were taken off fast-jet training after being deemed 'more suited to helicopters'. In Jonathan's case, his insubordination, illustrated by that low flying incident over his parents' home and a tendency to take unneccesary risks, were believed to be behind the decision.

It is estimated that training one pilot for three years on fast jets costs at least £3m, so the RAF tended to be very choosy about whom they invested in.

Jonathan Moyle was bitterly disappointed to be dropped as he had his heart set on being a 'top gun'. He had shown great skill as a fast-jet pilot, but his instructors were concerned about his gung-ho attitude. 'Jonathan flew by his own rules and that just doesn't work with jet fighters,' explained one fellow trainee.

Flying is one of the most testing and exhilarating experiences one can have. Jonathan adored swooping down into valleys and getting a real sense of speed from the hillsides on either side. But when flying over water, a wise pilot does not push his aircraft too low because the surface could be so calm it becomes extremely hard to distinguish between water and sky.

The RAF's decision was a big blow to Jonathan's ambitions. It wasn't in his nature to accept such a decision without question and he badgered his instructors for days to find out precisely why he had been dropped from fast-jet training. They insisted that he still had a worthwhile career ahead of him as a helicopter pilot. But he was told in no uncertain terms to stop complaining, otherwise that opportunity might pass him by as well.

Once again, Jonathan's impulsive recklessness had spoilt his control — and it foreshadowed events to come.

* * *

Jonathan and Steve Airey were despatched to Shawbury, near Shrewsbury, to start helicopter training on the Wessex and Gazelles.

Although Jonathan was still smarting over his failure to make the grade as a fast-jet pilot, he was now entitled to fly some of the most sophisticated helicopters in the world. He was still supremely self-confident, a quality which every pilot needs in abundance. Flying these technologically advanced aircraft was a bit like playing video arcade games — for real.

Jonathan's new instructors also feared that he was 'about to become a coffin' — RAF jargon for crashing. Back at base, where every practical manoeuvre had to be replayed over and over again, it became clear that Jonathan still believed he was a law unto himself.

One instructor even went so far as to tell the young airman, 'Your number'll be up sooner than any of us want if you're not careful. No one wants their name on the bullet.'

*   *   *

The rotors of the Westland sliced through the cold November air as it touched down in the long grass.

'Good luck, lads,' beamed the flight crew as Jonathan Moyle, Steve Airey and two other trainee pilots jumped out on to the muddy verge and moved towards a nearby clump of bushes for cover.

The Westland hovered momentarily before surging upwards and veering off towards the valleys beyond. Jonathan signalled to Airey and the others to follow him down to a nearby stream. As the hum of the rotor blades dispersed, an eerie silence enveloped the hillside.

Jonathan, Airey and the others had entered a gloomy twilight world in the middle of nowhere that was to be their home for the next week. They had just begun one of the RAF's toughest one-week survival tests.

Twelve young pilots were to be split up into teams of four and they were given just one chicken to eat between them. Helicopters dropped the teams on an isolated hillside in the middle of the Welsh countryside and left them to it. At the briefing, all the pilots looked as if they dreaded the exercise — all except Jonathan.

The four men built makeshift shelters with the intention of trapping rabbits for food. After three nights they moved into some nearby caves. During the exercise, Jonathan began to talk openly about his life to Steve Airey.

'He mentioned his earlier work at that unit inside the MoD,' says Airey. 'Johnny said some of the senior officers had been very disapproving because he was still a university student and not even a commissioned officer.'

Jonathan was very casual about his involvement with the strategic studies unit and laughed when Airey said to him, 'So you were a spook, were you, Johnny?'

But none of that mattered on a bleak deserted Welsh hillside. What most impressed Airey was Jonathan's ability to adapt to the terrain. 'He thrived on it,' says Airey.

When the team of four ran seriously low on food after only two days, Jonathan constructed a longbow out of some pieces of wood and started hunting rabbits.

Within hours, Jonathan came back through the woods with a stag over his shoulders. The other pilots were astonished.

Jonathan also proved to be the only one in the party capable of catching fish in a nearby stream — simply because he'd decided to pack a fishing line in addition to their standard kit. Jonathan's oak-bark tea proved very popular. 'He put chunks of oak bark in a pot and stewed it. We drank it through our teeth because there were so many bits in it, but it was delicious,' remembers Airey.

Jonathan had actually learned how to make all sorts of weird and wonderful concoctions at home. His regular attempts at acorn coffee brought groans from his mother and father at breakfast time.

There was undoubtedly some method in Jonathan's madness as far as his fellow trainees were concerned. For he knew full well that the best way to avoid hypothermia was to be well fed. He also led his team to the base-camp meeting point ahead of everyone else by following streams from the top of the hills. In fact, they actually had to go out and rescue their commanding officer himself when it became clear he had become lost.

Meanwhile, Jonathan's driving was taking on yet more legendary proportions. During one hairy ride down to the West Country from Yorkshire with fellow airman Steve Airey in the passenger seat, the engine of Jonathan's Saab caught fire.

Jonathan calmly pulled into a lay by and used some clothes to put out the blaze. 'Then we let it cool down and it started again first time,' says a still bemused Airey. 'Johnny wasn't in the slightest bit bothered about it.'

Back home in Dorset one weekend, Jonathan confronted local MP Paddy Ashdown when he was electioneering in their village. Jonathan stunned a gathering of people in the village hall by barracking Ashdown's claims over defence spending.

Even his father admits today, 'Jonathan hadn't got the sense sometimes to keep quiet and not argue. He believed that Ashdown's facts and figures were incorrect because he had completed his MSc by this stage. He just couldn't let go even though it was Ashdown.'

*   *   *

Jonathan Moyle got off to a good start in his helicopter training, finishing top of his class in the first year of flying. Technically, he could not be faulted, despite his reckless nature. It was decided that Jonathan should be put on an advanced training course for Gazelles, with a view to being posted eventually to Northern Ireland. Some of his instructors had doubts because of his 'irresponsibility', but they were overruled by those who believed in his so-called free spirit.

On the advanced training course, Jonathan continued to

achieve top marks, but his old carefree habits were never far away.

Jonathan's final pilot training test at RAF Shawbury before becoming fully qualified involved flying a Gazelle across a dense forest without being 'shot down' by the enemy after being 'spotted' on radar. It was a classic wartime scenario.

Jonathan carefully examined the map of the area and noticed a logging track that went right through the middle of the forest. Jonathan was the only trainee pilot that day not to be shot down because he flew his Gazelle 15 feet above the ground along that track. But his adventurous spirit got him in an enormous amount of trouble.

He was given an 'almighty bollocking' by his commanding officer and was failed on his helicopter pilot's test. Jonathan was surprised because he felt he had taken the only logical route. 'It's a wartime scenario, sir. I'm the only one who got through,' was his honest response.

Jonathan thought he'd been very unfairly treated and had built up quite a resentment against the way some RAF instructors were treating him. It made him all the more determined to go out on a limb and show the world what he was made of. His 'failure' would mean being permanently grounded and that was the kiss of death as far as he was concerned.

Desperate to get the decision reversed, Jonathan even appealed to the AOC and was sent to Biggin Hill to be reassessed. After a number of complex tests, the examiners recommended him as a first-class pilot, but his flying instructor would not back down and the AOC chose to support their decision to fail him.

Jonathan was given a fine reference by his commanding officer except that it had a proviso at the end which stated, 'I wasn't sure if one day I would have to call his parents to say he had flown into a mountain.'

Intriguingly, Jonathan's instructors at no time actually

tried to curtail his exploits or encourage him to channel his energies in a more responsible direction.

Behind the scenes, a desperate scramble was going on for Jonathan's services. It can only now be revealed for the first time that he was *deliberately* failed because the MoD wanted him to work as a full-time operative for the security services.

One of his instructors — who has since retired from the RAF — was Rick Howell. He says today, 'They didn't want him to become a pilot in the first place because he was too valuable with his background.'

Howell added, 'This happens all the time. People can be fixed to be chopped just because they don't fit in or because they are required for other jobs. Jonathan Moyle had been earmarked for something more important.'

Jonathan had already been put under immense pressure by his security service handler and others at the MoD to agree to quit flying long before his test failure. He had turned them down before but now they believed he had no choice.

Shortly before Jonathan was failed, instructor Rick Howell had lunch with him in the officer's mess at Shawbury and the young airman said categorically, 'They want me to go back to the MoD and work in a strategic job.'

Howell looked surprised. Then Jonathan added solemnly, 'If I can't fly I don't want to know about this other job. I'll leave the Air Force.'

Tony Moyle never forgot the conversation when he met with his son's commanding officer. 'I can get paid killers any time. We want Jonathan's brains,' Tony was told.

As Jonathan told another friend, 'I don't want to sit at a damn desk. I'm not a back-room boy. I wanted to be out and about in the skies.'

7

Somerset

'Airmen have few possessions, few ties, little
daily care.
For me, duty now orders only the brightness of
the five buttons down my front ...'

T E Lawrence

When Jonathan Moyle flew at low level, he had a mental picture of what the world should look like. And if that picture changed in any way, there was an overwhelming temptation to restore it to its familiar state.

If the trees below seem to grow smaller, the pilot's natural instinct is to bring the gently rising plane back closer to the ground — the picture is then 'normalised'. But Jonathan knew that objects 'shrinking' below him could not be trusted — it was a well-known optical illusion which was made quite clear to everyone during pre-exercise briefings.

In many ways, this distortion effect was how Jonathan viewed his position and subsequent rejection by the RAF. He knew he'd been a high-flier, and that he'd tested the boundaries a little at times, but he believed that he'd adjusted his situation skilfully enough to lay the foundations for a long and honourable RAF career.

*   *   *

Jonathan had difficulty in coming to terms with not being wanted as a pilot and could not accept the alternative jobs on offer at military intelligence following his attachment to the MoD.

He told his mother of his disappointment one sunny spring day when he took her up for a flight in a one-engined Slingsby near the family's West Country home.

As the flimsy aircraft twisted and turned at 5,000 feet over Exmoor, Jonathan tried to use the opportunity to explain to Diana his feeling over his apparent 'failure' as an RAF pilot.

He even took the Slingsby into a few rolls and dives just to prove his point. Diana admits she was 'a little worried, but Jonathan wanted to show me all the tricks of the trade so I didn't complain.'

Jonathan took the aircraft down low over a wooded area just a few miles from the family home 'to look for good dog walks'. It was typical of him that he thought about such practical things as new places to take the family dogs.

Jonathan and Diana flew down and followed the pathways to see how good they were. For some minutes they virtually skimmed the tree-tops before Jonathan pulled the plane up again.

It was almost as if he was trying to prove his flying skills and how he could still exert some control over his life, despite being dealt such a severe blow by the RAF.

Both of Jonathan's parents were deeply hurt by the way the RAF had failed their son as a pilot. Tony says, 'Jonathan was a bloody good pilot and immensely confident and competent. We never worried when we went up with him. He was so careful he checked every instrument in triplicate. He would even go round the engine himself, checking very,

very carefully.'

Neither of them realised that there had been another more sinister reason for their son's failure as a pilot.

*   *   *

Jonathan Moyle dated dozens of girls after splitting up with his first love, Annette Kissenbeck, who had qualified as a doctor and moved back to the German town of Tuebingen to begin training as a paediatrician.

Jonathan's romantic experiences veered from one disaster to another. There was an Army officer's daughter called Lydia who was so religious that when he unintentionally swore in front of her, she burst into tears. Then there was Jenny, an interior designer who begged Jonathan to marry her. Kate and Elizabeth were two other marriage contenders.

Jonathan was considered by many of these women to be a good, safe catch. He was solidly reliable, completely and utterly faithful and very attentive. 'He was the sort of man you marry, not the type to have a wild, sensual affair with,' recalled one of Jonathan's women friends.

'Jonathan was old-fashioned about women. He expected to take them out for candle-lit dinners and deliver them home in one piece, and perhaps snatch a kiss on the doorstep. He never expected to go to bed with them instantly.'

One girl — who looked just like tennis player Steffi Graf — became so obsessed with Jonathan that she'd regularly turn up on his doorstep unannounced. His parents would offer her a cup of tea and pretend their son wasn't at home.

Throughout all this, Jonathan and Annette Kissenbeck's relationship survived on a brother-and-sister level. As Jonathan stumbled from one disastrous relationship to another, he gradually came to the conclusion that Annette was the only one he truly cared about. In 1987, he began writing to her much more regularly and the sentiments in his letters made it clear that he wanted the romance between them to start again. But for the moment they simply remained nothing more than good friends.

Annette believes that she and Jonathan never actually fell out of love with each other. 'I knew he was having relationships but I also knew that one day we would be together again,' she says today.

The main stumbling block was that they they lived so far apart. But Jonathan was gradually and carefully breaking down the emotional barriers between them. Eventually, he hoped to move back into her life for ever.

He was trying to find his feet in the real world, a million miles away from his safe, solid upbringing. He had met a whole variety of people at university and in the RAF. But now he had to embark on a new career at an age when most people were already well established.

*   *   *

Before leaving the RAF, Jonathan was given a month's terminal leave and cleverly swung an RAF trip to Washington with a pilot friend. He spent a few days in the American capital, visiting art galleries and museums. He particularly liked the works of an American artist from the 1890s called Thomas Wilmer Dewing, whose works were showing at the Freer Gallery.

Jonathan slept on the floor of an expensive hotel room in Washington, where his pilot friend was posted as a member of the RAF resident crew on stand-by.

But Jonathan's real reason for hitching the ride to the United States was because he knew that his friend was scheduled to take an aircraft down to Belize. Jonathan was fascinated by what he had heard about the jungle, caves and deep-sea diving of the tiny Central American country.

On arrival in Belize, Jonathan hooked up with an RAF

Puma helicopter squadron and flew sorties over the dense jungle that dominates the inland areas of the country. He also flew to an archeological site deep in the jungle called Caracol.

The 1,000-year-old city created and then abandoned by the Mayans fascinated Jonathan. It had only been rediscovered in 1937 and was being excavated by a group of American university students.

Jonathan joined the archaeologists for a few days and worked on a number of sites with them. He dug up some pottery and bones, but was particularly intrigued by a pyrite necklace and a jade-inlaid tooth.

About a week after arriving in Belize, Jonathan attached himself to an RAF diving expedition on a small desert island 60 miles off the coast, called Half Moon Caye.

The party camped on the island for two weeks and encountered numerous iguanas and land crabs as they slept each night on the deserted beach. His days were spent diving in and around one of the world's longest coral reefs where he also came across sting-rays, turtles and sharks.

After returning to the mainland, Jonathan spent a week in the jungle with the Gurkhas. The young airman was particularly interested in how the troops trained for jungle survival and joined them on a one-day trek through dense undergrowth. This mini-expedition had to rely on compass bearings because no maps of the area existed, and a sweat-drenched Jonathan consumed seven litres of water en route.

For four days, Jonathan found himself commanding a Land Rover with four Gurkhas on a patrol into north Belize, an area populated by many drug traffickers and Guatemalan guerrillas. Jonathan was outraged to discover that drug barons were arming the rebels in exchange for protection. But the Gurkha Major commanding the patrol informed Jonathan that they were unable to become involved because Belize was an independent country.

After returning from that patrol, Jonathan joined a

caving expedition with a group from the USA. It involved a 15-mile walk into the jungle carrying a pack weighing over 100 pounds. At one stage, Jonathan almost toppled over the side of a huge crater after losing his footing.

The caving involved a great deal of swimming in underground rivers using tyre inner-tubes. Jonathan was staggered by the pure white stalactites and rivers of white crystal. After five days, Jonathan emerged back into the jungle and had a close encounter with a jaguar.

Towards the end of his six-week adventure in Belize, Jonathan found himself dreaming of cups of tea and chocolate biscuits and knew it was time to come home.

Jonathan's trip to Belize was, in many ways, like the contents of a *Boy's Own* annual — complete with crocodile-infested rivers. It seemed to indicate that Jonathan's boyish enthusiasm would see him through the crisis of his rejection from the RAF. He was determined to bounce back and had already turned his final months in the services to his advantage.

Once back in London, Jonathan realised he had to get a job. He went up to London for an interview at the Ministry of Defence for a position he told his parents was 'highly sensitive'. But he was disappointed when the Ministry turned him down because he was allegedly 'over-qualified'. Then he heard about an editor's post at a publication called *Defence Helicopter World* which sounded ideal. The magazine's publisher, Alexander Shephard, favoured ex-RAF pilots as editors because of their extensive knowledge of 'the kit' as the military aircraft industry describes modern weapons. The fact that Jonathan had no journalistic experience was not considered important. 'It was his contacts and technical knowledge that Shephard wanted. The writing could come later,' explained one former Shephard Press employee.

During his interview for the job at the publisher's offices in Slough, to the west of London, Jonathan was told he'd be expected to visit trade fairs and weapons shows all over the world to find stories. His brief was to expand the magazine's coverage to give it a worldwide readership. It sounded marvellous to the ever-enthusiastic Jonathan; an ideal opportunity to put all those disappointments about the RAF firmly behind him ...

8

Farnborough, Hampshire

'Take risks — be accountable.'

Colonel Jack Folley

A Harrier Jump-Jet was doing formation dancing just after a MiG performed a handful of *Boy's Own*-type stunts in the skies above the oldest airshow in the world. But to most of the deal-makers below, these displays didn't even merit a brief glance.

Among the dozens of stands at Farnborough that September in 1988 was one run by Shephard Press, publishers of *Defence Helicopter World*.

The military market for helicopters was (and still is) fiercely competitive and specialist magazines like *DHW* were immensely influential. Articles they published were capable of making or breaking a deal which could spell the survival or destruction of an entire workforce.

There were also other more salacious elements at work at Farnborough; undercover agents from all over the world keeping an eye on the latest lethal arms developments; second-hand arms dealers offering cut-price weapons; even unscrupulous helicopter salesman trying to broker deals by using grisly snapshots of crashed rival aircraft to prove that their product was safer and more commercially viable than anything else.

Then there were the highly respected test pilots, like Sikorsky helicopter specialist Nick Lappos — a cool, confident character who, between flights, strolled around the show in his khaki silk flying suit.

A Greek-born US citizen, Lappos — with his jet-black hair and olive complexion — also enjoyed another role as a freelance writer for *DHW*. He was therefore delighted to be asked to the magazine's stand at Farnborough to meet their new editor, Jonathan Moyle.

Jonathan's 'intellectual curiosity', however, bothered Lappos so much at first that he thought Jonathan might have a hidden agenda.

'I thought to myself, this fellow wants to know so much about what's going on that I had to ask myself his motive,' he later recalled.

Lappos felt as if he was being pumped for technical data by the new editor, who asked non-stop questions about Sikorsky's latest helicopter projects.

Lappos was so concerned that he laid a few traps in the conversation to see if Jonathan would rise to the bait. 'I wanted to know if he was cross-checking or serving as a data-gathering source.'

After a half-hour chat, Lappos concluded that Jonathan was a highly intelligent, knowledgeable man who might well be working for intelligence gatherers. Lappos certainly knew about such things, as he'd regularly worked with the US security agencies. But Lappos knew that if Jonathan was any good at his job he wouldn't have been able to trick him, anyhow.

Farnborough was Jonathan's first official duty as editor of *DHW*. His 'curiosity' about certain aspects of the military helicopter business was entirely understandable, considering his new job. But he did cause a few raised eyebrows at Farnborough by asking Lappos and others highly detailed questions about night flying and the weapons systems on the latest attack helicopters. Jonathan clearly wanted to know how the aircraft behaved in different terrain and weather. He was also deeply concerned about the visibility and agility of helicopters and how they were developing.

At Farnborough, Jonathan was introduced to his deputy editor Peter Donaldson, whose overriding memory of that day was that Jonathan was 'wearing a deeply unfashionable brown suit'. He also met former *DHW* founding-editor Paul Beaver, who was very impressed by the young ex-RAF officer and promised to feed him some big stories for the magazine.

Journalist Frank Colucci, *Defence Helicopter World*'s North American correspondent, also encountered Jonathan at Farnborough in 1988.

'Farnborough was like a test for Jonathan. After we all had lunch together, I was asked by publisher Alexander Shephard what I thought of him and I said he seemed fine. He was very enthusiastic and knowledgeable,' says Colucci.

There were many potential 'perks' for the editor of a magazine like *Defence Helicopter World*. Shortly after being appointed, Jonathan met an arms dealer who said he had 20 Russian MiG 21s for sale. If Jonathan could find a buyer, he'd get five per cent commission. Jonathan refused, but he couldn't help presuming that someone would eventually help such a character.

Just a few months after Farnborough, Jonathan flew to the United States to attend some test flights and joined up with North America editor Colucci for two nights in Phoenix and Tucson, Arizona.

Frank Colucci, 42 years old, is clean-shaven and taciturn, with a grey short-back-and-sides combed straight forward on to a high forehead. Of medium height and solidly proportioned, he has an intense stare that gives him a professional air.

The two dined together and one night, after a few beers, Jonathan admitted to Colucci that he had been 'targeted' by the secret services and he had carried out some 'undercover' work.

*   *   *

There are estimated to be thousands of people in Britain who are, in effect, tailor-made for undercover assignments. These freelance operatives are cultivated and approached after much careful consideration.

They include serving officers in the RAF, the Ministry of Defence and the Nuclear Security Department, as well as civilians.

Jonathan Moyle had already been given authorised access to information supposedly protected under the Official Secrets Act, which he used in the MoD version of his university thesis. And he had occasionally supplied scraps of information to his security services handler on a freelance basis. This included facts and figures about aircraft weaponry and defence systems.

But shortly after joining *Defence Helicopter World*, Jonathan became friends with a former Intelligence Corps Staff Officer who had progressed to the MoD where he was working as an operative for MI6. There were plans to expand Jonathan's role as a spy.

'What attracted them to Moyle was that he was travelling to all the big air fairs and was being kept constantly up-to-date on military weaponry,' explained one ex-intelligence gatherer.

Two other sources have confirmed Jonathan's involvement with MI6, and even pointed out that numerous journalists are used as freelancers in similar situations. Jonathan's role was well known within certain circles.

'Jonathan Moyle was a useful informant as he had access to a lot of sensitive information,' explained one of the sources.

Ironically, the security services had discovered to their cost in recent years that journalists were often provided with top-secret information by arms manufacturers desperate for new business.

'Often, the security services are the last ones to know and that's what's made the Jonathan Moyles of this world so important,' added one source.

In December 1988, Jonathan received a telephone call from the agent identifying himself as a Ministry of Defence official and mentioning the name of another MI6 contact of Jonathan's at the MoD. They had heard he'd joined *DHW* and thought it was important that they meet. After a brief conversation, it was agreed that Jonathan should report to a Whitehall address the following week.

Jonathan was confused by the approach because he thought that his earlier freelance espionage work was the full extent of his duties. In fact, the RAF had been overruled by MoD security officers because of Jonathan's superb academic record and his extensive knowledge of highly-sensitive military data.

At precisely the appointed time, a nervous Jonathan entered the old War Office building in Whitehall and reported to the security receptionist. After a cursory search, he was escorted by a smartly-dressed secretary to the interview suite, comprising two or three small, sparsely furnished rooms.

Jonathan was then introduced to two officials from MI6. For a few minutes they chatted about the weather, before getting down to serious business.

Jonathan was asked various questions about his experiences as a pilot, the types of aircraft on which he was rated and how many hours flying he had achieved. But the area of his knowledge that most interested the spymasters was Jonathan's new job on the magazine.

He remained in that interview room for more than an hour, during which time he was asked if he would undertake more specific work investigating illicit arms deals. Jonathan was also given a briefing about how dangerous some media employees were, and how their subversive attitudes were a threat to the security of the nation.

At the end of the meeting, it was agreed that Jonathan should return at a later date to finalise operational arrangements.

Less than a month later, Jonathan returned to the same interview room and was introduced to his new operational controller or 'handler'. Discussions were confined solely to general aspects of Jonathan's future work and whom he would be looking out for. He was also told that no debriefing would ever be held at a Ministry location. It was stressed that he was to concentrate on the illicit sales of military helicopters and their armaments. Certain obvious targets were mentioned, such as Iran, Iraq and Libya, and special telephone numbers were provided.

Rapidly, the ground rules were spelt out by the handler. No records were to be kept, even his closest family members were to be kept ignorant of what he was engaged in, and naturally he was not to discuss his work with *anyone*. Moyle's handler said the investigation into illicit sales of helicopters and their armaments was known inside the MoD as Operation Valkyrie, after the Norse myth.

Arrangements were made to meet at regular intervals and Jonathan's handler suggested they pick quiet country towns rather than bustling city centres. He warned that a number of debriefing sessions would be held at places such as terminal buildings at London's Heathrow Airport and nearby towns. On each occasion, Jonathan would be treated to a meal by his handler, during which various aspects of his work would be discussed.

Initial encounters with his handler proved to be fruitless because Jonathan simply wasn't getting close enough to any truly sensitive material.

In the early days of his editorship of *DHW*, Jonathan wrote extensively about subjects such as the Soviets' tests on ejector seats for helicopters — a revolutionary concept. He was fascinated how the Soviets would be able to create seats that could survive ejection beneath rotor blades. But none of this interested the security services.

They were more concerned with the material he revealed in *DHW*'s regular 'Defence Hoverview' column, which included brief items on subjects such as news that the US Army had just spent $16.2m on buying Apache helicopter flight simulators and how an Israeli company had just pulled off a deal to overhaul all its heavy helicopters used in Israel. It was Jonathan's constant up-to-date knowledge that would help keep the British security services informed. They wanted to know just as much about their allies as their enemies, and they expected him to tell them all this well before publication in the magazine itself.

It was not uncommon for Jonathan's handler to produce various drawings and photographs and ask Jonathan to identify someone, or a particular model of helicopter or whatever. Jonathan was concerned about the open nature of his debriefing.

'Often Moyle had little or nothing to tell his handler,' explained one former MoD official. 'Moyle also found it difficult to take seriously his handler's almost paranoid insistence on secrecy.'

At almost every meeting his handler would ask Jonathan if he was certain he hadn't been followed. When Jonathan laughed off the suggestion, it brought a dead-pan response from his handler.

On one occasion Moyle tried to bounce certain information off his handler and he became infuriated after calling one of the 'hotline' numbers only to be told his operative was 'unavailable'.

In the short time since Moyle had begun passing on information, he'd already discovered that intelligence gathering had many drawbacks.

*   *   *

Early in 1989, Jonathan met up with former *DHW* editor Paul Beaver, who said he had a very important long-term story for the magazine. Beaver said he couldn't reveal the details yet, but he'd be in touch after the fast-approaching Baghdad Airshow, in Iraq.

That was how Jonathan first became involved in the most dangerous situation of his entire life.

9

Baghdad, Iraq

> 'Do not follow where the path may lead ... Go
> instead where there is no path
> and leave a trail.'
>
> *Anon*

Former *Defence Helicopter World* editor Paul Beaver soon found what he was looking for at the Baghdad International Exhibition for Military Production as he wandered around the show in April 1989. It was a kit that could turn a civilian Bell helicopter into a potentially lethal gunship. It was the first piece of concrete evidence of the sensational story he'd promised to Jonathan Moyle a few weeks earlier.

The proposed conversion kits were the brainchild of Chilean arms manufacturer and dealer Dr Carlos Cardoen, already renowned as one of Saddam Hussein's chief suppliers of weapons throughout his country's brutal eight-year war with Iraq. After receiving a doctorate in metallurgic engineering from the University of Utah, US-educated Cardoen had founded his company, Industrias Cardoen, in 1977 to manufacture mining explosives. But when the USA implemented an arms embargo on Chile, Cardoen had effortlessly begun expanding into armoured vehicles and many other types of military equipment. It was a truly remarkable business success story. In 1983, Chile had no arms exports at all. By 1987, the country was exporting $170m worth of arms and, by the following year, that figure had mushroomed to $280m, making Chile the world's fifteenth-largest arms exporter.

Self-made businessman Carlos Remigio Cornejo Cardoen cut an impressive figure. A three-times-married father of seven children, he favoured pale-coloured linen suits, but his business methods were anything but light-weight.

His project PDR-8706-01 proposed to turn any Bell 206L-2 LongRanger helicopter into a single-pilot cockpit aircraft, capable of a variety of uses. He intended to fit it with a Lucas gun turret for an M60 machine-gun and weapon stations for 2.75-inch rocket pods. Defence expert Paul Beaver discovered that the project had been in development since 1987 — at the height of the Iran–Iraq conflict. There was even talk on the arms circuit that Cardoen had carefully calculated his profit margins and only went ahead with developing the project after an assurance that Iraq would order at least 100 of the converted Bells.

The West German MBB BO 105 helicopter had originally been intended as the craft which would be converted by the Cardoen 'kit'. However the West German company pulled out of an agreement with Cardoen because they feared that if they agreed to join forces with Cardoen, his inferior helicopter gunships would flood the market, effectively ruining business for their 'original' models.

Defence journalist Paul Beaver was particularly interested in the Cardoen scheme because he knew that Saddam Hussein was the biggest single potential Middle Eastern buyer.

At the Baghdad Airshow, the only evidence available at the Cardoen stand were vague plans that included a general diagram. 'It seemed to be at the very early stages,' explained Beaver.

Many journalists and arms dealers who attended the airshow presumed that the new helicopters would be equipped for military use. But Cardoen publicly insisted that the aircraft were intended for use as crop-spraying aircraft.

A source at the airshow even secretly fed Paul Beaver with military specifications for the aircraft that made it clear what the helicopters would really be used for.

What Paul Beaver did not realise was that, just a few months earlier, Cardoen bought into a small company called Global Helicopter Technology based in Hurst, Texas, to ensure that his converted Bells would receive full airworthiness certificates. FAA certification was essential because it proved that the aircraft had been tested and certified as safe and reliable, thereby boosting world market sales. The idea was that Global would convert the aircraft from their original shells and then get them licensed on behalf of Cardoen.

Cardoen secretly boasted to Global Helicopter's President, Clem Bailey, that he already had a handshake deal with Saddam Hussein to sell hundreds of the converted Bells to Iraq. 'Each one would be priced at least $2.5m. He was very proud of it,' explained Vice-President of Global, Dan Pettus.

Ironically, Pettus was so concerned about the eventual destination of the converted Bells that he cornered Cardoen at a meeting in Chile during early negotiations with the arms manufacturer before he bought into Global. Pettus was worried that the helicopters should never be produced in Chile, which was still suffering a strict arms embargo by the US government.

'Mr Cardoen, I've got some doubts about your market

projection,' Pettus said to Cardoen.

'You build the aircraft and I'll worry about the market,' replied the Chilean businessman. The question was never raised again.

Cardoen saw the Bell conversion kits as his final swan-song before pulling out of arms dealing and manufacturing and he was determined to go through with it.

*　　　　　*　　　　　*

President Saddam Hussein was an ambitious man with an obsessive quest to become the 'Sword of the Arabs'. He believed he was destined to dominate the Arab world just as Gamal Abdel Nasser of Egypt had done a generation before. Saddam saw himself as the head of an Arab superpower, controlling much of the world's oil supplies. One American news magazine called him 'the most dangerous man in the world'. Some CIA analysts estimated that, during the 1980s, Saddam spent as much as $50bn on the international arms market, making him the world's single biggest buyer of weaponry. Indeed, his progress in purchasing technology from abroad was so startling that by the end of the 1980s, US experts had halved their estimates — from ten years to five or less — of when he would finally have a nuclear capability. With 10 per cent of the world's petroleum reserves to finance him, Saddam's military endeavours knew few bounds. As is now well known, by mid-1988 Saddam's military advisers had already drawn up provisional plans for an invasion of Kuwait.

Saddam Hussein claimed to be not only a descendant of the Prophet Mohammed, but also heir to the legend of Nebuchadnezzar, king of the ancient Babylonians. Nor was it just imaginative lineage that linked Saddam with antiquity. He had the same military style as the ancients he admired so much. Saddam (the name means 'One Who Confronts') could match and surpass them. It was not without reason that he was known as 'the Butcher of Baghdad', a man who had gassed restive Kurds and left the corpses of political opponents to float in the capital's canals. More than a million Iraqis had dared to criticise his régime, and international agencies claimed that torture, even against children, was commonplace. The devastating eight-year war between Iran and Saddam's Iraq had ended only months before, and the West had suddenly switched from supporting Iraq to awarding it pariah status because of fears that Saddam was stock-piling weapons in preparation for a new conflict.

*   *   *

Almost every Western nation had military experts at the Baghdad exhibition. It was the job of these personnel to look out for the unusual, and try to find out more.

Dozens of supposedly home-grown weapons were unveiled at the show. There were the prototypes of two new six-wheel-drive, self-propelled cannons which had actually been developed with the expertise of the Belgian office of the Space Research Corporation, headed by the controversial Canadian 'supergun' inventor Dr Gerald Bull. He had designed 155mm artillery which was supplied to Iraq via South Africa, and entered a joint venture with the Iraqis to buy an empty factory in Belfast and use it to manufacture a vast range of weaponry.

Meanwhile, Dr Carlos Cardoen had been continually supplying vast quantities of cluster bombs and other essential armoury to Saddam Hussein for use in the Iran–Iraq war. By 1989, it was estimated that he had sold 29,000 cluster bombs for a total of $300m. But even more ominously, Cardoen openly disclosed at the Baghdad show that he had supplied Iraq with the technology to manufacture fuel-air explosive devices capable of producing a blast up to ten times greater in force than any conventional explosive with an impact that extended over an area of several miles and was the equivalent of a small nuclear explosion.

Cardoen was so proud of his lucrative business that he proudly displayed a photograph of himself meeting President Saddam Hussein in his office in Santiago, capital of Chile.

Cardoen was surprisingly open about his dealings with the Iraqis and shortly before the Baghdad show even smugly pointed out to one reporter, 'While I read all kinds of stories about governments that are supposedly not supplying armaments to Middle East countries at war, I see every single company from the developed countries competing with me in Iraq. How their products get there I don't know.'

At the Baghdad show, Cardoen attended a dinner for foreign exhibitors hosted by the newly-appointed Minister of Industry and Military Industrialisation, Hussein Kamel (Saddam Hussein's cousin and son-in-law). At the end of the meal, Kamel gave a speech welcoming the foreign arms manufacturers to Baghdad and wishing them well in their business relations with Iraq. The minister sat down to a moment of embarrassed silence among the foreign visitors — no one had planned a speech in response. It was Dr Carlos Cardoen who graciously stood up to thank Kamel for Iraq's hospitality.

There was also Nasser Beydoun, a Lebanese-born exporter living in Florida, who had good contacts in Baghdad. He became Cardoen's agent in the 1980s and first introduced him to Saddam Hussein. The Iraqi leader was unsure about Cardoen's credentials until the Chilean showed him a photograph of himself with Chilean dictator General Augusto Pinochet. Soon afterwards, a deal to supply cluster bombs was struck. What Iraq liked most about Cardoen was that business was quick and discreet. 'Nobody knew about Industrias Cardoen. It was secretive and Iraqis, especially in their military dealings, are very secretive,' explained Beydoun later.

Cardoen even built the Iraqis their own cluster bomb factory just outside Baghdad and he became more than a manufacturer; he was also an intermediary through whom Iraq was able to obtain technology it couldn't get directly from manufacturing countries.

Even more frightening than Saddam Hussein's conventional military capabilities were the ample indications in 1989 that he had few qualms about using some of the less well-publicised weapons. 'I swear to God,' he said in a statement printed around the world at the time, 'we will let our fire scorch half of Israel if it tries to wage anything against us.'

Worse still, it had already become very clear that there was virtually no one who could restrain Saddam from his appalling impulses. He had been continually stubbing out rivals, real and imagined, like cigarette butts, and even pulled the trigger himself on a number of occasions. According to informed opinion, Saddam committed his first murder at 14, attempted his first political assassination at 22 and he clearly had not broken the habit. Anyone closely probing his dealings anywhere in the world had good reason to fear for their own safety.

Saddam's non-stop shopping for weaponry had bought him a fundamental change in the strategic balance of the Middle East. This transformation was as much a measure of his own ruthlessness as it was of the 'see-no-evil' arms dealers like Dr Carlos Cardoen who almost every time the capacious pockets of Iraq opened up, offered a friendly deal.

Cardoen used effective psychology to understand the mentality of his Iraqi customers. Initially he invited several Iraqi engineers to Chile, gave them lavish gifts and sent them to local nightclubs with the best girls and they soon believed that Cardoen was a generous host and wanted to help them.

Two million people died during the Iran–Iraq conflict but Cardoen openly — some would say proudly — proclaimed: 'I have no moral problems about making bombs.'

In Chile, Cardoen had a reputation for hiring and firing people very fast. People who worked with him did not trust him. He created a tense atmosphere. Despite this, by the late 1980s, Cardoen was challenging the world arms market from all directions. He felt powerful with the Iraqis behind him.

Many of his former executives found Cardoen a frightening figure, more akin to a hooligan than a businessman when he was crossed. He even threatened to ruin one senior employee when he decided to leave the company.

'You will never work again,' Cardoen told his erstwhile close friend. 'I will destroy you.'

Some stood up to him, but Cardoen continued to try and destroy them.

'Cardoen wouldn't hesitate to buy off reporters to get favourable publicity. Others were threatened and ruined by him,' says one former employee, who is terrified of being identified because of his fear of the Chilean entrepreneur.

He explained, 'Cardoen can be an unpredictable person. He is capable of anything. He was like the devil sometimes, especially against weaker people.'

Three years earlier, one of Cardoen's arms factories in the northern city of Iquique was virtually destroyed by a huge explosion which killed more than 20 workers. Despite the tragedy, Cardoen was soon increasing production of cluster bombs for his biggest customer, Saddam Hussein.

In many ways, Cardoen's lifestyle was more like that of a tin-pot dictator than a businessman. He had at least three bodyguards armed with machine-guns, and always travelled in an entourage of at least three limousines. He admitted to his colleagues he feared kidnapping or a hijack.

One story doing the rounds of Santiago at the time suggested that Cardoen had paid off leftist guerillas *not* to snatch him or his family. But then Cardoen had friends in high places, including the then Chilean dictator General Pinochet, as well as the heads of the Chilean Air Force and Navy.

Cardoen's close circle of 'advisers' were also capable of doing anything, although Cardoen did try to keep strict control over them all.

Naturally, Cardoen greatly valued his relationship with the Iraqis. After all, he was making hundreds of millions of dollars from Saddam Hussein's war machine every year. The Iraqis in turn were prepared to do anything to help seal the relationship.

*   *   *

Less than a month after the Baghdad military fair, *Defence Helicopter World* editor Jonathan Moyle met the magazine's former editor Paul Beaver for lunch in London. Beaver told him all about Cardoen's proposed plan to convert civilian Bells into gunships and suggested they should jointly launch a major investigation into the controversial project. If they could prove that the helicopters were being manufactured for military use, it would make a sensational story.

Both men were also curious about how Iraq would pay for the converted gunships. Jonathan and Beaver reckoned Saddam would pay with oil because they knew the Iraqis didn't have the cash available.

Beaver was so obsessed with the story that he enlisted the help of Washington-based defence journalist David Harvey, who in turn tried to establish some hard evidence that the kits were being manufactured for Iraq.

They didn't realise it at the time, but both men were on the verge of uncovering a story that would have very serious repercussions for all concerned.

'Accept the challenges so that you may feel the
exhilaration of victory.'

Anon

Test pilot Nick Lappos looked across at his co-pilot
Jonathan Moyle as he held the Sikorsky steady at
5,000 feet. He had decided to give the young editor
a choice as to whether he should perform a near-death-
defying stunt.

'We don't have to do it. We're running a little out of
time ...'

Jonathan smiled. 'Let's do it.'

Seconds later, Lappos turned the aircraft completely
upside-down and round again in one of the most
dangerous manoeuvres that can be undertaken in a
helicopter. The aircraft was literally inverted in a split-S
manoeuvre when it froze in mid-air momentarily before
completing the second half of the loop in a circular
movement. The Sikorsky then exited in a 180-degree move
in the opposite direction, having reversed vertically rather
than horizontally, resulting in a serious loss of altitude.

In order to execute the highly complex move, Lappos had to use the controls simply to rotate and pull and not lose orientation or gravity. He explained, 'Unlike an aircraft, a helicopter is unforgiving, and if you go past zero G and go through these negative Gs, it is a very unnerving manoeuvre.' Often with passengers, Lappos would opt for caution, only taking the aircraft half-way through and sweep back.

Once level again, Lappos immediately let go of the stick and said to Jonathan, 'Now, it's your turn.'

Jonathan grabbed it and repeated the manoeuvre without batting an eyelid. Lappos had complete confidence in the ex-pilot.

Only about ten per cent of pilots could handle a machine the way that Jonathan Moyle did that day. Nick Lappos had no doubts he was a good pilot, more than capable of controlling himself well even under the most threatening of circumstances. The tests carried out that day at the Sikorsky headquarters in Stratford, Connecticut, in the autumn of 1989, were very rigorous and there was absolutely nothing to suggest that Jonathan was anything other than a fine aviator. Lappos believed Jonathan to be one of the best.

Frustratingly for Jonathan, the RAF had earlier seemed to believe otherwise.

*   *   *

Jonathan Moyle had very little fashion sense — his shirts tended to be traditional collar-and-cuffs and always tucked neatly into his trousers. But he had a touch of vanity. His hair had been rapidly receding since his early 20s and every morning he would comb long strands on the left side of his head over to the right. The hope was to hide the bald spot in the middle. But there was a real sparkle to his narrow blue eyes and, when he wanted to switch it on, there was considerable charisma. His shoulders were always straight and his head held high. He was 5ft 8in, and he gradually developed the notion that he had some of the appearance and all the tenacity of a bulldog. He was quick to argue a point.

But all this disguised the fact that Jonathan was a complex character who somehow failed to see the frequent clash of his word and deed. His training as an RAF pilot involved an understanding of the art of killing, yet he was not a cold-hearted person.

Quietly spoken with friends, Jonathan could be argumentative and obstinate with his professional colleagues, especially when he encountered incompetence. Ill-tempered and impatient when subjects were slow to respond to his challenges, he sometimes found it frustrating dealing with civilians.

Jonathan got into the habit of working long hours, fretting over an article for his magazine because he had to get it absolutely correct. His writing in *DHW* read as if he was bursting with information but lacked the relaxed style that is easy on the eye, even though he was writing for a very specialised market.

Jonathan was also, in some ways, politically naïve, despite having dealt regularly with MI6 and many high-ranking officials at the MoD during his work at Michael Armitage's secretive strategic studies unit. 'He expected to be told the truth at all times and couldn't understand it when his inquiries went unanswered,' explained American colleague Frank Colucci.

By late 1989, Jonathan was finding his job as editor of *DHW* very demanding. He was staying later and later at the magazine's offices. Sometimes he even slept the entire night at the office when faced with an imminent deadline.

Colucci received a call one day after midnight British time and was surprised to find Jonathan on the other end of the line.

'What're you doing? Where are you?' asked Colucci, presuming that Jonathan had long since left the office.

'I'm in the office.'

'Why?'

'Why not?'

It then transpired that Jonathan had nowhere else to go that night and was faced with a heavy schedule for the magazine.

Jonathan also had other problems at the *DHW* office. His lack of journalistic training meant he still found it hard to concentrate on writing in a crowded, open-plan office. Eventually, he asked publisher Alexander Shephard if a screen could be put up so that he did not have any distractions while he tried to work. At first, Jonathan's colleagues were a little upset by this apparently anti-social behaviour. But then Jonathan explained that it was the only way he could concentrate enough to write his articles.

Shephard had great faith in Jonathan Moyle because of his RAF background, enthusiasm and his detailed knowledge of the technical side of the military helicopter business. But hiring journalistic novices to edit his magazines did sometimes put added pressure on the rest of the Shephard Press staff.

There were other complications, too. One day, Jonathan was reprimanded by Shephard for swearing, even though it was a rare lapse of manners. A company memo was even issued by Shephard insisting that such behaviour would not be tolerated in the office. Later, Jonathan was also spoken to for using the telephone too much. Telephones are a journalist's most valuable tool, so Jonathan found that particularly frustrating.

Executives at Shephard Press were also concerned that their new editor did not seem to have a permanent home in the London area. During his first year, Jonathan commuted between the office and his parents' home in the West Country, or slept on the floors of various friends and relatives.

He eventually became a lodger at his aunt Pat's home in Kingston, the same house where his father Tony had been brought up during the Second World War.

It wasn't easy at Pat Moyle's but one bonus was that his aunt — a matron at nearby Kingston Hospital — was able to provide him with a non-stop supply of pretty young nurses to go out with.

Pat Moyle saw both sides of her nephew; the brilliant young ex-serviceman-turned-journalist, and the slightly shy man with a childlike curiosity.

She noticed that her nephew had not lost any of his early patriotic passion. 'He loved Britain and wasn't afraid to tell anyone that,' she says today.

Jonathan was well aware that lodging at his aunt's house and then spending weekends with his parents wasn't a very suitable arrangement for an adult. After a childhood spent living in comfortable rented properties, he had always dreamt of owning a beautiful big house in a pretty village somewhere in Devon ...

*   *   *

Just north of the village of Branscombe, in Devon, on the main A3052 road, is the Hangman's Stone. According to legend, a man, having stolen sheep, paused in his exertions to rest against this stone while he recovered his breath. Whereupon the sheep, alarmed at the situation, jumped frantically about on the end of the imprisoning rope, and dealt him rougher justice than he really deserved by entangling the rope around his neck and strangling him.

Branscombe nestles in a valley which runs through the centre of high hills at the foot of three branching coombs close to the South Devon coastline. It features a couple of farms, an old pub called the Fountain Head, thatched cottages, an old bakery and a forge. Most gardens have well-cultivated flower beds and vegetable patches. It is quintessentially rural England: rolling green hills, containment and security; the kind of setting one escapes from or never leaves.

The name Branscombe comes from the saints of St Branwellanus, St Branwalader and St Brendan, who all had connections with the area almost 2,000 years ago. A saint is said to have been buried somewhere in the village in a stone coffin during the 4th century. King Alfred mentioned the village in his will by referring to it as 'Brancescombe' and, in the Domesday Book, renamed it 'Branchescoma' because it was the place where the coombs' branch could be found. At one stage, the Danes even landed nearby and tried to seize the village, but locals swiftly forced them back to the sea.

Overlooking the village on a hill, with green lawns gently sloping towards a wooded valley, was Highcliff House. It was a large, ivory-white Georgian house, with a pillared patio and a balustrade along the shallow roof. The windows displayed perfectly proportioned sashes, and the columns were fluted. In alcoves on either side of the front door stood stone vases hung with carved drapery, and ivy and maidenhair fern tumbled over their rims. A gravel sweep would have been better but the carriage drive was still without an even surface. The tubs and troughs clustered on it held bay trees and yellow cypress, red fuchsias in full bloom, orange and cream arbutus and pink pelargoniums. In contrast, the flowerbeds contained only bare, turned earth without a single weed.

Its impressive pillared entranceway led into a hall with ornate Victorian tiles, and to the right was a vast drawing-room with elegantly stripped floorboards. Flagstones dominated the large kitchen, complete with an Aga gas-fired cooker in the corner. Up the galleried staircase were five bedrooms and two bathrooms. There was even a smaller staff staircase leading to the kitchen.

During the construction of Highcliff House in 1832, a

murder took place on the premises and the new owner never actually moved in. The crime was so grisly that when the farm was sold on to a family, they immediately renamed it Cox's Farm to ward off the bad luck.

When Jonathan Moyle and his parents decided to buy the house jointly in 1988 for £210,000, they ignored such superstitious stories and immediately restored the original name.

Highcliff House was the property they had been waiting for all their lives. It was their very own dream mansion.

For the Moyle family this was to be the perfect retreat, a place which Jonathan and his parents would renovate with their own hands. They looked on Highcliff House as their home for life. Even the family dogs, Smudge, Shula, Fancy, Rosie and Polly, took to the place within days of the family's arrival.

The first job for Jonathan was to plant 275 assorted trees including oak, beech, field maple, ash and birch. After that, they'd concentrate on converting the grounds into a picturesque landscape.

Jonathan couldn't wait to get started.

11

London

'Do what you can,
with what you have, where you are.'

Theodore Roosevelt

'Checkmate!'

Jonathan Moyle looked really irritated as he surrendered a game of chess to his work colleague Martin Pace one evening at Pace's flat in Chiswick, West London.

Pace, who worked as the advertising manager for Shephard Press, never forgot how desperately Jonathan tried to win that game.

He'd never seen anyone more annoyed at losing. Jonathan had tried everything to put Pace off his game; he frequently changed the conversation and pressurised Pace to move quickly. He even tried advising Pace wrongly because he would not accept he'd been beaten fair and square. It was all very unlike Jonathan and it stuck in Pace's mind for years.

The problem was that the young editor of *Defence Helicopter World* was feeling a great deal of pressure at work. He was also finding his assignments for the intelligence services increasingly strenuous. Basically, Jonathan was an old-fashioned, honourable character, but the stress of life was manifesting itself in such a way that he was becoming even more tense.

Pace witnessed this side of Jonathan after he began regularly turning up at his small flat to stay the night on the floor, rather then go back to his aunt Pat Moyle's home in nearby Kingston. He was extremely fond of her but felt he was getting a little too old to be lodging with his aunt.

'He became more serious. His mind was always on other things,' says Pace.

The two men played tennis and badminton together and Jonathan was just as competitive in those sports as he was at chess. Jonathan made up for in energy what he lacked in skill with gutsy determination. In tennis he was obsessed with serving aces.

He threw himself blindly into everything. When he went running with Pace most mornings, Jonathan always pushed himself harder if they'd been drinking the night before.

Once he turned up late for work after driving his Saab 900 Turbo through a flooded section of roadway under a bridge. Anyone else would have driven gently through it, but not Jonathan. He simply put his foot down and sped through the water which was sucked into his engine and caused it to seize up.

At the Shephard Press offices near London, Jonathan earned a reputation as a hugely enthusiastic workaholic. The job did have its perks, such as the regular trips abroad. Martin Pace went on a number of these trips with Jonathan on behalf of Shephard Press.

The first time was to Greece. It turned out to be a typical Jonathan-style roller-coaster ride. Pace explains, 'The first three nights Jonathan was lecturing me on Greek mythology and Byzantine art.

'Eventually, I told him I'd had enough and wanted to find some women. I managed to get us a date with two girls for a meal. But Jonathan would only come along for a drink because he'd met another girl earlier that evening and didn't want to let her down. He was so bloody honourable.'

Later, Pace even denied having a girl back to his hotel room because he feared that Jonathan would disapprove.

On the same trip, Jonathan booked a massage at the hotel and was outraged at Pace's suggestion that it might mean something more than innocent muscular relief.

During another foreign trip with Pace more than six months later, Jonathan angrily admonished another masseuse who offered to masturbate him for more money. He started lecturing the woman on why it was immoral to behave in such a way.

On one trip abroad, a woman took a liking to Jonathan but he refused to get involved with her because she was married. 'Jonathan had a rigid set of rules when it came to women and married ones were definitely out of bounds,' explains Pace. 'He always said he couldn't tolerate that sort of behaviour.'

During this period, there is little doubt that his day job combined with work for the intelligence services and family concerns about him settling down and marrying had quite a profound effect on Jonathan. In the background was his first and only real love Annette Kissenbeck, and he wanted to prove that he was getting closer and closer to being able to run his life in a very responsible fashion.

Pace noticed this attitude in relation to how Jonathan dealt with strangers. 'People seemed to feel more uncomfortable with him than he did with them. He was happy to talk about anything but ultimately he was not a brilliant listener. He sometimes struggled socially and could be terribly clumsy.'

As the pressure at work mounted, Jonathan admitted to Pace he was still finding it hard adjusting to civilian life, more than a year after leaving the RAF.

'He just would not compromise on any issue. He wanted to do the job his way. Jonathan felt he knew best even though his journalistic experience was so limited,' recalls Pace.

Jonathan told Pace that he eventually intended to give up journalism to sell antiques in the West Country.

Jonathan drove a company Montego on a trip to Paris with fellow *DHW* staff journalist Peter Donaldson. 'Jonathan's driving was terrifying,' recalls Donaldson. But Jonathan did teach Donaldson how to navigate by the sun using his own wrist-watch and spent hours explaining the Greek myths in painstaking detail.

On another trip to Bordeaux in France with *DHW* photographer Patrick Allen, Jonathan proved that some of his childhood obsessions had stayed with him when he and a group of defence journalists found themselves stranded for four hours at the local airport because their flight back to London had been delayed.

The writers set up camp in the VIP lounge and started ordering drinks. At first they talked amongst themselves, then Jonathan suddenly made an announcement: 'If we've got nothing better to do over the next two hours, I can always give you "The Charge of the Light Brigade".'

'What the bloody hell are you on about, Jonathan?' asked journalist Mike Gething.

'It's something I did at Cranwell when I was in the RAF.'

'Alright then,' replied Gething, still slightly bemused by what the young editor meant.

For the following hour-and-a-half, Jonathan set out matchboxes and various magazines and turned the floor of the VIP lounge at Bordeaux airport into a re-enactment of The Charge of the Light Brigade.

*   *   *

One morning, Jonathan walked into the office at Shephard Press looking deeply depressed. No one had the courage to ask him what was wrong. Then young production assistant Rhoda Parry — who had got to know Jonathan through Martin Pace — plucked up courage.

It turned out that one of Jonathan's former girlfriends called Tania had been killed in a horrifying accident when she parachuted into the rotor blades of a helicopter.

Jonathan became quite close to Rhoda Parry and she became the only person, other than Martin Pace at Shephard Press, in whom he confided. Jonathan even defended Rhoda admirably in the office when she was reprimanded for wearing trousers to work.

Many employees at Shephard Press thought that Jonathan was reckless. And he continued to be told off, on occasions, like a naughty schoolboy by publisher Alexander Shephard.

On the social front, Jonathan gained a reputation for being extremely generous when it came to paying his way. One drunken evening he admitted to Martin Pace that his generosity was linked to the fact that his parents had always struggled financially throughout his childhood, but managed to put a brave face on their lack of funds. He was determined to follow suit.

Although no longer in the RAF, Jonathan continued to dress very much like an officer. Even when he was being casual, he ended up invariably in a work shirt without a tie. And he always wore brown brogues or black Oxfords.

Only on rare occasions did he give away any clue as to his other secret agenda. Once, at Pace's flat in Chiswick, Jonathan admitted that he did some work for military intelligence, and then quickly changed the subject to politics. Pace didn't pursue the matter.

Jonathan considered Pace a bit of a 'lefty', and they would regularly engage in heated political discussions.

'He was always supporting the balance of power and I was saying they're all as bad as each other. He definitely believed in the government and military,' says Pace.

In many ways, Jonathan and Pace were complete opposites; Pace was always immaculately turned out in the latest fashionable suits while Jonathan stumbled along in a tweed jacket and cords. But they understood each other's attitudes and formed a loyal bond of friendship.

Jonathan's 'gung-ho' attitude even occasionally rubbed off on Pace. With Pace in his Alfa Romeo, and Jonathan in his dark-blue Saab, they would frequently race bumper-to-bumper on motorways. Sometimes they'd even nudge each other's cars in the outside lane while doing nearly 100 miles an hour. 'It was absolute madness,' says Pace, 'but that's the sort of thing he liked doing. He enjoyed being perceived as reckless because he was.'

Another more amusing habit of Jonathan's was related to his interest in antiques which had been encouraged by his parents' careful purchases as they moved from home to home when he was still a child.

Pace explains, 'Everywhere Jonathan went he used to value people's furniture. People were very irritated by this habit, although Jonathan thought it was all a bit of a joke.'

*   *   *

By the middle of 1989, Jonathan found himself being drawn back towards his old flame Annette Kissenbeck. He was convinced that she was the only woman he truly cared about.

Jonathan found the perfect excuse by dropping in on Annette at her home in Regensberg, Germany, on the way back from a skiing holiday with friends. The couple realised immediately that they wanted to be with each other and spent a romantic two days together before Jonathan continued his journey back to London.

'We had a wonderful time together. It felt as if we'd never been apart. I knew then we would stay together for ever,' Annette later recalled.

Annette had become a fully qualified paediatrician by this time and she had always felt equally enthusiastic about Jonathan. They found it easy to pick up the pieces despite the long break in their relationship.

In the late summer that year, Annette began spending more and more time in England, mainly at the Moyles' home in Branscombe, Devon. The couple were soon meeting virtually every weekend.

'I loved it at the house. We'd go on long country walks and build huge roaring fires. It was the happiest time of my life,' says Annette now.

Jonathan talked about the possibility of marriage but for the moment they both delayed making a decision since there was a natural reluctance on both their parts to rush into such a commitment. 'It was definitely on both our minds but we wanted to be settled in our jobs before actually marrying,' says Annette.

*   *   *

In late summer, 1989, a letter turned up at the Slough offices of *Defence Helicopter World* from the organisers of FIDAE '90 — an international air and space show to be held in Santiago, Chile, the following March.

Nobody at *DHW* took much notice of the letter from one of the airshow's organisers, Colonel Bruno Ugatti, offering to exchange a free stand at the exhibition for articles to be published in the magazine. Dozens of such offers arrived regularly from around the world, more than the magazine could cope with. But when Jonathan saw the letter on his assistant's desk he immediately realised that a trip to Chile would be invaluable as part of the ongoing investigation he had started with Paul Beaver into Carlos

Cardoen's helicopter conversion plans.

Over the following few months, Jonathan negotiated a deal with the airshow organisers whereby they would provide the air fare and hotel charges in exchange for full-page colour advertisements in the best possible position in *DHW* December/January 1990 and February/March 1990, plus extensive editorial coverage.

Jonathan's interest in Cardoen's Bell helicopter conversion scheme was insatiable. He made contact with British Intelligence once again and told them about his suspicions surrounding the Chilean's plans to sell the gunships.

Moyle's contribution to Operation Valkyrie was already proving invaluable, and he told his handler that the trip to Chile could provide him with the evidence to blow Cardoen's plans sky high.

12

Germany

'Happy the man, and happy he alone,
He who can today call his own;
He who, secure within, can say,
Tomorrow, do thy worst,
for I have lived today.

John Dryden (1697)

In November 1989, as the Berlin Wall was being dismantled and a 28-year-old nightmare came to an end, Jonathan Moyle was flying en route to Munich to see his beloved Annette Kissenbeck yet again.

On the flight, he sat next to a friendly old lady who sounded surprised when Jonathan said he wasn't yet married Annette. 'Oh, you must get married,' the woman told him. 'You might lose her.'

Those words preyed on Jonathan's mind and almost as soon as he arrived at Annette's home in Regensberg, he proposed to her. He even promised to be christened at the local church in Branscombe at Christmas so that the Christian ceremony would be completely legitimate.

The couple agreed that the wedding should take place the following summer. Jonathan then started talking enthusiastically about honeymooning on a jungle expedition back in Belize.

Annette was horrified so they agreed to something more civilised, such as a week in Venice. Jonathan was changing.

On the work front, Jonathan was setting up Shephard Press's long-awaited fighter-helicopter conference to be held in London in January 1990. As editor of *DHW*, it was his job to persuade military top-brass from east and west to attend.

Jonathan also continued to spend a lot of time in the United States. He went to an airshow in New Orleans with *DHW*'s Frank Colucci, who recalls that the young editor seemed very distracted.

He was continually being called away by mysterious telephone calls and at one meal in a restaurant, Jonathan seemed very moody after leaving the table to call 'a friend'.

Colucci adds, 'But throughout that trip Jonathan continued to show great interest in Carlos Cardoen's plans to convert the Bell helicopters. Jonathan seemed obsessed with Cardoen's scheme.'

But Colucci was particularly concerned by Jonathan's mysterious absences. 'Most mealtimes he disappeared to make calls. He also went to meet people he clearly didn't want me to meet with him.'

Colucci tried to corner Jonathan about his activities, but he was told it was nothing out of the ordinary. 'The message was loud and clear — I should mind my own business.'

Jonathan was secretly trying to organise a visit to Hurst, Texas, headquarters of Global Helicopters, the company in which Carlos Cardoen had bought a 51% share to get his aircraft the all-important FAA approval. Jonathan intended to visit Texas without Colucci. Eventually, he flew into Texas from New Orleans.

Jonathan had a tense meeting with Global President Clem Bailey, during which he asked the Texan ex-Bell test pilot outright if he knew that Cardoen intended to sell the converted Bells to Saddam Hussein for military use.

'Clem insisted he had no idea, but that wasn't true,' explained an ex-Global employee. 'Moyle was clearly trying to prove a link between Cardoen's converted helicopters and Iraq, and we didn't really want to know.

'Moyle just wouldn't stop asking questions about it and in the end Clem tactfully brought the meeting to an end and saw him out of the offices.'

Clem Bailey had carefully avoided telling Jonathan that air trials for the redesigned helicopter had already started at Global. Bailey feared that Carlos Cardoen was dragging the Texan company into some very risky areas but he wasn't about to tell a journalist about those activities.

Outside the Global office, two men in a dark-blue Ford LTD were secretly taking photographs of Jonathan as he walked towards his rental car in the blistering Texan heat. Neither Jonathan nor Bailey realised they were being watched.

The men were FBI agents who had already started monitoring Cardoen's movements inside the United States following a request from the special investigations units of the Department of Commerce and US Customs. They had long been concerned about the arms manufacturing activities of Dr Cardoen.

*   *   *

Jonathan Moyle's Fighter Helicopter Conference was held at the Novotel in London, on 18 and 19 January 1990. One of the main subjects tabled for discussion at the show was how to adapt helicopters for military missions, making them more agile and capable of performing practical air combat duties. It sounded like a blue-print for Dr Carlos Cardoen's plans to convert Bell 206 helicopters.

The conference itself attracted more than 300 military top-brass and arms industry executives from around the world. It also marked the first time that Jonathan was approached by the CIA.

The organisation had been observing Cardoen's Bell helicopter conversions with trepidation because they feared he was intending to supply Iraq with hundreds of the lethal gunships. But the Americans had been unable to prove conclusively that the helicopters were being produced for military purposes. They were first alerted to Jonathan when he was photographed while visiting the Texas headquarters of Global Helicopter Technology, the company preparing the helicopter for its FAA airworthiness certification. The CIA did not at this stage realise that Jonathan was already working as a freelancer for the British security services.

One of the CIA's most senior London bureau members approached Jonathan on the second day of the conference.

'Moyle was extremely reluctant to talk to us at first,' explained one of the CIA operatives who worked with the agency in London at that time. 'And he insisted we contact his controller first. That was when we realised he was already working on Operation Valkyrie.

'When we made it clear that we genuinely intended to block Cardoen's plans, Moyle agreed to talk. He told us about his meetings with Clem Bailey in Texas. We didn't mention we already knew he'd been there. Moyle also said that he had heard about Cardoen's handshake deal to sell at least 100 of the converted helicopters to Saddam Hussein. He agreed to keep an eye on what was happening.'

However it was emphasised by the CIA that any further approaches would only occur with the approval of Jonathan's British intelligence handler, to whom Jonathan had already relayed much of this information. The CIA agent told him: 'We'll probably make contact at the Singapore airshow next month.' He even gave Jonathan a confidential phone number to call if he had any more relevant information.

Jonathan's efforts to make the helicopter conference a success continued, even though he was finding himself stretched by his dual roles as a magazine editor and security services informant. His North American colleague, Frank Colucci, was very impressed by the number of important delegates who showed up. 'Much of it was down to Jonathan's superb powers of persuasion.'

Half-way through the conference, Jonathan scored a major coup by getting the Americans and Soviet military to sit down together at the same table for a discussion panel about helicopter armoury. This attracted widespread comment as the Cold War was still simmering at the time, despite the gradual collapse of many eastern European countries.

Sikorsky helicopter's chief test pilot Nick Lappos had by this time become a close acquaintance of Jonathan's, despite their first awkward meeting at the Farnborough Airshow 18 months earlier. Lappos even helped Jonathan approach some of the American military top-brass who attended the conference. But Lappos noticed that Jonathan seemed much more tense than usual. He also kept asking questions about Carlos Cardoen's plans to convert Bell 206s.

The conference was hailed as a great success for *Defence Helicopter World* with Jonathan as its chief architect.

But behind the scenes, Jonathan was extremely anxious for much of the conference because he was precariously balanced between his full-time job responsibilities as a magazine editor and his duties as a patriotic freelance intelligence operative for Britain and, now, the United States.

In some ways, Jonathan revelled in the pressure, but there were times when he wondered if he could handle the never-ending juggling.

Jonathan began thinking beyond his job and started making inquiries about getting his thesis on conventional warfare between the UK and Soviets published by a specialist military publisher called Brassey's. Despite the fall of the Berlin Wall and communism teetering on the verge of collapse, he still felt that his project might be of interest. He also told Annette Kissenbeck that what he wanted to do was to live in Devon, raise children, run an antique shop and get books on military strategy regularly published.

The thrill of working for the security services on Operation Valkyrie was undeniable but, ultimately, he wanted to settle down and lead a relatively 'normal' life.

13

Norway

'Between cowardice and despair,
valour is gendred.'

John Donne, Paradoxes, Problems and Essays
(1633)

A little after 1.00pm in the afternoon of 31 January 1990, the sky greyed faintly for an hour as the sun rose and set beyond the horizon, but this was only because there had been no cloud.

Suddenly, there was a deafening roar in the air. The Sea King Mark 4 helicopter was directly over Jonathan Moyle's head now ... hovering ... adjusting forward slightly ... now hovering again.

The rotors thrashed away, a shattering row, but hardly disturbing the fog. Jonathan could see the yellow haze of several helicopters' searchlights desperately trying to confirm the landing. He couldn't see the machines. And he knew they couldn't see him. They maintained altitude, for the moment.

Towards the centre of the strait, huge hummocks had begun to appear, windswept snow funnelled between the mainland and islands, now turned into pillars of ice. They loomed suddenly, disappearing up into the fog, very high. Helicopter after helicopter then streamed through the mist like a swarm of giant insects.

Jonathan's face was crusted with snow, his gloved hands numb as he moved across the landing strip. He could scarcely feel the little compass in his pocket. He took his gloves off, breathed on his hands and shone a torch on to the face of the compass. The wind was howling, snow blowing horizontally. He hunched through it, with his photographer Patrick Allen snapping away furiously.

To the right, everything seemed featureless. Another white plain, set above the sea. All the way along, the shore line shelved. Snowflakes were still whirling. Between the flakes and the snatches of mist he could see a star or two.

Ten minutes later, Jonathan and Allen were in the air talking to the pilots of the Sea King as it swept over a fjord and looped out towards the barren hills beyond. They were in Norway on an assignment for *Defence Helicopter World*. For Jonathan, it was a journey into the past, a reminder of what might have been if he'd remained an RAF helicopter pilot.

Military photographer Patrick Allen had fixed up the trip to visit 846 Squadron of the Navy Commandoes at their snow-swept base at Tretten, near Lillehammer. Jonathan had pushed hard to join the assignment which was normally only open to a photographer. Allen felt that Jonathan was trying to prove to himself that he could still have succeeded as a services airman. Jonathan was also fascinated by 846 Squadron's role in dropping SAS troops behind enemy lines during the Falklands War.

The trip to Norway began ominously two weeks earlier when Jonathan showed up late at RAF Yeovilton to pick up thermal gear for the trip, which included long johns, arctic anoraks and thermal vests. It was the same story at RAF Lynham where Jonathan only just arrived in the nick of time to catch a giant C130 Transport for Norway. Being late was one of his characteristics, which many put down to his 'only child' status within a loving, caring family who were always prepared to keep an eye on his time-keeping. In the outside world he sometimes had trouble adjusting.

The first full day in Norway consisted of watching troop movements and then travelling in a Westland to pick up three members of a survival unit lost in the white wilderness.

Jonathan clearly found it hard to get used to the fact he was no longer a serving officer and many at the base were irritated when he kept behaving as if he was.

'Jonathan was a bit odd in Norway. It was completely out of character. He was so different from what he'd been like before. He was drinking quite heavily and seemed troubled,' says Allen today.

One drunken night in the officer's mess, Jonathan was even drawn into a heated discussion with a group of servicemen about how the RAF was far superior to the Navy. He insisted that the RAF would have done a far superior job of dropping those SAS troops inside Argentina during the Falklands War. He told the navy pilots he would have relished taking part in that escapade in the southernmost tip of South America.

As Allen later explained, 'A lot of it was a wind up on his behalf, but he did definitely regress into what I would call classic RAF officer mode.'

But any complications Jonathan might have felt about being in Norway were put aside when he was introduced to the Norwegian manufacturers of the Penguin missile heads which were being used by the Royal Navy in Norway. The Penguin was a missile guidance system which enabled the weapon only to hit the particular target it was programmed to recognise. It also executed a deliberately confusing 'dog-leg' turn before finally hitting its target.

The Norwegians were particularly proud of the Penguin because the US military had just paid out tens of millions of dollars for it. However, they were very sensitive about giving away too many trade secrets in case it upset their American customers.

During a specially arranged interview with the manufacturers, Jonathan startled the reserved Norwegians by asking highly technical questions about the Penguin. To start with, they accepted that he was simply doing his job as editor of *DHW*, but then he began probing about complex data that no one would need for a standard magazine article.

Eventually, Allen advised Jonathan to 'Lay off!' because it was clear that the Norwegians were becoming unnerved by his incessant questions.

Jonathan completely ignored his colleague's advice. He clearly had an agenda to find out as much as he could about the missile guidance system. Whether for his magazine or as part of Operation Valkyrie was not clear.

During the trip, Jonathan briefly mentioned his work for the MoD when he said to Allen that he had worked as 'an intelligence gatherer'.

Allen says now, 'That was all he said, but I remember thinking at the time that being the editor of a magazine like *DHW* would be the most brilliant cover. You go everywhere in the world at someone else's expense. Johnny was classic spy material. He was an incredible patriot always barking on about Queen and country. He also had so much technical knowledge.'

Jonathan knew he had 'been a right pain' during the trip to Norway and even called up Allen to apologise a few days after they returned to Britain.

'But he never really explained what his problem had been. I didn't really think much of it until much later,' recalled Allen.

*   *   *

Dublin-based defence journalist Adrian English first encountered Jonathan Moyle when he was delivering some copy to the *DHW* office in Slough. Jonathan offered English a lift to Aldershot in his Saab. English accepted and deeply regretted it from the moment he climbed into the passenger seat. He explains, 'Moyle was cutting in and out of traffic and I was relieved to get to Aldershot in one piece.'

One evening in early 1990, Jonathan was supposed to meet English for dinner at a hotel near the *DHW* office, but bailed out at the last minute because he couldn't get an article finished in time for the magazine's press deadline and had to spend the entire night at the office completing it.

English later recalled, 'I didn't know he'd cancelled until I rang him. He complained about being overloaded by Shephard Press and apologised.'

Jonathan actually found writing for the magazine much harder work than being an RAF pilot.

'War is an ugly thing, but not the ugliest of
things. The decayed and degraded state of moral
and patriotic feeling which thinks that nothing
is worth war is much worse.
The person who has nothing for which he is
willing to fight, nothing which is more
important than his own personal safety, is a
miserable creature and has no chance of being
free unless made and kept so by the exertions
of better men than himself.'

John Stewart Mills

Martin Pace was annoyed. He'd been waiting in a
crowded restaurant in downtown Singapore for
more than an hour and Jonathan had failed to
show up. Pace couldn't understand it because Jonathan
had suggested the meal in the first place. They'd pretty
much stuck together since arriving for the South-East Asia
Airshow three days earlier in mid-February 1990.

What Pace didn't realise was that as Jonathan left his
hotel to meet his friend, he was approached by the same
CIA agent he'd met at the *DHW* conference in London the
previous month. The American wanted to know if
Jonathan had any more information on the Cardoen Bell
helicopter conversions, because they were convinced that
the Chilean was about to start supplying them to Saddam

Hussein. They even gave Jonathan a photo of the aircraft in flight taken secretly by US investigators observing trials in Texas.

'We wanted to know every single detail about Cardoen, almost down to the colour of his socks. Every single piece of information was to be assessed and then eventually used against him,' explained a CIA source who worked closely with senior agency officials in London.

'Moyle might have seemed small fry, but there were dozens of versions of him around the world feeding us information.'

Jonathan cautiously informed his CIA contact that he had nothing new to tell but he would keep them informed of any developments through his British security services handler.

'See you in Chile,' were the CIA agent's parting words.

Moyle looked surprised that they knew so much about his movements. As the CIA source later explained, 'It was our business to know everyone's movements, and that included Jonathan Moyle.'

*   *   *

Throughout the Singapore Airshow, Jonathan was picking up information about projects like a vacuum cleaner. He even engineered a lunch with Bob Letter of Bell Helicopters on St Valentine's Day 1990, and deliberately excluded Martin Pace from the meeting. Jonathan questioned the Texan closely about the Cardoen deal. Letter told him categorically that Bell was not involved. However, he noted Jonathan's close and rather unsubtle line of questioning.

Martin Pace's overriding memory of Singapore was that Jonathan insisted on carrying his tatty briefcase everywhere they went. 'It was as if he was hiding something in it. He just wouldn't leave it at the hotel.' Pace was so irritated by the briefcase and Jonathan's continual concern for its whereabouts that he took a photo of Jonathan clutching it so he could tease him about it later.

Pace was puzzled by the briefcase behaviour because it was so out of character. Jonathan rarely remembered to lock his car, yet he was being so obsessively careful with his briefcase. In fact, Jonathan was carrying around the photo of the converted Bell provided by the CIA, plus dozens of documents he had gathered over the previous few months. He was worried about losing them.

Pace and Jonathan cemented their close friendship during the Singapore trip by spending many hours talking together. At one stage, the subject of suicide came up and both came to the same conclusion that there was far too much to live for. Jonathan said he was outraged by the notion of suicide and even told a story about how the father of one of his own father's pupils at school in Yeovil had hanged himself and what a cowardly act that was.

Pace saw many sides of Jonathan's character and considered him a 'friend for life, warts and all'.

On one occasion, they were in a run-down Chinese restaurant in Singapore when the subject of Annette came up. Pace said to Jonathan, 'Why don't we forget all this and just go travelling for a year? You, me and Annette. We'll just take off. Blow a few thousand, tour Europe and then head for Australia.'

'Annette would love that,' Jonathan replied. But he knew in his heart that he was so entrenched in mortgages and marriage plans by this stage that he could never make such a trip.

On the flight back from Singapore, Jonathan found himself sitting near his old friend and former *DHW* editor Paul Beaver. The two men had been so busy at the airshow they hadn't had a chance to meet.

'We've got to talk, Jonathan,' Beaver told his colleague once the Jumbo had taken off. The two men found an empty row of seats in the business-class section and began swapping the latest information about Cardoen's Bell conversion plans.

Beaver believed it was significant that Cardoen's converted helicopters were not in evidence at the Singapore show. Both men knew that Cardoen wasn't interested in the Asian market. His primary aim was to persuade Saddam Hussein to purchase the converted helicopters as part of the dictator's ominous re-arming schedule for Iraq. And there were strong rumours that second-hand helicopter dealers were trying to buy up used Bell helicopters. The implication was that they were being collected to be converted into gunships using Cardoen's 'kit'.

Beaver told his friend that he had established that Cardoen intended selling his converted Bell for just under $3m, compared to the $9m-$13m for new rivals like the Apache, $7.5m for a new Bell (called the LH), and $4m for the Agusta A-129 Mangusta. The price would include an air–surface weapon system which was claimed to have a range of 2,000 metres. Jonathan was captivated by this new information. He wondered how Cardoen could develop such a sophisticated system without some highly knowledgeable technical advice.

A sale of 100 models to Iraq would raise $300m in revenue, but Beaver and Jonathan suspected that many more than that would eventually be sold to Saddam Hussein. Beaver had gathered much of his information through sources inside the arms industry and via freelance defence journalist David Harvey, based in Washington.

By the time the Singapore Airlines 747 touched down at Heathrow, Jonathan had punched out six pages of data about the converted Bells on to his lap-top computer to pass on to his handler as part of his information gathering on behalf of Operation Valkyrie.

*   *   *

On 22 February 1990, Jonathan took his aunt Pat out for dinner near her home in Kingston, Surrey. It was a belated thank you for putting up with having him as a part-time lodger over the previous year or so.

Just before they left the house, Pat Moyle noticed that her nephew seemed slightly on edge. He even followed her into the kitchen and started talking about his trip to Chile for an airshow the following month.

Jonathan mentioned that he had been working on a story about how civilian helicopters were being converted into gunships.

'Jonathan told me it was completely unacceptable because it gave Iraq a dangerous advantage,' Pat later recalled.

Jonathan told his aunt he was going to check up on the Bell situation while he was in Chile. It sounded as if it was the main purpose of his trip.

Two days later, on 24 February, Jonathan travelled to Germany for a week of skiing with fiancée Annette. He was exhausted after many months of intense work for *DHW* and the intelligence services. It was a much-needed break.

On the train back from the ski resort, the couple talked excitedly about their wedding plans. When Jonathan briefly mentioned the trip to FIDAE in Chile, Annette suddenly felt an overriding feeling of gloom. 'I had a feeling I wouldn't see him again after he went to South America. I was so worried about him,' recalled Annette.

Annette tried to keep her fears to herself on that train journey, but Jonathan noticed that his fiancée seemed upset by something.

'What's the matter?' he asked Annette.

'I'm so afraid about you going to Chile.'

Jonathan looked puzzled. 'You don't want me to go?'

Annette sensed something in his tone. 'Why? Shouldn't you go?'

'I won't go then,' replied Jonathan.

Then Annette snapped out of her mood of self-pity. 'No, this is stupid. You should go.'

But she couldn't help feeling that Jonathan knew he was facing something very dangerous.

*   *   *

Besides his re-ignited love for Annette Kissenbeck, Jonathan's other great passion had become the family home at Highcliff House at Branscombe, Devon. He adored the property and spent virtually all his free time working on improving it.

One freezing winter day, Jonathan bought a motorised fountain for the pond at the front of the house and dived into the icy pond in his swimming trunks just to install the pump.

The cliffs near Branscombe were lofty, imposing and extremely beautiful, with rocks festooned in ivy and creepers offering perfect nesting for gulls on their ledges. Two weeks before his departure for South America, Jonathan strolled along those same windswept cliffs with his mother on a sunny March morning. They talked about the house, the garden, the weather, but carefully avoided the one subject uppermost on both their minds — the forthcoming trip to FIDAE in Chile.

Diana Moyle didn't feel it her right to probe too deeply, but she needed some reassurance as they headed back towards Highcliff House on the public footpath that twisted its way through the valley of Branscombe. Chile sounded remote and dangerous, even though she was under the impression that he was travelling to South America on *DHW* business.

'Do be careful, Jonathan. I'm so worried about your trip.'

Diana had always been impressed by the way her son was so sure of himself, so committed. He was indestructible, or so it seemed. Despite the set-backs, everyone considered Jonathan one of life's achievers. After all, he had admirably bounced back after leaving the RAF.

This time, however, Diana Moyle had nagging doubts.

'There's nothing to worry about, Mum,' breezed Jonathan. 'I'm planning to do an article on a Chilean arms dealer called Carlos Cardoen. He's made a fortune out of weapons and I'm going to find out all about him.'

Jonathan sounded so up-beat about it all.

Diana didn't really want to know any more. She didn't want to tempt fate.

'Have you told Annette about what you're doing?'

'Not really,' replied Jonathan. 'I didn't want to worry her about it.'

He paused for a moment as they crossed the village high street.

'D'you think I should tell her?'

Diana didn't reply, and they walked the rest of the way home in silence.

*   *   *

On 18 March 1990, Annette flew over from Germany for an interview for a job as a paediatrician at Queen Charlotte's Hospital in West London. The couple also managed some much needed pre-wedding preparations.

Annette stayed with Jonathan at his aunt Pat's house in Kingston while she was away in Romania. They enjoyed candle-lit romantic dinners together and even went to the West End to look for a ball gown for Annette to wear at her wedding reception. Jonathan encouraged Annette to choose a traditional-looking gown because he did not particularly like the bright colours which were the fashion at the time.

Annette's interview for the paediatrician's job went so well that she was immediately offered the post. Everything seemed to be falling into place perfectly for the couple.

They also began looking for a flat in the Chiswick area of West London. It was near the M4 motorway, which was Jonathan's route out of London to Branscombe, Devon. Jonathan and his parents had hopes of eventually converting a barn in the grounds of Highcliff House which would then become the young couple's weekend home.

On Friday afternoon, 23 March, Jonathan escorted Annette to London's Victoria Station where she was to catch a train to Gatwick Airport for a plane to Munich.

As the train pulled away from the platform, Annette mouthed the words, 'Take care' to her fiancé. She hid her tears so as not to upset him, but she couldn't hold them back as the train gathered speed. She cried most of the way to Gatwick.

*   *   *

The only other person to see Jonathan the day he departed for Chile was close friend and work colleague Martin Pace.

Jonathan showed up at Pace's flat less than an hour after seeing Annette off at Victoria Station. He parked his car up outside his friend's flat in Chiswick and knocked on the door.

Pace was surprised to see Jonathan, who charged straight past him muttering, 'I'm dying for a crap.'

A few minutes later, Jonathan emerged from the bathroom and told Pace he had been looking in Chiswick for properties with Annette. Then he slung the clothes he'd kept at Pace's flat into a bag and headed outside to hail a passing taxi to Heathrow Airport for the flight to Chile.

In his Saab parked outside Pace's flat, Jonathan left a half-finished box of chocolates given to him by Annette just a few hours earlier.

*   *   *

Jonathan was to fly to Chile by Iberia Airlines because his Chilean Air Force hosts had a special fare discount with the Spanish company.

From Heathrow, Jonathan's flight went first to Madrid to pick up the connection for Santiago, Chile. While waiting in Madrid, Jonathan called Annette in Germany to make sure she had arrived home safely. It was a touching gesture — ample evidence that while Jonathan rarely considered risks to himself, he never stopped worrying about others, especially Annette.

Twelve hours later, the captain of Iberia flight 905 switched on the seat-belt signs before warning passengers that heavy turbulence was expected over the Andes during the 747's gradual descent into Santiago. Jonathan looked out of his window seat at the huge expanse of snow-peaked mountains below and noticed the tiny dots of a mountaineering team scaling a peak that seemed almost as high as the plane, which pitched wildly in the air.

But the bumpy ride on board the Jumbo that morning of 24 March 1990, was nothing compared to the turbulent times ahead for Jonathan.

Part 2
The Cataract
of Death

'I see the Past
Lying beneath me with its
sounds and sights ... And hear
above me on the autumnal blast
The cataract of death
far thundering from the heights ...'

Henry Wadsworth Longfellow,
Mezzo Cammin

'My words are not spoken in bitterness, but in disappointment. There will be a moral judgement on those who have betrayed the oath they took as soldiers of Chile ... They have the might and they can enslave us, but they cannot halt the world's social processes, not with crimes, nor with guns ... May you go forward in the knowledge that, sooner rather than later, the great avenues will open once again, along which free citizens will march in order to build a better society. Long live Chile! Long live the people! Long live the workers! These are my last words, and I am sure that this sacrifice will constitute a moral lesson which will punish cowardice, perfidy and treason.'

The last words of Chilean President Salvador Allende, part of a radio address on 11 September 1973, just before his own air force jet fighters bombed the Presidential Palace in Santiago and Allende apparently committed suicide.

Santiago, Chile

'Therefore is the anger of the Lord
kindled against his people,
and he hath stretched forth his hand against
them, and hath smitten them:
and the hills did tremble,
and their carcasses were torn
in the midst of the streets.'

Isaiah, 5:25

Santiago during the early months of 1990 was a melting pot of gossip and innuendo centring around shady arms dealing. During years of oppression and political killings under the strong-arm leadership of General Augusto Pinochet, Chile had become an armaments *entrepôt*, not just for Latin America, but for much of the Developing World — a back-door route for arms sales to practically any country having difficulty buying from the four leading producers: the United States, the USSR, Britain and France.

In early March 1990, after 16 years of military dictatorship, Pinochet finally moved out of the Presidential Palace to make way for the democratic government of Señor Patricio Aylwin Azocar. But Chile's new democracy immediately had to come to terms with the blatant evidence of human rights violations.

There were regular television news bulletins about the recently discovered mass graves of Pinochet's political opponents. Often, dozens of bodies were found huddled together on the outskirts of villages. Tens of thousand of people had been killed or just disappeared.

Certainly, the streets of Santiago's city centre were clean. On the surface, the population seemed well fed, healthily preoccupied with work and relatively happy with their lot. But on the poor side of town, unemployment was rife and you could still hire a hitman for just US$500.

General Pinochet lost a plebiscite and, although still head of the Army, had been forced to stand aside for democracy. Chile was looking abroad, trying to rehabilitate its international reputation. One result of this was the new government's continued sponsorship of an airshow called FIDAE, even though it had been set up ten years earlier by the Chilean Air Force's Chief-of-Staff under the Pinochet régime. Even under the repressive military dictatorship, 13 countries, including Britain and the USA, were represented at the first show in 1980. It was a sort of Latin-American Farnborough.

By March 1990, FIDAE featured 568 stands with more than 190 exhibitors from 22 countries.

Chile was on the verge of becoming a model of growth and stability, largely because of its emphasis on international business.

Tucked between the towering Andes and the wide Pacific, this narrow strip of country might be excused for being insular. But, despite its geographical isolation, Chile capitalised on international trade and investment like no other country in the region.

With a population of only 13 million, Chile was well aware that it wasn't a big enough market for many of its own companies to survive. Export revenues were increasing every year. Chile's total trade — imports and exports —

represents more than 40% of gross domestic product.

To gain advantages in the lucrative US market, Chile even began lobbying in Washington to join the North American Free Trade Agreement (NAFTA).

Meanwhile, newly elected President Aylwin pledged to set up a Commission for Truth and Reconciliation to investigate the human rights violations between 1973 and 1990.

'The Commission is part of an effort to establish the truth in Chile,' explained Commission member José Zalaquett. 'We are there to return to the country a chapter of its history that was stolen from it. In the Greek myth you find you know that the father is going to search for the body of the son to give him a proper burial. It's a basic aspect of civilisation, it's deep inside all ourselves that we want to honour our dead, to give them a decent place of rest and this has been denied to people. People were executed and then buried in unknown places. Now these places are coming to the surface.'

However, others suspected the killings were still going on.

Santiago

'Never turn your back on a threatened danger
and try to run away from it. If you do that,
you will double the danger. But if you meet it
promptly and without flinching,
you will reduce the danger by half.
Never run away from anything. Never!'

Winston Churchill

The goose-stepping guards in their knee-high brown
leather boots and khaki uniforms were changing
over in front of the President's Palace in the centre
of downtown Santiago when Jonathan Moyle's black-and-
yellow taxi passed on its way from the airport. It was an
impeccable piece of military drill by members of the
paramilitary Carabiñeros force, one which had taken place
like clockwork since General Pinochet seized power in
Chile 17 years earlier. True, there was a new
democratically elected government, but the ceremony still
remained the same.

Jonathan's taxi drew up at the Carrera Hotel, a vast
piece of 1930s architecture whose huge grey walls
dominated one side of the Plaza de la Constitucion.
Nearby, the restored beauty of the President's Palace
belied the events of 17 years ago, *el Presidente* Salvadore

Allende died as British-made Hawker jets dive-bombed his living quarters. The hotel's imposing entrance with its uniformed staff gave off an air of colonial grandeur. That week it was bristling with arms merchants, journalists and official brass.

At the hotel's front entrance, at least three American limousines were constantly available for hire as taxis. During the worst years of oppression, locals became convinced that the drivers were members of the Pinochet secret police keeping a close watch on foreign visitors.

Jonathan made his way towards the hotel lobby, past the Carrera doormen in their green double-breasted trench coats, as piped muzak wafted across the marble floor. At reception, he handed in his passport (Number 816218), complete with a 30-day visa issued from the Chilean Embassy in London.

Jonathan then headed for the art deco elevators with their multi-coloured wood and ornate brass fittings. His room, 1406 on the 14th floor of the Carrera, was located at the end of a long corridor next to the service elevator, which had been used many times over the years by guests secretly smuggling girls into their rooms from the side entrance in the narrow street below.

Room 1406 was spacious with an entrance hallway, a desk and chair, television, mini-bar fridge and a closet almost large enough to walk into. The only slight irritation was that the room overlooked the narrow side-street of Bombero Salas, where the noise of motorbikes and trucks provided a permanent cacophony day and night.

Jonathan then went up to the roof of the Carrera to see the swimming pool and restaurant. He was going to try to swim a dozen lengths most mornings. Up on top of the hotel you could see between the skyscrapers of downtown Santiago to the rich residential area of Las Condes miles away and, beyond, the foothills of the Andes. The roads became much wider outside the city centre and patches of green sprouted up in the suburbs where the houses ran in rows between the avenues.

Other hotels in the small city centre were also packed with free-spending arms dealers, government officials and military personnel from more than 50 countries. But the place with the most important guests was the Carrera. The Chilean Air Force even hired their own security guard, Señor Juan Bascunan, to keep an eye on the VIPs.

One of the largest contingents was from Iraq. And with those official delegates came other, more shadowy figures from the intelligence and security services, including Saddam Hussein's feared Mukhabarat.

Jonathan met up with fellow defence journalists Tony Robinson and Adrian English soon after checking into the Carrera.

A couple of hours later the three went for a walk on the herring-bone-bricked sidewalks of downtown Santiago. English was surprised at how energetic Jonathan seemed to be, despite only having just got off a plane from Europe.

The journalists walked up a busy street called Augustinas past the banks, boutiques and office blocks, and stumbled upon two hole-in-the-wall bars where they tasted the delights of the local speciality, Pisco Sour, a lethal concoction of spirit made from white grapes mixed with fresh lemon, sugar and crushed ice cubes. The origins of Pisco had caused a heated debate for hundreds of years between Peru and Chile, which both claimed to have discovered the unique-tasting grape in two towns both called Pisco.

On the way back to the hotel, Jonathan and Robinson were almost run over by one of the careering dirty yellow-and-white Mercedes buses that surge through the city streets at peak times. Paid on the number of times they can circuit the city, the drivers were renowned for taking no prisoners.

The group of Britons also stopped at the Café de Brasil

on the corner of Moneda and Morande, near the Carrera Hotel, where dark-haired waitresses in black micro mini-dresses, high heels and flesh-coloured stockings provided *cortado* coffees and glasses of mineral water for weary city businessmen.

Back at the Carrera early that evening, Jonathan phoned his parents in Devon and Annette in Germany to tell them he had arrived safely.

He then had a quiet supper with Tony Robinson in the hotel restaurant before retiring to bed. Jet-lag had finally caught up with him.

The following day, Jonathan made his way to El Bosque airfield on Gran Avenida, in Santiago's southern suburbs, for the opening ceremony of FIDAE. El Bosque was a pilot cadet training base which had been transformed into South America's largest air fair over three months of careful preparation.

At the opening, Jonathan was introduced to Pedro del Fierro, the Chilean freelance journalist for the magazine *Defence Weekly*. Jonathan asked del Fierro about Dr Carlos Cardoen's Bell helicopter conversion plans. He was particularly interested in how weapons would be carried on the aircraft and their capabilities.

Pedro del Fierro, known as Peter, was a strange combination of journalist and arms dealer — a dark-haired, dark-eyed charming character with a Latin habit of staring intently into people's eyes when speaking. He and Jonathan hit it off immediately, but he warned Jonathan that digging up new information on Cardoen would not be easy.

On the walls of del Fierro's office in the Santiago suburb of Providencia were posters of MiG 29s, Colt Python pistols and Smith and Wesson .38 Specials. There was even a dent where the 6ft 2in del Fierro had punched the wall in anger and, rather incongruously, there was also a drawing by one of his young children of a helicopter on a bombing mission.

Del Fierro was intrigued by Jonathan because he

seemed so determined to dig up some exciting stories for his magazine.

Jonathan toasted his trip with del Fierro and British journalist Adrian English by drinking a large Pisco Sour at the opening ceremony. This was followed by large helpings of beef and fruity Chilean red wine at a special luncheon. However, English couldn't help noticing that Jonathan almost constantly gravitated towards the military personnel rather than the arms company executives.

'I told him to watch his back. He laughed at me. But I knew the danger of getting too close to those sort of characters,' says English today.

Carlos Cardoen turned up for the opening ceremony with his close friend, the new Chilean President Patricio Aylwin, further evidence of the arms entrepreneur's power and influence in Chile. Also present was the British Ambassador Alan White.

Jonathan was fascinated by FIDAE because it was such an unlikely combination of civilian and military products. The Americans had the largest number of stands in their own special hangar but the French, British, Israelis and South Africans were also highly prominent. As Jonathan wandered from hangar to hangar he came across many familiar faces from the airshow circuit.

The most impressive British product at FIDAE that year was the Harrier Jump-Jet which had made such a huge impression during the Falklands War when the Chileans aided the British against their Argentinian neighbours. A Harrier GR.3 was specially flown in by the RAF from Belize. Throughout the first day of FIDAE it made regular demonstrations of its vertical flight capabilities. But there was almost a very serious accident when the Harrier cut its engines on landing and came down so hard that its undercarriage nearly collapsed.

During that first day, Jonathan also met a friendly Chilean Air Force helicopter pilot who was so impressed by

Jonathan's RAF credentials that he asked him if he would like to join him and some VIPs for a 1,500-mile flight south to the military port of Punta Arenas for a helicopter trip to Antarctica later that week. The pilot decided that Jonathan's RAF background qualified him for the trip, unlike the other journalists. Some of the other defence reporters had already begun to resent the way Jonathan was being treated.

'In many ways, he was acting more like a member of the military than a journalist,' recalled one of the British journalists at FIDAE that year. 'He was constantly asking highly technical questions, and one got the impression he was involved in things at a different level from the rest of us.'

At FIDAE, Jonathan also came across another British journalist called Terry Gander. Gander was surprised when Jonathan began asking some rather tactless questions about Cardoen's Bell conversions. 'He was obsessed with its military capabilities even though no one was admitting that that was its function,' says Gander.

'If you delve too far into anything in this business you can become very, very unpopular,' added Gander. And he should know, as he has been frequently vetted by British intelligence since starting his career as a defence journalist 20 years earlier. 'They like to keep an eye on everyone.'

Jonathan wasn't particularly impressed by Gander's advice to tread carefully. The scene was set, now he intended to get down to the business of intelligence gathering.

16

Santiago

'You cannot put a rope around the neck
of an idea; you cannot put an idea
up against the barrack-square wall
and riddle it with bullets;
you cannot confine it in the strongest
prison cell your slaves could ever build.'

Sean O'Casey, Death of Thomas Ashe *(1918)*

On Monday, 26 March, Jonathan and Pedro del Fierro visited the Cardoen stand at FIDAE. Jonathan spent at least an hour inspecting a mock-up of the converted Bell helicopter. Cardoen was still insisting the aircraft had been developed for an agricultural role, even though the life-size model on display was painted in camouflage colours.

'Jonathan couldn't disguise his interest in the helicopter. He wanted to know everything about it,' recalled Pedro del Fierro. 'He kept walking round and round it. Many of Cardoen's people were watching us. I knew it was annoying them.'

At one stage, Jonathan questioned one of the Cardoen staff on duty at the stand at length and in some detail about the helicopter.

'This guy was obviously getting quite irritated with Jonathan. In the end, I pulled Jonathan away and told him to cool it,' says del Fierro.

Jonathan was surprised by the number of freelance 'technical experts' working on the Cardoen stand and he was particularly intrigued by one South African whom he knew worked full-time for a company in Cape Town.

Many of Cardoen's 'technical experts' were actually part of an exchange deal with a South African company co-producing bomb fuses with the Chilean entrepreneur. When journalist Terry Gander started asking awkward questions at the stand about the fuses he was delicately rebuffed. 'It was a real "secret squirrel" operation. Every time I tried to ask any questions about the fuses, I got the complete brush-off,' he later recalled. It seemed that Cardoen was happy to earn millions of pounds out of his home-produced weaponry, but he didn't want to reveal any uncomfortable details to the world.

Amongst those South Africans was a notorious Colonel in the South African secret police who was sent over on an 'exchange deal' with Cardoen Industrias. He was in Chile with a brief to keep an eye on what the enemies of apartheid were buying in the way of arms. He also happened to be a trained killer, responsible for the deaths of more than 50 people over the previous 20 years.

The Cardoen fuses were a classic 'turn-key' operation. Terry Gander explains, 'Cardoen would set up a factory to produce all the parts and then the customer would assemble it.'

It all sounded rather similar to those Airfix model planes Jonathan so lovingly constructed during his childhood.

*   *   *

At all the important stands at FIDAE, Jonathan enthusiastically handed his business card to everyone and persuaded dozens of people to sign up for subscriptions to *Defence Helicopter World*.

Throughout all this, he kept his briefcase constantly by his side just as he had in Singapore. He did not want to risk anyone else getting their hands on it.

Jonathan discovered from one friendly character on the Bell stand in the US Pavilion that the American company had rejected an approach from Cardoen in 1989 when he wanted to purchase at least 100 Bell 206s. They had been concerned that he might be planning to convert them into gunships for Saddam Hussein.

Cardoen was so annoyed by Bell's refusal to help that his representatives immediately began a worldwide search for second-hand Bells. 'They were told to find them anywhere. They were needed urgently,' explained a former Cardoen employee.

Also at Bell that day was Texan stand designer Owen Day. Jonathan bombarded him with questions about Cardoen's Bell conversion plans and the two men exchanged cards.

Owen Day's opinion of Cardoen was refreshingly candid. He told Jonathan, 'Cardoen's a wheeler-dealer alright. Why, his hangar looks like the K-Mart of weapons.'

Later that Monday afternoon, Jonathan visited the Bolivian consulate in Santiago to collect a visa for his *DHW* trip to accompany DEA helicopters in an anti-drugs operation in La Paz, Bolivia, the following week.

That evening, Jonathan dined at the Hereford Grill Steak House in the suburb of Providencia with Pedro del Fierro, his wife Soledad, a well-known local doctor, and other journalists including Adrian English, Tony Robinson and Terry Gander from Jane's *Defence* publications.

Jonathan was in good spirits and everyone drank numerous Pisco Sours. The party broke up at about midnight and Pedro del Fierro noticed that Jonathan was complaining of an upset stomach, but it didn't seem too serious. The other guests ribbed Jonathan because he appeared to be the first one of them on that trip to have caught 'Chileitis', a notorious stomach complaint usually caused by infected local drinking water.

*   *   *

Gossip was an inevitable part of a show like FIDAE and the following day, Tuesday, 27 March, Jonathan picked up on a story going around that Chile and Argentina were preparing to go to war over sovereignty of the Beagle Channel. It was well known in the defence world at the time that Argentina had the money to invest in a nuclear weapons programme.

One woman journalist from an American press agency was floating the idea that Chile was intending to manufacture its own brand of deadly nerve gas to counter Argentina's nuclear plans. Allegedly, they wanted to use the gas as a deterrent to Argentina and so avoid a nuclear attack.

Jonathan was convinced that the converted Bell helicopters were capable of being armed with chemicals and decided to visit the Cardoen stand again to check out the aircraft's specifications even more carefully. It was entirely feasible that the aircraft could be used to drop the nerve gas across the Argentine border.

Jonathan's close questioning of one Cardoen employee did not go unnoticed by senior executives of the company.

*   *   *

Early on the morning of Wednesday, 28 March, Jonathan telephoned the *DHW* offices at Shephard Press to confirm his travel arrangements for the trip to Bolivia the following

Saturday. He asked editorial assistant Dorothy Dawson to contact the US Embassy representative in Bolivia and confirm a meeting.

That day, Jonathan attended a lunchtime reception at Carlos Cardoen's vast stand at FIDAE. Guest of honour at the reception was Cardoen's relative-by-marriage, new Chilean President Patricio Aylwin.

Once again, Jonathan spent ages inspecting the full-scale mock-up of the converted Bell helicopter. He was particularly fascinated by the equipment mountings and fittings which could easily have been converted to military use. Jonathan had already picked up a suggestion that Cardoen was developing his own version of the sophisticated Helios weapons guidance system which would make the converted Bells even more lethal war machines.

The Bell 206 L-3 derivative was openly being touted by Cardoen and his people as an agricultural aircraft aimed at any country's domestic market. No mention was made of its military potential. And few dared to ask.

The principal modification entailed replacing the Bell two-man cockpit with a pointed, single-seat design that provided a wider viewing angle. Cardoen claimed an identical fuel and speed performance to the basic Bell 206.

Many onlookers at the show considered Cardoen's scheme to be a classic Mid-Life Update. 'You look at what's on the market and come up with a way of updating it, rather than buying the latest model,' was how one arms dealer put it.

Cardoen had only spent $6m developing the project, reflecting the low cost of manpower in Chile. He even proudly claimed at FIDAE that Bell had already agreed a component supply contract. But this was a lie. Bell had carefully distanced themselves from the project.

By the time of FIDAE '90, the helicopter was still undergoing air-worthiness certification tests in Texas.

At his reception that Wednesday, Cardoen proudly announced to guests: 'We have been working on this project for over four years and it means to Chile a large step into the technical capacities. We believe that the only way that Third World countries and developing countries are going to find their way in this world is by applying their imagination and putting it into service for the rest of the world.' Naturally, the good doctor's patriotic speech received rousing applause.

The Bell conversion was entirely the brainchild of Cardoen and no one could discourage him from turning his dream into a lucrative reality. Cardoen — with his annual revenue of at least $350m, despite a workforce of just 3,000 — seemed to be sitting on an even larger financial goldmine if the Bell project took off. There was no denying that it was a brilliantly simple idea.

Throughout all this, Cardoen saw himself as a perfectly legitimate businessman with the patriotic interests of Chile at heart. When he was cornered by one journalist about the morals of arms dealing, he coolly replied, 'People do not understand how this country makes business. We are respected because we produce guns.'

Cardoen was referred to as a 'Morena' — a dark-skinned white man — by other Chileans. His complexion was smooth, not the usual pitted surface common in his compatriots. His hair was thick and grey. He wasn't a big man, but you could tell by his cold stare that if he became angry, anything could happen.

British journalist Mike Gething was also at the Cardoen stand that day, and he actually asked Cardoen up-front about rumours that the converted Bells would be used for military purposes. Cardoen insisted the aircraft would primarily be used for light crop-spraying. But his 'reassurance' simply made Gething wonder if the helicopters were really intended for chemical warfare.

Towards the end of the Cardoen reception, Jonathan

and other magazine editors were given a Cardoen Industrias plastic calculator shaped like a yellow book of matches and an alarm clock radio embossed with the company's logo.

It was just after this that Jonathan cornered Cardoen and bluntly asked him exactly what the converted Bells would be used for. Cardoen squinted and looked straight at Jonathan with an inquisitive expression on his face but did not reply. Jonathan then pressed Cardoen about whether he had developed his own version of the sophisticated Helios weapons guidance system to integrate into the converted Bells. Any system based on Helios would significantly increase the machine's military capability.

Just then, Cardoen's nervy public relations chief, Raul Montecinos, appeared next to his boss and introduced himself. Montecinos was so neurotic at work that he was nicknamed 'El Gritopata' — the cryer — by colleagues. He was a nondescript man in his early 60s with a small nose and light coloured skin. His suits were always well fitted and his silver hair was very wavy and his eyes were brown. But Montecinos did not like to look anyone directly in the eye.

Cardoen was clearly irritated by Jonathan's detailed questions and seemed relieved when his greasy PR man interrupted Jonathan.

'Mr. Moyle. These are very important points you are making but it is too busy to talk about them here. Where are you staying?'

'The Carrera.'

'Perfecto. We will meet there tonight. Seven thirty?'

'Okay,' an irritated Jonathan replied. He hated the way Montecinos had cut him dead.

At Cardoen Industrias's impressive tower-block headquarters overlooking the river Mapocho in downtown Santiago, PR chief Montecinos had a reputation as a control freak. 'He shouted at secretaries and tried to cover his back whenever he made a mistake. He was also always calling up newspapers complaining about articles on Cardoen. One minute he was charming, then the next he was very angry,' recalled one former colleague.

Montecinos's links to the Iraqi secret police, the Mukhabarat, had been forged during more than half-a-dozen trips to Iraq with Carlos Cardoen. The Iraqis considered Montecinos to be Cardoen's most trusted lieutenant. He had, in many ways, become their eyes and ears inside the Cardoen corporation. Cardoen knew about this but chose to ignore it, on the basis that if it made his most important clients happy, then he had no problem with it.

Raul Montecinos was not an educated man by any means. He'd started work as a copy boy on a newspaper at 14 and sometimes he seemed more like an explosive bully than a highly-paid senior executive. That made him potentially a very dangerous man.

Montecinos feared that the huge financial deal to sell the converted Bells to Iraq would crumble if anyone fully exposed the military purpose of the aircraft and Cardoen's self-built version of the Helios weapons guidance system. It would also embarrass newly-installed Chilean leader Patricio Aylwin, whose successful presidential campaign had been bolstered to the tune of $1m by Carlos Cardoen.

*   *   *

Fellow journalist Adrian English saw Jonathan talking to Cardoen that afternoon. 'It was clear he was digging away at Cardoen and asking some damn awkward questions.' English also noticed the edgy state of Raul Montecinos.

Carlos Cardoen loathed bad publicity, especially when it concerned his beloved converted Bells, because he feared any negative coverage could jeopardise his chances of FAA certification for the machines.

The FAA was obliged to grant certification if the aircraft were not for military use. They were told that the converted helicopters would be for agricultural and firefighting duties. At this stage, neither Bell nor the CIA had been able to provide sufficient evidence to the contrary, despite all their efforts.

A few minutes after his meeting with Cardoen, Jonathan encountered Gordon Reid, the First Secretary at the British Embassy. Reid started backing away from Jonathan the moment Jonathan began asking awkward questions, such as which defence companies he believed had encouraged Cardoen to develop his own version of the Helios guidance system for the converted Bell helicopters.

'Moyle was quite indignant with Reid and it was obvious that Reid did not want to get involved. He actually looked quite embarrassed,' recalls one eye-witness who was at the meeting.

Jonathan took down copious notes at the Cardoen reception and even told local journalist Pedro del Fierro he thought it was outrageous that Cardoen could get away with developing his own versions of sophisticated weapons systems and then export them to Iraq.

'Jonathan seemed genuinely concerned. I shrugged my shoulders and tried to explain to him that Carlos Cardoen was so powerful he could do what the hell he wanted,' explains del Fierro.

Many of the defence journalists who visited the Cardoen stand that day were surprised there wasn't a working version of the converted Bell on display, considering it was obviously one of their most important exhibits. When Mike Gething tried to get a photo of a flying prototype aircraft, he was told none was available.

'It struck me as odd at the time,' says Gething. 'There I was, a Western journalist, wanting to know more about a new and interesting project which they said they wanted to market to the world, but there was not even a photo of it available. They just didn't really want to tell us anything about it.'

Jonathan did not have such problems. He had already been given a photo of the aircraft in flight, taken secretly by US investigators observing air trials in Texas.

Frustrated by the lack of hard information on the Bell conversions, Mike Gething asked Carlos Cardoen outright whom he was intending to sell them to.

'Whoever wants to do business with me,' came the unhesitating reply.

Gething also heard more rumours about Cardoen buying up dozens of second-hand Bell helicopters all over the world on behalf of the Iraqis. He presumed they were going to be converted by Cardoen.

More and more unscrupulous second-hand helicopter salesmen in the United States were being briefed by middlemen for the Iraqis and Carlos Cardoen to look out for any available Bells the moment they came on the market.

At the Cardoen stand at FIDAE, Jonathan was reintroduced to Clem Bailey, President of Global Helicopters, majority-owned by Cardoen and in the process of gaining FAA certification for the converted Bells. Ex-fighter pilot Clem Bailey cut a dapper figure with his tailored suits and neat, grey swept-back hair. But he rapidly became unnerved by the extent of Jonathan's questions. Bailey's alarm bells had been ringing about Jonathan ever since his visit to Global four months earlier.

But then Bailey had good reason to be fearful of any prying journalists. He was up to his neck in shady deals with Cardoen and had even banked vast sums of the Chilean's cash in various Swiss bank accounts.

'Clem allowed Cardoen to control him,' explained one former Global employee. 'But then without Cardoen's cash, Clem's company would have crumbled at that time. He had no choice but to play along with Cardoen.'

Clem Bailey had become part of Carlos Cardoen's inner

circle after the Chilean bought into Global. Cardoen recognised that, without Global's involvement, he would never get the Bell conversion scheme off the ground.

Jonathan asked Bailey if he knew the helicopters were going to be used for conventional and chemical warfare. He smiled and tried to change the subject. Carlos Cardoen was effectively saving his ailing company by injecting millions of dollars into it so he could get FAA certification for the machines. He did not want to hear such talk.

Ex-Global salesman Mike Robbins — now working for Bell in India — was present at the meeting between Jonathan and Bailey. 'Moyle was very interested in the Cardoen Bell programme. He was very knowledgeable about it,' is how the American remembers it today.

Jonathan wanted to know precise — and potentially embarrassing — details about the relationship between Global, Cardoen and Bell. He even mentioned to Robbins and Bailey that he thought Bell had set up the deal in the first place. The helicopter manufacturer has always strenuously denied this.

At this time there was no US ban on arms sales to Iraq, although Robbins thought that Global would not sanction the sale of the converted Bells to Saddam Hussein if Cardoen proposed such a plan. But did Cardoen care what anyone thought on such matters? Jonathan assumed he did not.

Within minutes of Jonathan leaving the Cardoen stand, Clem Bailey spoke to Cardoen's tense public relations executive Raul Montecinos. One journalist who was standing nearby heard Bailey tell Montecinos he was concerned that the wrong type of publicity would completely wreck plans for FAA certification.

'Both of them looked very worried,' that source later explained.

It was certainly true that Jonathan's inquiries were no different in substance from those of at least half-a-dozen other journalists at FIDAE. But Jonathan's work on behalf of Operation Valkyrie would cause Cardoen and Bailey far more concern. They were convinced that Jonathan had a hidden agenda.

17
Santiago

'One man with courage makes a majority.'

Andrew Jackson

As Jonathan Moyle strolled away from the Cardoen stand on 28 March, he was approached by two military attachés from the British Embassy called Captain John Finnegan and Group Captain Barry Hall. They'd earlier seen Jonathan talking to Carlos Cardoen about the Bell helicopter conversions.

Jonathan sat down and had a *cortado* with the two attachés at the coffee bar in the centre of the show. Finnegan and Hall knew about Jonathan's freelance status and his work on Operation Valkyrie and advised him to be careful.

One member of the embassy staff later explained, 'Their agenda at FIDAE was to keep an eye on all major arms developments, including sales and manufacture.

Jonathan's name had been passed to them by London and they wanted to ensure that he understood that the ground rules in Chile were a lot different from the UK.'

Nearby, two members of the Iraqi delegation, who'd also been at the Cardoen stand earlier, noticed the three men sitting together. They knew the two military attachés well, but they were concerned about the third man, Jonathan Moyle. Cardoen's PR man, Raul Montecinos, had already told the Iraqis that the young Englishmen had been asking too many questions, even for a journalist. Why was he now talking to the British 'spies'?

That afternoon, Jonathan told the two military attachés about the Chilean nerve gas story he'd picked up the previous day. He felt it was his duty to keep them informed of such developments.

Finnegan and Hall told Jonathan he would be contacted later that day by the same CIA agent that he had met at the helicopter conference in London earlier that year and later in Singapore. He was to offer the Americans all the information he had on Cardoen. It didn't even matter if much of the information was already known to them because they wanted to make their file on Cardoen airtight. They were looking for any extra clues that would enable them to come down on Cardoen heavily. Jonathan was surprised that the British were working so closely with the Americans.

Shortly after this, the Iraqis told Montecinos how they had seen the young journalist meet with the two British 'spies'. Montecinos was already angry about Jonathan's snooping because he knew he would get the blame from Cardoen if a journalist started causing trouble. But to hear that Jonathan might also be a spy was disastrous news.

That afternoon, Jonathan spent some considerable time at a number of the French companies at FIDAE trying to gather enough data to write an article about a new French-made helicopter warship for the following issue of *DHW*.

Later that same day, Jonathan was contacted by the CIA agent from London and two other men. One of them was CIA helicopter pilot Paul Bennett.

He recalled that Jonathan was very cautious about helping the Americans because he felt he should only be answerable to the British.

'He had some info and we had some info and we wanted to know his opinion on certain things,' says Bennett today. 'Moyle wasn't working full-time for British intelligence, he was a freelance. He was very meticulous with what he knew and pretty accurate, too.'

The Americans were particularly interested in any rumours about Saddam Hussein re-arming his forces in preparation to invade his considerably weaker neighbour, Kuwait. The end of the eight-year Iran–Iraq conflict had left Saddam the warmonger without a battle to fight, and they had no doubts he was planning a new offensive.

The purchase of hundreds of helicopter gunships would confirm the CIA's worst fears.

Jonathan also told the Americans he suspected that Cardoen had developed his own version of the sophisticated Helios weapons guidance system.

'That confirmed the CIA's worst fears about the military capability of those converted Bells,' explained a CIA source.

*   *   *

The spring of 1990 was a bad time for Iraq's weapon procurement network. They'd had enormous success in arming Saddam Hussein's war machine but were facing major setbacks at precisely the time Jonathan Moyle departed for Santiago.

Dr Gerald Bull, architect of the Iraqi supergun, was shot dead in Brussels two days before Jonathan arrived in Chile on 22 March. His killers were believed to be members of the Israeli secret service, Mossad. The Israelis felt they had to move to stop Saddam getting his hands on a weapon that would put them within easy firing range of Iraq. (In October 1992, Bull's son, Michael, publicly admitted that his late father had met Carlos Cardoen in Iraq when both men were working closely with Saddam.)

At this same time, trigger mechanism parts, believed to be for Iraq's nuclear programme, were intercepted at London's Heathrow Airport en route from the US to Iraq.

Saddam badly needed cheap battlefield helicopters, similar to the American Apache and the Russian Hind, and he hoped that Cardoen's plans to convert civilian Bells into gunships would prove the ideal solution. In addition, Cardoen's intention to provide his own version of the super-sensitive Helios weapons guidance and observation system made the helicopters an even more lethal proposition.

The Americans had been following the progress of the Bell conversions very closely, but had not yet gathered enough evidence to prove conclusively that Cardoen intended to sell them to Iraq. They had heard the rumours about vast commissions being offered to second-hand helicopter dealers in exchange for finding used Bells, but they needed cold, hard facts if they were going to pursue Carlos Cardoen successfully, as well as his US 'subsidary' Global Helicopter Technology.

*   *   *

Back at the Carrera Hotel early that evening, Jonathan telephoned Annette Kissenbeck in Germany. His call left Annette feeling anxious about her boyfriend's activities in Chile. Jonathan seemed quite tense and the call was very hurried. He said his stomach hurt. He also mentioned he had a meeting and was running late.

Minutes after putting down the phone, Cardoen PR executive Raul Montecinos came knocking at Jonathan's door. The young journalist was surprised he hadn't called from reception, but Montecinos insisted it was better they met in private. (Montecinos later told two other people what happened during that meeting.)

The edgy PR man explained to Jonathan that Cardoen was very concerned that Jonathan might be about to publish some kind of exposé on their Bell conversion plans.

Montecinos told Jonathan that Cardoen Industrias would not hesitate to take steps to 'prevent inaccurate reports about us being published', as he later recounted to an associate.

Montecinos's voice was virtually bellowing with anger by the time he'd finished. This surprised Jonathan, who hadn't realised that the 62-year-old PR executive was completely deaf in one ear and always spoke louder than anyone else.

Across the corridor, chambermaid Silvia Cabrera was so alarmed when she heard Montecinos's loud, angry voice that she thought a fight was about to occur. But then there was silence.

*   *   *

The stomach-ache that Jonathan had first started suffering during dinner on the previous Monday became much worse that same night.

At just after 8.00pm, Jonathan joined defence writer Adrian English and other journalists for a cocktail in English's suite at the Hotel Carrera before they travelled to Pedro del Fierro's home for dinner. English noticed that Jonathan was very distracted and frequently checked the doors to the room to see if anyone was behind them. 'He seemed very twitchy,' English later recalled.

At 8.30pm, del Fierro picked up his guests in his Citroën and drove them out to his three-bedroom home in the wealthy suburb of La Reina, south-east of Santiago. In the car, Jonathan was quiet. He was in the back seat planning guerrilla tactics concerning Cardoen. He barely noticed the light from the street-lamps bouncing off the wide, glassy boulevards, gently mirrored with softly falling rain.

The del Fierros' house was on an estate built exclusively for doctors and their families. The property was overlooked from the east by the brown foothills of the Andes, while to the west, the flickering lights of the city formed a dazzling sight. Outside, the *grillos* — crickets — were chirruping in the undergrowth, a sign of good luck in Chile. Jonathan noticed a colourful mural of a Bolivian farm which hung on one wall and couldn't resist asking about the numerous china ducks, which were part of a collection that had been given to Soledad del Fierro by her patients from the breast clinic she ran locally. All the guests noticed the constant buzzing of overhead military planes from a nearby airfield.

When tall, elegant, dark-haired Soledad del Fierro heard about Jonathan's stomach problems, she advised him to avoid alcohol and eat plain rice for dinner. He reluctantly agreed. During the early stages of the evening, Jonathan talked to Soledad about his trip to Punta Arenas and Antarctica. He seemed relaxed despite his illness.

Then, half-way through the main course, Jonathan became extremely pale and quiet. Soledad asked him if he was all right and he insisted he was fine. Then, just before she served her guests milky *cortada* coffees, Jonathan's head slumped forward and hit the table. He had virtually passed out.

The del Fierros helped Jonathan to a bed in one of their children's rooms. Two hours later, as the other guests were about to depart, they looked in on him. He was sleeping so heavily they decided not to disturb him.

The following morning, Jonathan seemed much better and even played football in the garden with the del Fierros' two young children, Ignacio and Francisca. Pedro del Fierro dropped Jonathan back at the Hotel Carrera and waited outside while he grabbed some things for the trip to Punta Arenas and Antarctica later that day.

It was raining hard as Jonathan climbed the steps to the hotel reception area. He rushed into his room, changed clothes and packed the long johns and a thermal vest he had used in freezing Norway the previous February. He'd always known they would come in handy one day.

On his way out of the Carrera, Jonathan bought some postcards at reception. A few minutes later, in del Fierro's Citroën, Jonathan wrote a card to Alexander Shephard, his publisher back in England. It was positive and up-beat. 'Off to Bolivia Saturday night and back Thursday.' His intentions to get home in one piece were clear.

At FIDAE that Thursday morning, Jonathan met one of Chile's few female air force pilots, an attractive 41-year-old blonde called Annette Vogt Aichel. He was amused that she shared the same Christian name as his fiancée and persuaded Aichel to pose for a photograph by a helicopter on display.

At lunchtime, Jonathan spent 8,000 pesos on a taxi ride to the Arturo Merino Benitez airport for the Chilean Air Force flight to Punta Arenas, 2,000 miles to the south of Santiago.

At the airfield, Jonathan was introduced to the brother-in-law of the Chilean Air Force Commander who had asked Jonathan on the trip earlier that week. Jorge LaFrentz, aged 33, spoke perfect English and accompanied Jonathan through the airfield. After checking in his luggage, Jonathan was violently sick. LaFrentz then lent him his jacket because he was shivering so badly.

Jonathan was reluctantly persuaded to go to the airforce infirmary for medication. A few minutes later, Jonathan Moyle shut his eyes tight as male nurse Jaime Alcides Navaro Soto plunged a syringe filled with Diazepam into his arm to kill the pain. He'd always hated injections.

18

Punta Arenas, Chile

'Life is either a daring adventure or nothing.
To keep our faces toward change and behave like
free spirits in the presence of fate is
strength undefeatable.'

Helen Keller, Let Us Have Faith *(1940)*

At the foot of the Andes, on the western side of the Strait of Magellan, lies the port of Punta Arenas. It is inhabited by more than 100,000 people. Founded in 1848, the city was originally a military garrison and penal settlement, which proved very convenient for dropping off unwanted criminals en route for California during the gold rush.

As the Chilean Air Force Boeing 707 carrying Jonathan Moyle and other dignitaries finally began its descent into Punta Arenas, the young journalist noticed the hilly terrain that looked so much like the Brecon Beacons in Wales, where he'd spent many a freezing night on RAF survival exercises. During the flight, Jonathan sat next to the late President of France's brother, Jacques Mitterand, head of Aerospatiale, one of the world's biggest defence manufacturers. They exchanged pleasantries but little more. Nearby, air force 'liaison man'

Jorge LaFrentz kept a close eye on his guests.

It was bleak, grey and rainy when the aircraft finally touched down at the Aeropuerto Carlos Ibanez del Campo. Jonathan watched from his window seat as the plane taxied to the tiny terminal hoping, praying, that he could get down the steps and out of the airport without any more nausea from his upset stomach. When the plane came to a halt, he noticed a number of dignitaries standing below him as sheets of rain swept across the tarmac.

Thankfully, Jonathan made it out of the airport without incident and accepted a ride into Punta Arenas with Jorge LaFrentz. Jonathan was booked into an old-fashioned hotel called the Cabo de Hormos, but as they drove into the city, LaFrentz persuaded Jonathan to stay at his father-in-law's house instead. He thought the Englishman might appreciate a night with a family, rather than yet another lonely stay in a hotel.

Shortly after arriving in Punta, it emerged that weather conditions were so bad in the Antarctic that the following day's trip was in jeopardy. As the locals knew only too well, when it rained in Punta there were usually blizzards to the south. Jonathan mentioned to LaFrentz that, as an alternative, he was very interested in visiting Puerto Williams, a tiny garrison where the SAS crashed their helicopter during the Falklands War. LaFrentz said he would try but Williams, 200 miles south, had similar weather conditions to the Antarctic.

The helicopter Jonathan referred to was a Sea King Mark 4 of 846 Royal Naval Air Squadron — the same squadron Jonathan had visited in Norway two months earlier. His interest in the SAS operation was fuelled by stories he'd heard in Scandinavia. The burnt-out shell of the Sea King was the only tangible evidence that the SAS had infiltrated into mainland Argentina during the Falklands conflict. The aircraft was found abandoned 11 miles south of Puerto Williams close to the Argentinian border. It had been stripped down clearly to undertake a long range, one-way mission. Later, the crew of three emerged from hiding after surviving unaided for several days in wild countryside. It is widely believed that an SAS unit went across the border and set up watching posts at Argentinian bases to give the British advanced notice of plane and ship movements.

Early that evening, as the strong sea breeze picked up strength and a fast-fading light dimmed the grey skies, Jorge LaFrentz took Jonathan on a driving tour of Punta Arenas, with its classical Spanish architecture and carefully cobbled side-streets. Jonathan even insisted on stopping to buy a gift for LaFrentz's mother-in-law Ruby as a 'thank you' for letting him stay.

That night, LaFrentz's father-in-law, Segunda Jose Marusich Ostoich, and his wife entertained Jonathan in the family's home on Jose Davet Street, in the Punta Arenas district of Ganaddero. Jonathan proudly told them of his marriage plans and the house at Branscombe. But he didn't stay up late because of his ongoing stomach problems.

The following morning, Ruby cooked Jonathan a hearty breakfast but he could only manage a couple of dry biscuits and herbal tea. LaFrentz confirmed that weather conditions were too bad for the Antarctic trip, but assured Jonathan that a flight to the helicopter crash site at Puerto Williams was possible.

During the 90-minute helicopter journey, Jonathan began talking to a friendly Chilean Air Force pilot who knew all about Cardoen's plans for converting the Bells. He told Jonathan it was strongly rumoured that Cardoen's aircraft would be capable of carrying chemicals for warfare. 'Why would he bother manufacturing such an aircraft if they weren't for a military purpose?' pointed out the pilot.

Puerta Williams itself was something of a disappointment; a small military settlement surrounded by thin tributaries and thousands of acres of knee-high grassy marshes. Jonathan wondered how on earth those SAS men managed to keep their sanity in such barren surroundings. As they flew over a small grassy verge four miles east of the garrison, the carcass of the Sea King emerged as a surreal sight looming up through the low-level mist. The helicopter did not land because the recent rain had made the marshes dangerously unpredictable. Jonathan tried to imagine what it must have been like to take part in a secret operation in such unfriendly terrain.

At lunchtime, Jonathan flew back to Santiago still feeling groggy from his upset stomach. He had only had a slice of cheese and a glass of mineral water on the plane and mentioned to LaFrentz that he was looking forward to calling his fiancée and parents later that evening.

Minutes after the air force Boeing 707 touched down in Santiago, Jonathan caught a taxi to FIDAE on the other side of the city. There, he was disappointed to find that four of his closest journalistic colleagues, including Adrian English and Tony Robinson, had departed at 10.00am that morning for a short flight to the coastal town of Vina del Mar in a brand new BAe 146 mini-airliner.

Jonathan visited the Cardoen stand yet again and encountered PR head Raul Montecinos. There was an uneasy truce between the two men at first, but then Jonathan asked Montecinos if Cardoen Industrias would deny 'on the record' that the helicopters could be equipped with nerve gas.

One journalist who was standing nearby at the time later explained, 'I couldn't believe it when I heard Moyle. He was asking for trouble.'

Montecinos became infuriated. 'He wasn't used to being treated so disrespectfully by a mere journalist,' added the witness.

However, Montecinos reluctantly bit his lip. This was neither the time or the place to be seen arguing with Jonathan.

That afternoon, Jonathan ran into Italian marketing executive Guissepina Arrigoni, whom he had met a few weeks earlier at the Singapore Airshow. The couple wandered around dozens of stands together and then stopped for a *cortado* at the FIDAE coffee shop.

Jonathan told Arrigoni he had to go to a Chilean Air Force reception at the Hotel Carrera early that evening but perhaps they could meet after that.

Not long after this, Jonathan also bumped into *Defence Weekly* journalist Mike Gething, who was staying just two rooms away from Jonathan at the Carrera. He also told Gething he was going to the air force reception. Gething was quite envious when Jonathan mentioned he'd been down to Punta Arenas.

'You lucky sod,' said Gething. 'I wish I'd been.'

Jonathan smiled.

19
Santiago

'Far better it is to dare mighty things,
to win glorious triumphs, even though
checkered by failure, than to take rank with
those poor spirits who neither enjoy much
nor suffer much, because they live in the
grey twilight that knows not
victory nor defeat.'

Theodore Roosevelt

Night had come by the time Jonathan got back to his hotel. The streets of downtown Santiago were bustling with vendors and commuters leaving their jobs for the weekend. The dark-coloured Chevrolet Caprices and Ford Taurus taxis were parked opposite the entrance to the Carrera as usual.

As Jonathan walked up the steps to the reception area he saw Raul Montecinos rise from an armchair in the lounge area. He was wearing a dark grey suit. There seemed to be another man with him but he did not get up, so Jonathan could not be sure if they were together.

Montecinos strode quickly in Jonathan's direction.

'Mister Moyle,' he called from behind.

'Hello.'

Montecinos was approaching fast but cautiously. He had one hand in his pocket.

'We must talk. Come.' He held out a hand and smiled. But instead of allaying Jonathan's fears, he made him uneasy. Montecinos led the way to the hotel bar. His head moving from side to side was less a gesture of human kindness and more like the sway of a cobra marking distance. Montecinos was pleased with himself, though. He knew that Jonathan was going to the Chilean Air Force reception at the hotel and had decided to arrive early in the hope of catching Jonathan on his way in.

Montecinos later admitted he had instigated the meeting to put the record straight with Jonathan about Cardoen's activities and to try to placate the young Englishman after their meeting that afternoon at the Cardoen stand.

'Moyle seemed obsessed with the helicopter conversions. He wasn't like the other journalists. He seemed only interested in one thing,' Montecinos later told a friend.

With a monthly budget of $50,000, Dr Carlos Cardoen took his public image very seriously and he expected Montecinos to counter any negative publicity effectively.

Jonathan and Montecinos sat down on the padded wicker chairs in a quiet corner of the wood-panelled bar. Montecinos tried to be polite at the beginning but Jonathan was only interested in one thing.

Montecinos explained away his earlier aggressive behaviour in Jonathan's room by saying that so much money was at stake over the Bell conversions that any negative coverage might effectively end the project. Montecinos continued to insist that the helicopters were not intended for a military purpose, but he did concede that some of them might end up in Iraq.

'Are you trying to tell me these helicopters will be used for crop spraying by Saddam Hussein?' Jonathan asked almost mockingly.

'Certainly that is the case, Mister Moyle,' replied Montecinos.

'He must have lots of farms.'

'He has plans ...' Montecinos stopped himself in his tracks and got up abruptly.

Jonathan's eyes widened. Everything the Americans had told him was suddenly clicking into place.

'He's going into Kuwait, isn't he?'

'Goodbye, Mister Moyle,' Montecinos spat out the words.

As he turned to walk away, Montecinos stopped again.

'Stop all this wild speculation. It can only cause you harm.'

Montecinos left without saying another word.

Three separate people in Santiago have since said in tape recorded interviews that Montecinos told them about this meeting. He even told them the exact words of his conversation with Jonathan.

'I tried everything to stop him printing bad stories about Cardoen. But his mind was fixed on certain subjects. He just would not listen to my advice,' said Montecinos.

Montecinos was shaking with rage as he walked away from that meeting with Jonathan Moyle at the Hotel Carrera. He knew that the Bell conversion scheme would be wrecked if Moyle revealed that Saddam was planning to buy the helicopters in preparation for an invasion of Kuwait.

'Montecinos had heard the rumours about Kuwait from his own contacts inside the Iraqi secret service,' explained one colleague. 'But Carlos Cardoen would never forgive him if he ever heard what had happened at the meeting with Moyle. Montecinos was also terrified that Moyle had secretly tape recorded the conversation.'

Montecinos went straight to a public phone near the hotel elevators and called his Iraqi Mukhabarat secret service contact, who was staying at a nearby hotel.

The agent wasn't in, but Montecinos knew he'd see him at the Chilean Air Force reception that evening. He'd tell him about Jonathan then.

As Montecinos later told a friend, 'The Englishman would not leave things alone. He thought he was so clever. But he underestimated how important the Iraqis were to us. I thought that if I warned him to keep away he would appreciate the danger but he didn't seem to care.'

Upstairs in his room, Jonathan was feeling very annoyed by Montecinos's attitude. But he knew there was little he could do about it, so he decided to plan his evening instead.

He telephoned a Chilean woman called Anna Marie Yrarrazabal whom he had briefly met at a concert at the Louvre in Paris the previous November. The two had enjoyed a meal together after the concert, but their relationship was entirely platonic. She wasn't in, however, so Jonathan talked to her sister Fransisca who later recalled Jonathan speaking to her for five minutes about his impressions of Chile. 'He seemed charming,' she said.

Jonathan then went down to the Chilean Air Force reception which was being held in a large, high-ceilinged room at the rear of the hotel.

As Jonathan entered the reception, he immediately noticed Montecinos talking to Carlos Cardoen. Jonathan nodded tersely, accepted a Pisco Sour from a drinks tray and then stood awkwardly with the two Chileans for a short time. Montecinos gave Cardoen the impression that he and Jonathan were the best of friends.

Jonathan soon moved away from them when he spotted Tony Robinson across the room. He was horrified to hear that Robinson had been mugged in a street near the hotel a couple of hours earlier.

Jonathan avoided talking with Cardoen and Montecinos throughout the remainder of the reception. But seeing them watching him made him feel vulnerable. Sometimes they seemed to be smirking in his direction. Jonathan remembered the warning the two British military attachés had given him earlier in the week.

Later that evening, Jonathan met up once again with Guissepina Arrigonni. But he was not as relaxed as he had been earlier in the afternoon. As the couple were walking across the dimly-lit Plaza de la Constitucion in front of the hotel, Jonathan became very distracted by two men standing nearby.

'What's wrong?' she asked Jonathan.

'I think they're following us,' he replied, but he refused to elaborate.

After a few minutes, the two men turned off and Jonathan never mentioned them again.

It had been an exhausting day for Jonathan and he felt so tired and worried he did not stay long with Guissepina, returning to his room to sleep.

*   *   *

Just two miles away at a seedy hostess bar called Emmanuell on El Bosque street in the suburb of Provedencia, Jonathan's neighbour on the 14th floor of the Hotel Carrera was in his element. Spaniard Antonio Terol was enjoying Pisco Sours and ogling beautiful girls trying to be picked up by wealthy foreigners just like him.

They didn't come cheap either; a minimum of 15,000 pesos ($40) for drinks before they could leave the club and a further 80,000 pesos ($200) for sex, plus the cost of a hotel room of their choice.

Inside Emmanuell were numerous fake columns and velvet drapes, designed to look vaguely like the inside of Caligula's palace, but the effect was ruined by one entire wall of mirrors complete with flashing Christmas-tree-style fairy lights. And the dozens of hostesses tended to favour black-seamed stockings and leather mini-skirts rather than Roman togas.

Terol eventually homed in on two dark-haired women and was soon informing them in hushed tones that he was an arms dealing spy.

'I'm here keeping an eye on things,' he boasted to the girls.

Thirty-four-year-old Irene del Carmen Severino del Fuentes sat on Terol's lap, while her friend Lenka Ximena Amelia Zullivich Rubio, 27, held his hand. There was certainly something rather sinister about the 6ft 4in 33-year-old Spaniard with his soulless eyes and razor-sharp short-back-and-sides.

But Irene and Lenka were more concerned that Terol had enough cash to have sex with both of them and buy the cocaine he had asked them to supply.

*　　　　*　　　　*

Back in his room at the Carrera, Jonathan woke up after a few hours' troubled sleep and lay motionless on the bed for a while, not really knowing what was wrong. He'd pushed his luck earlier with Montecinos but surely they wouldn't dare do anything to him. It would be too obvious.

Jonathan had once read a book of stories by a man named Frederic Brown. In one of them he quoted the tale of a peasant walking through a haunted wood, saying to himself, 'I am a good man and have done no wrong. If devils can harm me, then there isn't any justice,' and he heard a voice behind him say, 'There isn't.'

Despite his misgivings, he was determined not to drop his investigation into Carlos Cardoen. He was leaving for Bolivia the next morning so the problems here would soon pass, and once he got back to London he would put the finishing touches on the whole investigation.

Jonathan got up and turned on the light. He decided to

go for a walk and took the service elevator down to the staff exit where he slipped out into Bombero Salas. It was surprisingly cold and the Carabiñeros riot-control truck, which usually hung around the narrow street in daytime in case of any problems amongst the locals, had long gone.

Across the street, two men were parked in a dark-coloured car. They watched the hotel carefully and when Jonathan emerged from the side exit they presumed he was going somewhere important. Their instructions were to continue observing and not to approach the subject under any circumstances.

At 4.00am there wasn't even a dog out investigating the litter on the Plaza de la Constitucion. The grey pavements of the square were deathly quiet, and the flowerbeds were dotted now and again with small white flowers that barely shone in the yellow lamplight.

Jonathan turned into Augustinas and passed an all-night news vendor. As the street narrowed, high crumbling buildings emerged through the darkness and Jonathan contemplated whether he should contact either Hall and Finnegan or the CIA men in the morning to tell them about Iraq's intention to invade Kuwait. He then doubled back up Bombero Salas towards the Carrera Hotel. High above the tower blocks of downtown Santiago, green-and-red neon lights flashed on and off, advertising Banco de Sud Americano. On the street, only the occasional, rusting Chevy pick-up rumbled by.

Jonathan returned to his room 15 minutes later, but his head was still no clearer. He turned off the light and sat on the bed, thinking and shivering. He felt quite chilled, so he put on the thermal long johns that he'd taken to Punta Arenas. Still he could not sleep, and the shivering was becoming worse. After a while, he switched the light on again in the hope he might find it easier to sleep.

When Jonathan woke up less than an hour later, he felt as if he was in a lot of trouble. He had a blinding headache, but was wide awake and his mind was functioning with almost startling clarity, as though he'd been fed some sort of stimulating drug. Again, he thought about what had happened with Montecinos a few hours earlier and turned it over and over, looking at it from every angle. He concluded that he was in danger.

Then he picked up his airline tickets on the bedside table as if for reassurance. He was due to fly with Lloyd Bolivia Airlines flight 964 from Santiago to La Paz at 2.50pm that afternoon. He was booked into the Plaza Hotel in the Avenida 16 de Julio for two nights.

Then on 3 April, he would be flying to Santa Cruz from where he would catch a flight to São Paulo, Brazil, for the connecting British Airways flight 244 to Heathrow.

It wouldn't be long before he was safely home. Jonathan got out of bed and went to the bathroom where he looked out of the window in the opposite direction to the Plaza de la Constitucion. The side-street below stretched downtown before him, flanked by street lights and occasional smudges of neon, glowing throughout the night in the windows of hole-in-the-wall bars and nightclubs.

Jonathan splashed his face with water and looked at his watch. It was 5.31am; the perfect time to call Annette in Germany which was six hours ahead.

Annette was not in, so Jonathan called his parents at Branscombe, Devon, at just after 10.30am British time. He told them about his trip to Punta Arenas and his bad stomach. But his mind was really on home.

'Did you manage to plant the grass seed in the front garden, Dad?' he asked.

'Not yet. I'm still levelling it off,' came the reply.

'Don't worry, I'll give you a hand when I get back next week.'

Jonathan mentioned to Tony that he intended to take Annette's father flying at Dunkeswell, Devon, the following Saturday.

Jonathan also said that his illness had left him feeling terribly tired. He sounded to Tony as if he was literally fading away. He also seemed worried about something.

At 5.46am, Jonathan replaced the receiver and went over to the small desk near the door to room 1406, took a sheet of hotel-headed notepaper and began writing a letter to a friend he met in Belize telling her of his plans to get married. He dated it 1 April, as he presumed he wouldn't finish it until after he got to La Paz, Bolivia.

Jonathan wrote for about ten minutes at the desk. Then he heard a knock at the door. He was startled by it, and dropped his pen. He got up and opened the door ...

20
Santiago

'Death cancels everything but the truth.'

Anonymous

Chambermaid Silvia Cabrera, well into her 40s, was not the kind of woman to take life as it comes. Her husband had abandoned her years ago to bring up their daughter alone in a tiny one-bedroom apartment. She struggled to survive on a paltry weekly wage and rarely left her home except for the ten-minute walk each day to the Hotel Carrera for the start of yet another ten-hour shift. Television was Silvia's main source of entertainment. She never read newspapers because that required too much effort. That week, Silvia was exhausted from cleaning more rooms than usual because the hotel was packed with officials, businessmen and journalists visiting FIDAE.

After four hours of tormented sleep, twisting and thrashing amid dreams of death and destruction, Silvia got up, made herself a *cortada* coffee and set off for the Carrera.

The streets of downtown Santiago were quiet at that

time on a Saturday morning. The gloom seemed right for that day. Silvia recalled how, as a child, it had always rained on the Easter weekend, especially the day before — Good Friday — the day they had crucified Christ. Her mother told her that the sky would get dark around 3.00pm, the time He might have died, and it frequently did that all Easter weekend. Those were the days when she dreamed of becoming a nun and used to dress up in white sheets and roam around the house when everyone was outside. Those were the days before she had to fend for herself and bring up her own family. Silvia never stopped praying and dreaming of becoming a person who could lead a happy, carefree life.

So when she clocked in for work at 7.47am, her only concern was to get through the day in one piece. She hated the mess these airshow people left in their rooms. They never picked up their towels; underwear was strewn all over the floor; not to mention the soiled and stained sheets, unflushed lavatories and condoms.

During that week, Silvia had built up a mental picture of many of the occupants of those rooms through their personal belongings and standards of hygiene. Often, in the middle of the day, some guests would return to their rooms and she was pleasantly surprised by how accurate her images of them would be.

But Silvia's overriding responsibility was to get into each of the rooms, sweep through them, grab sheets and towels as quickly as possible and deposit them in the laundry room at the end of the corridor. Her duties were to clean rooms 1402 to 1414 on the 14th floor. Little else really mattered.

*   *   *

At 8.00am, Silvia knocked hard on the door of room 1406. 'Maid! Maid!'

There was no reply, so she used her master key. The security chain was not on. Perhaps the guest had already checked out.

Silvia sighed with irritation when she saw the chaos on the floor and an empty suitcase in the corner. She picked up the newspaper from the floor and put it on the bedside table. Then she looked for the laundry bag to see if the guest had any washing he wanted done. It was on the floor by the bed, twisted up like a rope. Silvia picked it up. It felt wet and had a strange smell, like perspiration. But it was empty. There was no point in cleaning the room until he checked out, so she moved across the hall to room 1405.

A few minutes later, Silvia heard a muffled sound coming from either 1406 or the corridor outside the two rooms. The door of room 1406 opened and closed. Then there was silence. Silvia peeped quietly out of her room but saw nobody. She presumed the guest in 1406 had returned to his room.

At 8.35am, Jonathan Moyle's Chilean friend, Anna Maria Yrarrazabal, phoned the Hotel Carrera in response to the call he made to her home the previous evening. The operator insisted that Jonathan was not in, so she left a message for him to call her.

At 9.00am, a bellboy called Vladimir arrived at room 1406 with the telephone message for Jonathan. He knocked hard. Receiving no answer, he left the note by the door.

As Vladimir passed Silvia Cabrera, he said 'Good morning.' She didn't respond, as she was thinking how strange it was that the guest in 1406 had left the room once again, and so quietly.

At 11.15am, Silvia returned to Jonathan's room. The security chain was still unfastened. She picked up the message and put it by the phone next to the newspaper she had placed there earlier.

Silvia again cursed under her breath because the room still looked like a mini bomb site. Clothes remained on the floor. Some trousers were hanging over a chair. A briefcase and a silver wallet lay open on the desk by the door. An empty suitcase was perched at a strange angle in the corner. Hand-written notes were scattered on the desk. In the white-tiled bathroom, damp towels were spread across the floor. She also inspected the mini-bar which was untouched, as it had been all week.

Then Silvia noticed a syringe on the table. Maybe the guest was a diabetic. There could have been a thousand reasons why it was there. It wasn't her business to care. She didn't want to touch it just in case.

She cleaned the bathroom thoroughly before returning to the bedroom, where she noticed that the top sheet of the bed had been twisted up tightly like a length of rope. And on the bottom right-hand corner of the under-sheet was a small bloodstain. The only reason it registered with Silvia was because most stains on beds tended to be in the centre or top-half of sheets for reasons she did not like to think about. Silvia also wondered why there was no cover on the pillow case.

Silvia realised there was little point in cleaning the room completely until the guest had finally checked out, so she left it as it was.

When Silvia returned at just after 3.00pm, she was very irritated that the guest had still not left. She noticed that the clean bathroom towels were untouched. But the strangest thing was that the silver wallet and the syringe she had seen earlier were no longer there, and the papers she had earlier noticed strewn across the desk had been gathered up and put in the open black-leather briefcase. Perhaps the guest had rushed in and out earlier?

Silvia's main concern was that the occupant would return at any moment and she had not completed her job. She changed the bedclothes. While vacuuming, she picked up numerous peso notes that were lying on the floor and put them on the desk. She didn't notice the torn photo of a military helicopter lying on the floor just under the bed.

As she was about to leave room 1406, she noticed that the door to the built-in closet was slightly ajar, but the light that should come on automatically was off. She presumed it would need a new bulb.

Silvia pulled the handle of the closet door and swung it open. There was something strange inside it. She leaned forward and gasped.

Slumped in the closet, his neck hooked to the clothes rail by a shirt, his legs bent slightly behind him, was the body of Jonathan Moyle. His head was hooded by a pillow case. His body was crooked because he seemed taller than the height of the cupboard itself. He was naked from the waist up with transparent plastic covering what appeared to be a nappy-like garment over his genitals, which was fitted over a pair of white long johns. White underpants hung around his ankles as if he had been desperately trying to kick them off.

Silvia didn't scream. She just stared at the corpse for a few moments. It didn't seem real. She gingerly moved forward and touched the body. She knew immediately he was dead.

Clutching her uniform with one hand, she made the sign of the cross.

She was afraid. Trembling, she ran towards the telephone.

She phoned the head of hotel security, Señor Roberto Campusano. It was 3.07pm.

'Come quickly. There is a body in the cupboard,' she gasped in Spanish.

Roberto Campusano, a 33-year-old ex-policeman, immediately alerted the hotel reception manager, Frederico Echaiz, and asked to meet him in room 1406.

Minutes later, the two men opened the closet door with an air of dreaded expectation. Campusano carefully touched the arm and then the neck, but he already knew the

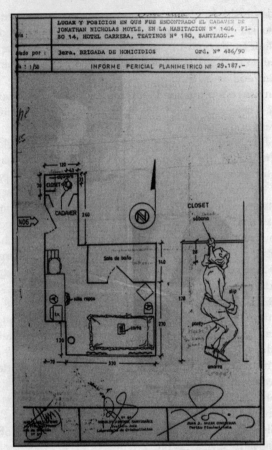

A police artist's plan of the scene

man was dead.

He then gingerly pulled up the hood. 'His face looked so restful, so content,' recalled the security man later.

Campusano then closed the door gently, almost as if he didn't want to wake the dead. He went to the phone and called an old colleague from the Carabiñeros called Lt Urmeneta.

Chilean Air Force security official Carlos Enrique Montenegro Gonzales arrived at room 1406, just as Campusano and Echaiz were leaving. He agreed that nothing should be touched until the police arrived.

*   *   *

They filled the place, it was so small; the air force security men, the photographer, the uniformed officers, every one of them dispensable, but each believing they had an important, specific task. Everyone noted that, strangely, there was no smell.

First on the scene were the Carabiñeros, the uniformed paramilitary force considered to be part of the armed forces. During Pinochet's reign in Chile, they were the ones in control of law and order and their black-and-white patrol cars struck fear into many citizens.

But in the new democratic Chile the Carabiñeros were obliged to call in the civil police's Brigada de Homicidios de la Policia de Investigaciones, if any suspicious deaths occurred. Perhaps not so surprisingly, the two forces loathed each other and frequently set up rival investigations for the same crime.

Brigada de Homicidios Inspector Marco Arellano Rojas and his colleague Mario Torres Salgado arrived at the Hotel Carrera in their unmarked blue Fiat Uno, possibly irritated that their Saturday afternoon had been disturbed because of some foreigner.

Arellano marched past the hotel reception with Torres struggling to keep up. The two detectives looked similar in their black suits. But Arellano's head clearly made him the man in charge — it was shaped like a square loaf of store-produced bread.

Arellano had a full mane of black hair and drooping

eyelids that were sad and smiling at the same time. His skin was dark but not by race, or the sun. He had the look of a dusk-to-dawn drinker; Pisco Sours were a certainty. He wore no wedding band and his white shirt was too wrinkled, even for a policeman, with one too many stains poking out from underneath his black suit jacket.

It was 4.50pm by the time Arellano and Torres appeared at the doorway to 1406 and the place was teeming with all those people who had no business being anywhere near the body of Jonathan Moyle.

Arellano looked at everyone with a smile that could have been a mourner's valiant attempt to console a bereaved widow.

21
Santiago

'Somehow, our sense of justice
never turns in its sleep till long after the
sense of injustice in others
has been thoroughly aroused.'

Max Beerbohm, 'Servants', And Even Now (1920)

'Everybody out!' screamed Detective Arellano, whose irritation was compounded by the fact he'd been happily watching his son playing soccer just an hour earlier.

His sidekick Torres — a swarthy-looking fellow with carefully gelled, swept-back dark hair, a large round head and pin-prick dark brown eyes — immediately began herding the cattle out of room 1406.

Arellano and Torres found no evidence of a struggle and decided that the half-finished letter on the floor by the bed was conclusive evidence of suicide, even though neither of them could speak English, let alone read it.

Within an hour, Arellano was on the phone to local magistrate Mano Carroza Espinoza, requesting an order giving detectives permission to remove the body. '*Este claramente un caso de suicidio,*' Arellano told the magistrate in a matter-of-fact manner. It was an open-and-shut case of death by hanging. Espinoza authorised a death certificate over the phone and agreed with Arellano that there was no point in sending a pathologist to the scene for such an obvious suicide.

As a police photographer snapped away, Detective Torres reminded him not to take too many photos as the *Investigaciones* were trying to keep their costs down.

Arellano picked up Jonathan's passport which was next to his watch and a glass of water on the desk. It was a newish passport, in the dark red-and-gold binding of the European Union. The detective held it open at the photo page and looked at the figure in the cupboard; in spite of the effects on his face of the strangulation, the swelling and the cyanosis, he looked as if he had fallen asleep. His hair was still swept across his head, which made a wide frame for his face. There were no rings on the hands and no earrings.

'Jonatan Moyley,' Detective Arellano pronounced in a heavy Spanish accent as he compared the name in the passport with the mask of death. 'Looks like he's been dead a few hours,' he added matter-of-factly. 'The pathologist will tell us more when he gets to the morgue.'

Then, as an after-thought: 'Looks pretty straightforward to me. The foreigner gets depressed and kills himself.'

*   *   *

On Saturday, 31 March 1990, Diana Moyle drove to her local hairdresser in Sidmouth, Devon. As she entered the salon, she was overcome with a feeling of dread and collapsed in tears.

It was 12.00 noon GMT. At approximately the same time in Santiago, Chile, her son was being hauled from his bed across the floor of his hotel room to the closet, and hanged by his own shirt from the clothes rail.

That night, at home in Highcliff House, Branscombe, Tony Moyle tried to reassure his wife. But she was highly agitated and kept seeing Jonathan's sleeping face every time she shut her eyes, even for a moment.

At 11.00am next day, a police car arrived at the house. The moment Tony opened the front door to the nervous young police constable, he knew it was Jonathan.

'I have some bad news, sir.'

'What?'

'Your son has died.'

Tony stood there and stared in disbelief for a few moments.

'That's impossible. I only talked to him yesterday morning.'

'The police in Chile have been in touch with us. They don't suspect foul play.'

Tony recovered his composure and looked straight at the policeman.

'What do you mean?'

'He took his own life, sir.'

'Suicide?'

The officer nodded.

'Not my son,' said Tony. 'Not my son.'

On the evening of that same day, Sunday, 1 April, the phone rang at Annette Kissenbeck's apartment in Bonn, Germany. She hurriedly lifted the receiver. There was a long silence. She shouted, 'Jon! Jon! Is that you?'

A moment passed, then a voice. 'No. It's Tony. I've got the most terrible news for you.'

Not surprisingly, Annette was devastated.

*   *   *

Detectives Arellano and Torres should have kept an open mind about the death of Jonathan Moyle from the moment they walked into room 1406 at the Carrera Hotel. The golden rule for any police investigator is never to jump to conclusions because nothing is ever as it first appears.

They weren't helped by Silvia Cabrera's efforts to clean and tidy the room before Jonathan's body was discovered. That unfortunately destroyed valuable evidence as to what really happened in the room.

But the police failed to carry out any forensic examination of the room because they did not consider Jonathan's death to be suspicious. They also thought that much of the evidence would have disappeared after the chambermaid had cleaned the room.

Worst of all, Jonathan's body was taken down just one hour after the *Investigaciones* appeared on the scene. 'The corpse should have been left untouched in that cupboard while a search was made for any forensic clues,' says British ex-murder squad detective Jim Hutchinson.

He has outlined all the other mistakes made during the first hours of the police involvement:

1. Removing the twisted shirt that hanged Jonathan without first preserving the knots to determine if Jonathan had tied them himself.
2. Taking clothing off the body after removing it from the closet. The corpse should have been preserved as it was found with head, hands and feet bagged up in plastic.
3. No attempt was made to carry out a detailed search of room 1406 for clues. The detectives should have made a route to the body working their way across the carpet, collecting any objects in their path. They should also have used an electrostatic lift for footprints.
4. Police did not even bother to fingerprint the room using superglue, aluminium powder or iodine, depending on the surfaces.
5. Jonathan's body was laid down directly on the carpet by officers, instead of being put straight into a bodybag which could have preserved insect life

inside the corpse, revealing a more accurate time of death and whether he was killed elsewhere.

6. Every single item in room 1406 should have been bagged and kept for later forensic examination.

7. The inside of the walk-in closet should have been given an inch-by-inch examination for fingerprints, scuffs, marks, hairs, saliva, semen — anything that might reveal what actually happened to Jonathan in the minutes before he died.

8. Every single person who walked into room 1406 should have had their shoes covered to prevent important evidence being destroyed.

9. No one even bothered to take a temperature reading in the room, which would have helped the pathologist to establish the exact time of death.

10. Police did not attempt to interview the other guests on the 14th floor of the Carrera Hotel until three days later, by which time many had flown home.

11. Detectives did not even question the fact that Jonathan's 'suicide' happened from a virtually impossible angle in a cupboard that was shorter (1.70 metres) than the man himself (1.78 metres). Also, it seemed strange that Jonathan's dead weight had not snapped the flimsy wooden clothes rail in the closet.

Under pressure from the Chilean Air Force security official staying inside the hotel, Inspector Arellano issued an order to everyone to maintain silence about Jonathan's death. Bad publicity for FIDAE was the last thing anyone wanted.

Hotel security chief Roberto Campusano did not break that order of silence until March 1996. He said, 'I was very scared about what happened and I still don't like the idea of the authorities knowing I have said anything about Moyle's death.'

But he admitted to this author, 'I thought there was something suspicious about his death from the start, but no one was interested in my opinion.'

Neither of the investigating officers were curious about the notes and brochures in Jonathan's briefcase, which mentioned Carlos Cardoen's Bell helicopter conversion plans. Among these notes were highly technical specifications on weapons, vehicles and the geopolitical situation in Chile and Argentina. When a scruffy, torn photograph of the only flying prototype of the converted aircraft was found on the floor, one of the detectives picked it up and simply threw it back into the black-leather briefcase.

The hood over Jonathan's head should have alerted the police, because hitmen in certain parts of South America are renowned for using hoods as a mark of respect for their victims. They also dislike seeing their victim's face at the moment of death.

Hired assassins have also even been known to use a nappy-type garment to prevent body fluids exiting the body immediately after death. This is supposed to give the killers more time to flee the scene of a murder.

The hapless detectives Arellano and Torres even failed to locate the bloodstained sheet, because Silvia Cabrera had already taken it to the laundry to be cleaned. Neither did they bother to check the rubbish which had been removed from the room, but which was still on the maid's trolley.

The only items taken out of the room during the early hours of the investigation were beers and Cokes from Jonathan's mini-bar fridge. Various personal items belonging to Jonathan also went missing, including the Cardoen Industrias alarm clock radio which Jonathan was given during his visit to the Cardoen stand at FIDAE. It was never established if these items were taken from the room just before he died, or by a light-fingered policeman or hotel staff member following the discovery of the body.

Downstairs in the hotel bar, the other journalists were oblivious to the news of Jonathan's death, until one German reporter mentioned to defence writer Adrian English that he'd heard that a guest had died inside the hotel.

English immediately approached one of the Chilean Air Force men at other end of the bar. They told him it was Jonathan Moyle.

'Suicidio.'

News soon filtered through to the other journalists, including those staying in the nearby hotels. 'It was bewildering news. No one really new how to react, especially since they were saying he'd killed himself,' explained one writer.

Upstairs in room 1406, Jonathan's body was covered with a beige hotel blanket. They didn't even look at the soles of his feet to see if he had been dragged into the cupboard. They took the body by stretcher to the service elevator and then out of the back entrance in Bombero Salas to a waiting coroner's van.

Jonathan's body was taken to the Servicio Medico Legal — the city morgue — on Avenue La Paz in an area north of Santiago called Recoleta.

The old, run-down, white-washed three-storey building was built in the 1920s and featured vast windows and a 12-foot-high double doorway with the words 'SERVICIO MEDICO LEGAL' in big letters above it.

Inside the building, tearful relatives of the dead were scattered along the dark corridors, waiting to identify their loved ones. Moving amongst them were immaculately-dressed young men in dark suits offering their services as funeral directors. They promised modest-priced coffins and tasteful gravestones, which could be produced at a workshop across the street in under two hours. The city's largest graveyard — the Cemeterio General — was just three blocks from the Servicio Medico Legal building.

No wonder the locals long ago christened this area *La*

Empresa de la Muerte — the enterprises of the dead.

*　　　　　*　　　　　*

A couple of miles south of the Servicio Medico Legal building, Mr Gordon Reid, First Secretary at the British Embassy, and his wife Marianella, were attending a reception hosted by the National Congress of Chile.

Reid — tall, dignified and bearded, in his mid-30s — bumped into an old acquaintance from the Santiago diplomatic circuit called Patricio Frez. As the two men and their wives sipped politely at their cocktails, Reid mentioned in passing that he had been in contact with a young journalist called Jonathan Moyle at FIDAE during the week. He remarked that Jonathan was a very 'interesting fellow'.

At no time did he mention that Jonathan had just died. In fact, Reid talked about Jonathan in such glowing terms that Frez presumed he was someone very well known to the British Embassy in Santiago.

*　　　　　*　　　　　*

In Anaheim, California, *DHW* deputy editor Ian Parker, his publisher Alexander Shephard and North American correspondent Frank Colucci were attending a trade show at the huge exhibition centre in the city.

Colucci had just been out for a walk before breakfast that Sunday, 1 April, and was returning to hotel reception when Ian Parker approached him.

'I've got some bad news, Frank.'

Colucci stopped in his tracks. 'What?'

'Jonathan's dead.'

Colucci waited for the punch line but it never came. 'You're kidding me! Is this some kinda sick English April fool's joke?'

'No. It's true. Apparently he's taken his own life.'

'I don't fucking believe it!' Colucci could not accept the news.

A few minutes later, the two *DHW* men met with Alexander Shephard at the hotel coffee shop to discuss the tragedy. The same question kept on surfacing again and again.

Why?

Shephard then announced he was intending to travel to Chile to find out what really happened.

'There's no point. You don't speak the language and what could you achieve?' Frank Colucci pointed out.

All three men sat in stony silence contemplating the fate of Jonathan Moyle. They didn't utter another word until they left the coffee shop five minutes later.

*   *   *

It wasn't until Tuesday, 3 April, that Chilean police bothered to send a message to the British Embassy in Bonn, Germany, asking them to pass on the bad news to Annette Kissenbeck. It further compounded the anguish to get a call when she already knew her fiancé's fate.

That week, Annette received a letter Jonathan had written five days before his death.

In it he wrote, '*You can't imagine how much I love you. I can't wait until I get home and we will be back together.*'

In London, Tony Moyle called the Foreign Office for a fuller explanation of what had happened to his son. Initially, he was kept hanging on for more than five minutes, then a brisk man called Brian Hammill finally came on the line. He kept repeating the obvious.

'The fact remains that your son killed himself, Mr Moyle.'

'I don't believe it,' Tony replied.

'The police say his clothes were even neatly folded on

his bed.'

'That's rubbish. My son was the most untidy person in the world.'

But Hammill would not be deterred.

'There was also a note from a girl jilting him and saying she was getting married in two months' time.'

'Nonsense!'

[Fact: The note had not been properly translated and the maid had cleaned the room after Jonathan died.]

From that moment on, Tony Moyle decided he could not trust anyone connected with the death of his son and he would tape all future conversations. He was disappointed that the Foreign Office seemed disinterested in uncovering the full facts surrounding his son's death.

At home in Devon, Diana Moyle was plunged into a virtual nervous breakdown at the news of her only child's death.

For the first seven days, she drank vast amounts of whisky to try and dull the pain. For a modest drinker, it did nothing but make things worse.

Often, Diana would stop dead in her tracks as she was walking round the house and just start screaming. She'd get louder and louder until Tony appeared and calmed her down.

A few days after Jonathan's death, she suffered a full-blown panic attack when Tony was five minutes late while out walking the family dogs.

Dressed only in a nightgown with bare feet, Diana rushed out of the house and sped off in their Saab to try and find her husband.

Driving at high speed through the rainswept narrow twisting country lanes, she frantically searched for Tony. She was terrified she was going to lose the only other person in her life.

Diana could not find a way of coming to terms with her son's death. She didn't want to believe it had happened and kept imagining Jonathan walking through the front door, safe and well. She'd always believed she could cope with just about everything other than losing Jonathan. It wasn't supposed to happen that way. The parent was meant to die before the child.

She found herself constantly thinking, 'Please, God or whoever you are, make sure Jonathan is safe. I don't want him to suffer. How can life be so unkind? How can it be so cruel? I haven't just lost my past, I've lost my future.'

*   *   *

The Monday morning newspapers in Santiago all reported Jonathan's death prominently but stated that it was an open-and-shut case of suicide.

In Britain, the case merited only the briefest of mentions in the newspapers of Monday, 2 April.

A typical report was one that appeared in *The Times*:

JOURNALIST FOUND DEAD IN CHILE

SANTIAGO: An English journalist, Jonathan Nicholas Moyle, aged 28, attending an aerospace exhibition organised by the Chilean Air Force, was found dead on Saturday night in a Santiago hotel, police said yesterday. He was found hanging in a cupboard. Police said no note was found and they did not know who Mr Moyle worked for. *(Reuter)*

Just as the Chilean detectives had insisted, it looked like a straightforward suicide.

22
Santiago

Pathologist Dr José Belleti reached his office at Santiago's Servicio Medico Legal at 8.30am on the morning of 2 April 1990. Just as he was walking into the morgue, he paused mid-way along the corridor, puzzled. Parked at a haphazard angle near the dented stainless-steel refrigerator door was a trolley bearing the body of Jonathan Moyle.

Checking the toe tag, Belleti read Jonathan's name, and looked around. There was no one inside his office or the main room. He opened the autopsy suite and found his assistant dressed in overalls and dialling a number on the phone. He quickly hung up and greeted Belleti with a nervous 'Good morning'.

The trolley was then pushed to the centre of the suite where it transpired that the body was not going to succumb easily to an autopsy. Dr Belleti moved to the side of the trolley to help. He and two assistants secured the body under the arms and waist while an attendant held his legs. Then they heaved it on to the autopsy table. The body was naked. A scruffy plastic bag with the clothes he was wearing in the cupboard lay nearby.

Jonathan Moyle's medium-brown hair was still carefully swept across his head, even in death. Belleti noted he was well built, and that he had been an extremely fit young man. Belleti then manipulated his head and neck to feel for fractures. There were none. He placed the back of his hand against the cheek and struggled to turn him. He was cold and stiff from 36 hours of refrigeration. The skin did not blanch when pressed. He had been dead some considerable time.

Belleti — a slim, neatly-dressed man with a perfectly trimmed moustache — then wedged a block under Jonathan's neck to keep the head from lolling and got down to work. He did not see any obvious injuries, no bruises or broken nails. His nose was not fractured. There were no cuts inside his lips and he hadn't bitten his tongue.

Belleti's assistant did not take any X-rays because there were no machines available at the Servicio Medico Legal. However, Belleti did go over the front of the body with a lens. But he failed to notice a tiny red mark on Jonathan's shin which was almost certainly made by a needle. Very fine needle marks are difficult to see if administered by an expert. However, on later examination in Britain, that mark was clearly seen.

By this time, it was more than two days since Jonathan Moyle's death, making it virtually impossible to trace all the relevant substances in his body.

Dr Belleti did find drugs in Jonathan's stomach; Bromacepam and Diazepam, both tranquillizer-type medicines, possibly sedatives which could have formed a drug cocktail and been injected. However, the pathologist did not have the correct instruments to measure these drug traces, so he had no idea what quantity was present in Jonathan's body. He later claimed that the drugs were not relevant to the investigation. 'It is possible that the Diazepam could have been the remnants of what Moyle was given when he was injected following those stomach complaints earlier that week,' admitted a British medical examiner. 'But that still leaves a question mark over the Bromacepam.'

But most startling of all, Belleti insisted that virtually no contents were found in the stomach. Yet Jonathan ate on the plane from Punta Arenas and was seen drinking Pisco Sours at the Chilean Air Force reception the night before he died. Alcohol should remain in the bloodstream for much longer than 48 hours. 'The pathologist was either mistaken, or Moyle's body was irrigated by his killers to ensure that the massive traces of tranquillizer would not be found,' explained one post mortem expert.

Dr Belleti did not even carry out a full internal examination of the body.

One of the world's leading pathologists, Professor Iain West, believes that marks left on Jonathan's neck by the shirt which was used to hang him could disguise evidence that he was strangled before being put in the closet. 'Moyle could well have been garrotted before being hanged in the cupboard, but the indent of the shirt wrapped around his neck would have disguised the real injuries sufficiently. It is entirely plausible that he was strangled before being hanged in that cupboard,' says West, who — after analysing documents, photos and reports on the case — proclaimed it to be a very 'sloppy investigation'.

Dr Belleti always maintained that Jonathan Moyle killed himself. But he conceded to this author, 'It's always possible I was wrong and that Moyle's killers simply did a good job.' Belleti refused to elaborate any further on that comment.

*   *   *

On Monday, 2 April, chambermaid Silvia Cabrera nervously

walked past the plain clothes policemen in their dark suits and sunglasses, who had congregated outside the main entrance to the dilapidated Brigada de Homicidio de la Policia de Investigaciones building on Condel, in downtown Santiago.

A few minutes later, Silvia told detectives in vivid detail about the movement she heard in room 1406 shortly after 8.00am on the morning of Jonathan's death.

She made a statement to police saying that she saw a man in his early 60s leave Jonathan's room the previous Wednesday evening after voices were raised.

'They were very angry and I was startled by them but I didn't understand what they were saying because they were speaking English,' Silvia later recalled.

Silvia also insisted that a man who went in and out of Jonathan's room the morning of his death was Spaniard Antonio Terol, who was staying in the room next to Jonathan's. 'I heard the doors to both men's rooms open and close, so the Spaniard must have been involved,' she told police.

Detective Inspector Arellano did nothing about Silvia's claims at the time because he felt they were not relevant to Jonathan's death, which he firmly believed was suicide.

The only thing the police and pathologist Dr Belleti could not agree on was the time of death. Belleti claimed it was at least ten hours before Silvia Cabrera's grisly discovery, despite the police telling him about the phonecalls Jonathan was known to have made during the early hours of Saturday morning.

The detectives' main priority was to wrap the case up as quickly as possible. Certainly, they wanted to be seen by their superiors to be as efficient as possible because Jonathan was a prominent British citizen, but they did not want to linger on a simple *suicidio*. They had many other crimes on their books which still lay unsolved.

There was one powerful figure, however, who was not

satisfied with the way the *Caso de Moyle* was progressing.

*   *   *

The Palacio de Tribunales office of the 5th Precinct of the Santiago Police Department was located in the northern part of the city, near the Estacion de Mapocho. A three-storey, fading, red-brick building, it housed the crumbling, chaotic office of the precinct's investigating judge Alejandro Solis.

He was handed the file on the Moyle case by his Chief of Detectives on Tuesday, 2 April. Solis was intrigued the moment he started reading about Jonathan's background. He also found it hard to believe that anyone would chose a small cupboard to commit suicide in. Something about the case did not add up. And when he reached Silvia Cabrera's statement, he was certain the case needed further investigation. Solis immediately decided to issue an *Ordre de la Investigaciones* insisting that the police look more closely at the case.

Solis, in his 40s with shoulder-length, wavy dark hair and a friendly face, had a reputation for impartiality which was second to none, even in the bad old days of dictator General Pinochet. He also had a penchant for wearing brightly-coloured socks with his highly-polished Cuban loafers.

Perhaps surprisingly, Judge Alejandro Solis always retained a pleasant demeanour in or out of his robes. In fact, he didn't really look like a judge at all.

What he looked like, sitting behind the desk of his untidy office, was a middle-aged advertising executive. An advertising executive or a movie director dressed in dark-coloured shirts buttoned up to the top and loose-fitting jackets. The top of his forehead, where it disappeared into his hair, was marginally lighter than the rest of his face. He had the smile of someone used to being in charge. He often sat with his hands behind his head, leaning back in his chair. Most visitors to his chambers could only see his raised arms, elbows sticking out, and his head, his hair shining in the fluorescent light. On the wall behind him were framed photos of his wife and family.

Solis told his Chief of Detectives he wanted them to interview Pedro del Fierro immediately, because a fax to him had been found amongst Jonathan's belongings, and Anna Maria Yrarrazabal, who had called Jonathan's room the morning of his death. He also wanted to interview the guests on the 14th floor, as well as FIDAE officials.

'Then I want to interview every single person who met Moyle in Santiago,' Solis told an irritated Detective Arellano, who couldn't understand why the judge refused to accept his suicide theory.

Solis also insisted that a full internal examination of Jonathan's body should be carried out by a civilian doctor as soon as possible.

Detective Arrelano rolled his eyes skyward as he listened.

*   *   *

Just a few days after the discovery of Jonathan's body, Cardoen PR executive Raul Montecinos admitted to journalist Pedro del Fierro he had seen Jonathan at the Hotel Carrera the night before he died.

'I had to call him up about another story and he just threw it into the conversation,' recalled del Fierro. 'Montecinos was very casual about it. He just said, "I wasn't surprised Moyle died. I met him at the Carrera the night before he was found and he seemed really depressed. We talked in the bar and then I saw him across the room at a reception. He wasn't a happy man, you know. Very depressive type." When I tried to ask him more about Moyle he just changed the subject and said there was nothing more to say.'

But when Montecinos later heard that del Fierro had told some colleagues that he had said he'd seen Jonathan at the hotel, he warned del Fierro to stop spreading lies about him.

In an attempt to reprimand del Fierro further, Montecinos later made a formal complaint to *Defence Weekly* about one of del Fierro's articles in which he claimed the converted Bells were being developed for the military. Jonathan's death had already sparked off a surge of interest in the subject which had not existed before he died.

Montecinos's letter to *Defence Weekly*'s publishers, Jane's, said: 'This [the helicopter story] is untrue since its multi-purpose characteristics have strictly civilian purposes. It is absolutely false that the future production of the helicopter is an essential part of an agreement with Iraq.'

Del Fierro believes to this day that the hidden message behind Montecinos's letter was that del Fierro should keep his nose out of the Bell story. The letter also proves that Montecinos was perfectly willing to continue lying about the helicopter's real military role.

*   *   *

Back in England, at the Slough offices of Shephard Press, staff were desperately scrambling around for some evidence of what really happened to Jonathan. They found it impossible to accept that Jonathan had committed suicide. But, like his family, they were told by the Foreign Office that there was no point in travelling to Chile because it was an open-and-shut case.

The company even re-examined all the travel arrangements concerning Jonathan's trip to Chile and then to Bolivia on the anti-drugs patrol with the DEA.

Senior manager of Shephard Press, John Hamer, then contacted Chip Barclay, a senior diplomat at the US

Embassy in London, who had helped to set up the trip to Bolivia a few weeks earlier. However, Barclay was not forthcoming and told Hamer that, officially, the US could not get involved.

Shephard Press were disappointed by the US Embassy response since they had been so helpful previously. But the Americans knew more about Carlos Cardoen and Jonathan Moyle than they were willing to admit.

Shephard Press remained in a severe state of shock over Jonathan's death for some months. One member of staff admitted in a letter to Jonathan's friend and Sikorsky test pilot Nick Lappos that 'the news of Jonathan has been hanging over this office like a rain cloud.'

*   *   *

In Santiago on 11 April, following Judge Alejandro Solis's specific orders, civilian pathologist Soledad Arredondo Bahamonde re-examined Jonathan's body at the Servicio Medico Legal. She confirmed that the stomach was empty after removing certain vital organs, commented on the good condition of Jonathan's teeth and promptly recommended that the body should be returned to the family for transportation to Britain.

No one, it seemed, other than Solis, was prepared even to concede that Jonathan's death was suspicious.

Neither pathologist will acknowledge to this day that they should have held on to the corpse for longer, and then the mystery of what happened to Jonathan Moyle might have been solved much sooner.

> 'Government is not reason. It is not
> eloquence. It is a force, like fire;
> a dangerous servant and a terrible master.'
>
> *George Washington*

Spring had just come in the gardens of Highcliff House; flowers were coming into bloom — daffodils, zinnias and crocuses. All the renovation work at Highcliff House stopped the day that Jonathan died. The garden he had spent so many hours lovingly restoring was left untended, and many of the rooms in the vast property remained unpainted and covered in dustsheets.

Inquisitive reporters began turning up at the house at all hours of the day and night trying to find out more about Jonathan. Had he told Tony and Diana Moyle he was a spy? What was the real reason he was in Chile?

The constant attention and intrusion prolonged Diana's bereavement, even though Tony remained convinced that the only way to get to the bottom of his son's death was to stay in constant touch with the media.

When Jonathan's body was flown home from Chile, a local pathologist examined it and gave evidence at the opening of the inquest in Exeter, Devon. The brain, stomach and all vital organs had been removed by Chilean practitioners, and he could come to no firm conclusions.

The inquest was opened and adjourned to await the result of inquiries by Chilean judge Alejandro Solis.

Tony was becoming more and more frustrated by the Foreign Office's apparent lack of interest. Immediately after Jonathan's remains had been examined in Britain, Tony put forward a whole series of questions and comments that the undertaker, and Jonathan's aunt Pat Moyle, a nurse, had made.

'There was a bruise on his shin and certain vital organs were missing. I wanted to know what had happened to them. But the Foreign Office sounded completely uninterested. They just didn't seem to care,' explained Tony Moyle.

*   *   *

In Santiago, the main daily newspaper *La Tercera* quoted a police source close to the investigation who claimed that Jonathan had been murdered by hitmen connected to a Western intelligence service. Another linked his death with a deal between the Chilean Air Force and a German defence company.

As these reports started filtering back to London, some newspapers began investigating the claims. Increasing numbers of journalists turned up in Branscombe to interview the Moyles.

A typical piece at the time was published in the *Daily Mail* headlined: THE DRUG BARONS MURDERED OUR SON, SAY PARENTS.

It centred on remarks made by Tony Moyle in which he speculated about whether his son's trip to join the DEA anti-drug patrols in Bolivia might have been linked to Jonathan's death. As Tony told the newspaper: 'I would swear on my own life that Jonathan would not top himself.

It was not in his repertoire. He was a determined type, a real action man with everything to live for. He was in absolutely top spirits when I last spoke to him.'

These early claims about drug baron assassins were a long way off the mark, but the newspapers were at least waking up to the fact that Jonathan's death was very suspicious.

As Fleet Street reporter Richard Holliday explained, 'Moyle's death hardly caused a ripple of interest at first, but then stories about his background started circulating and we all began to sit up and take notice of it. Something fishy was going on.'

*   *   *

Jonathan Moyle's cremation took place at 12.00 midday on Thursday, 26 April, at the Exeter Crematorium in Topsham Road. His parents had decided that their son's ashes would be laid to rest under a memorial stone in the graveyard at St Winifred's Church in the centre of Branscombe, where many of his friends and family gathered following the ceremony.

The interior of St Winifred's was filled with an orange haze which dimmed to a blue twilight towards the high vaulted roof.

Outside, barely audible, the sounds of the Devon countryside, occasionally filtered through.

St Winifred's has nestled in the centre of Branscombe since it was built in the 13th century. Saxon herring-bone carving at the base of the main tower provides a graceful, square turret. The central chamber of the church was once a priests' room, and the ornate Elizabethan oak gallery has an unusual three-deck pulpit.

Among the mourners at St Winifred's was journalist Paul Beaver, who felt overwhelmingly guilty about Jonathan's death since it was he who had encouraged the young magazine editor to pursue the Cardoen Bell helicopter story. Beaver, though, like everyone else, had no idea that their inquiries would end so tragically.

'I felt dreadful about what had happened to Jonathan. It seemed such a tragic waste,' he later recalled.

Once the funeral was over, the Moyles and Annette Kissenbeck had to try to start coming to terms with what had happened. Annette's response was almost to move into the Moyle family home in Branscombe. She arrived from her job in London every weekend for months after Jonathan's death.

Annette tried in a bizarre way to take over from Jonathan as the Moyles' child. She constantly attended to heartbroken Diana Moyle, and Diana found herself, in turn, mothering Annette in her time of grief.

Often, the two women would link arms and walk off into the woods near the house for hours on end thinking, talking and weeping over Jonathan.

At one stage, Annette became so emotionally disturbed by the loss of her fiancé that she insisted on climbing into Diana's bed whenever she woke up in the middle of the night.

'The only way I could get her back to sleep was to read her the same bedtime stories that Jonathan had enjoyed as a child,' explained Diana later.

Tony and Diana eventually realised that, while Annette's motives were perfectly understandable, her behaviour was having a crushing effect on them. They felt overwhelmingly trapped by Annette's turmoil and, after months of mourning, they pleaded with Annette to get on with her own life and let them try to pick up the pieces of their own ruined existence. She reluctantly agreed.

*   *   *

The British media interest gained momentum as more and

more reports emerged from Chile. On Sunday, 29 April, the *Sunday Express* published an article headlined 'WAS BRITON MURDERED BY HITMAN?' which put pressure on the Chilean authorities to look more closely at the case.

Then *The Times* seized the moral high ground in an editorial:

MURDER MOST FOUL?

The Foreign Office should heed the Moyle family's protests at the British Embassy's refusal to exert pressure on the Chilean authorities to treat the case as one of murder. Those responsible for Jonathan Moyle's death may well have nothing to do with the firm of Industrias Cardoen SA or its owner. The Iraqis, however, would clearly have had a motive. Few will have confidence in Chilean justice until Jonathan Moyle's death has been thoroughly and impartially investigated.

On 26 April 1990, the day of Jonathan's funeral in Devon, Labour MP George Galloway asked the then British Foreign Secretary Douglas Hurd if the Government was fully satisfied that the Chilean authorities were properly investigating the death of Jonathan Moyle. He also asked for a report from the UK Ambassador in Santiago and a statement from Mr Hurd. Neither was forthcoming.

Galloway claimed that junior Conservative Foreign Minister Timothy Sainsbury cornered him in the House of Commons lobby and tried to convince him that the UK Government had no idea about the circumstances of Jonathan's death.

Weeks later, Galloway again raised a question in Parliament by asking Defence Minister Archie Hamilton if he would list the capacities in which the late Jonathan Moyle served Her Majesty's Government.

Hamilton replied that Jonathan had served in the Royal

Air Force but he made no reference to his 'other' work for the Ministry of Defence or Michael Armitage's top secret strategic studies unit.

Galloway questioned the Foreign Office closely about the investigation and was assured that the British authorities in Santiago were doing all they could, and that the Chileans were 'vigorously investigating' the death. He also asked Douglas Hurd for a statement to the House. The Government replied: 'It's for the Chilean authorities to investigate ... ready to assist in any way ... embassy totally diligent ...' Galloway remarked sardonically, 'This is the worst case of suicide I've ever heard of.'

Meanwhile, at Foster's, Jonathan's old school, news of his death stunned staff and pupils. They ran a moving obituary in the *Fosterian* magazine:

> JONATHAN MOYLE ('72-'79) Many old Fosterians will have learned with shock of the tragic death in peculiar circumstances of Jonathan Moyle. Jonathan, after serving as a pilot in the RAF, was editor of the magazine *Defence Helicopter World*. At the time of his death he was in Santiago, Chile, planning to fly to Bolivia with the CIA on an anti-drugs mission. Though it has not been possible to prove it legally, it is practically certain that he was murdered. All who knew Jonathan were impressed by his boundless enthusiasm and it is very sad that a life of such promise should be so tragically brought to an end at the early age of 28. To his parents and his fiancée, Annette Kissenbeck, we send our deepest condolences.

Jonathan Moyle's death was touching many people and would continue to do so ...

24

Santiago

'God is good, there is no devil but fear.'

Elbert Hubbard, The Note Book (1927)

People connected with the *Caso de Moyle*, as it was known in Chile, rapidly closed ranks by the end of April 1990. Many, like chambermaid Silvia Cabrera, were terrified that their evidence might cost them their lives.

'Everyone at the hotel was very scared. The authorities ordered us not to speak publicly about the case. I was scared for my life. I had seen things that people didn't want me to see,' Silvia later recalled.

All the staff at the Hotel Carrera were told not to talk about the death and British diplomats were ordered by the Foreign Office to say nothing publicly about the case.

The British Embassy in Santiago accepted the suicide verdict and responded to every press inquiry with a terse explanation: 'It is believed this is a case of suicide.' The staff at the embassy had even advised journalists 'off the record' that they had reasons for believing Jonathan to have discussed suicide with his family.

The source for these claims was a five-page letter which Jonathan's fiancée Annette sent to the Foreign Office in London, setting out her reasons for believing that Jonathan had been murdered.

She asked them to forward the letter to Chile. But when she discovered that the embassy intended to fax a shortened version of the letter, Annette abandoned her plans to go the 'official' route and sent the letter herself. The Foreign Office official refused to explain why they wanted to 'edit' the letter.

Annette eventually faxed the letter to the British Embassy in Santiago herself, but she never received a response.

In her letter, Annette wrote: 'He always detested the idea of suicide and mentioned this several times. He once heard of a pupil's father [a pupil of Tony Moyle's] who had been found hanged in a garage, and he said that he could neither understand nor accept such "cowardice" under whatever circumstances.'

For some bizarre reason, this reference alone was interpreted by the embassy as implying that Jonathan Moyle had suicidal tendencies.

Two weeks after this, ITN journalist Ian Williams visited the embassy during his inquiries into the case and was told categorically that Annette's letter included a suggestion that Jonathan had discussed suicide.

When Williams asked to see the letter for himself, he was told by an embassy official that he shouldn't even be telling Williams about it and it was 'out of the question' that he could allow the journalist to see the letter.

Williams later explained, 'There was absolutely no doubt that he wished to convey the impression that there was evidence of suicidal tendencies contained in that statement from Annette.

'He went out of his way towards the end of our discussion to highlight this aspect of the letter but all the time emphasising that while he shouldn't even be telling us this, there was no way that he could breach confidence and allow us to see the letter physically in which this was supposedly contained.'

Later, British Foreign Office Minister Timothy Sainsbury denied that the embassy had deliberately tried to mislead journalists about Jonathan's 'suicidal tendencies'. But he could offer no reasonable explanation of the embassy's behaviour.

*   *   *

In Chile, Judge Solis found out that Silvia Cabrera saw blood on the sheet of the bed in room 1406 and the existence of a syringe in the room when he interviewed Silvia himself on 17 May — this was more than six weeks after Jonathan's death. None of this had been mentioned in her earlier statement to detectives. She later claimed she had omitted to mention it because she was so scared for her life.

Judge Solis then assigned a team of detectives from OS7, Chile's FBI, to the case because he was angry that the police investigation had been so sloppy. By this time, the police who had originally led the case did not even have the confidence of their own chief, General Toro. In a television interview just a few weeks after Jonathan's death, he described his own force:

'What's happening inside the force is a reflection of what's happening outside. There's immoral behaviour from many policemen, pressure, extortion, collusion with crime and unlawful harassment of prisoners.'

Fifty-five of General Toro's own force were then under investigation for human rights violations, but 21 of those officers had used false identities while questioning prisoners and were therefore untraceable. Police files had even been burned to avoid implicating certain high-ranking officers in the atrocities.

There were also other forces trying their hardest to block Judge Solis's attempts to re-investigate the killing of Jonathan Moyle.

The judge spent six weeks waiting for the British consulate to call him back with the home address of Jonathan's parents. In frustration, he began asking journalists to take the Moyles' lists of questions because he so distrusted the British diplomats in Santiago. The embassy insists to this day that it was 'due to simple inefficiency' that Judge Solis's calls were not returned.

But the judge's biggest battle was with his own police force. They steadfastly refused to concede that Jonathan's death was anything other than suicide. They insisted that the tidy state of the room was ample evidence of Jonathan's state of mind, conveniently forgetting that Silvia Cabrera had tidied the room before looking in the closet.

*　　　　　*　　　　　*

Calling in OS7 — Order Y Seguridad (Order and Security) — was a controversial move by Judge Solis. An undercover force of investigators run by the paramilitary Carabiñeros, they only ever probed drugs and murder cases. Even the name of the head of OS7 was kept a secret, as was the location of the force's headquarters in Santiago.

OS7 carried out a detailed investigation but were hampered by having lost so many weeks of valuable inquiry time. Witnesses such as Silvia Cabrera, the hotel chief of security Roberto Campusano and other hotel staff were intimidated by the level of publicity the case had attracted and the tough reputation of OS7. And OS7's rivals in the Investigaciones did not lift a finger to help.

Officers from 0S7 soon established that Jonathan's wallet, briefcase and two files were missing from room 1406 by the time detectives arrived at the death scene.

They told Judge Solis that anyone could have walked

into the Carrera Hotel unchallenged through the front, or the tradesman's entrance alongside the hotel, because there were no security checks on people coming in or out of the hotel.

The OS7 taskforce soon became convinced that Jonathan was murdered. However, there was pressure from above to clear up the investigation 'quickly and cleanly'. One senior OS7 officer, Angel Garida, revealed that he was ordered to conclude it was a suicide. Garida said that Chile's Interior Ministry issued the orders over the head of Judge Solis. 'They wanted it all swept under the carpet. They did not want any bad publicity. That would be bad for Chile,' claimed Garida.

On 8 May, 1990, Alan Whitmore of the British Embassy — which was still publicly insisting that Jonathan had committed suicide — sent a letter to Judge Solis requesting all the police papers and photos taken at the scene of Jonathan's death. In London, a file had already been opened on the Moyle case at the MoD.

Tony Moyle appointed a lawyer called Jorge Trivino, a young, ambitious attorney who was outraged by what he saw as a travesty of justice. Within days of taking on the high-profile investigation, Trivino was threatened with death in a series of anonymous phone calls.

'They told me to stop causing problems on the *Caso de Moyle*,' recalled Trivino. Trivino's slightly nervous, lisping, high-pitched voice disguised a determination not to be intimidated.

'Someone was trying to stop me investigating Moyle's death. The caller was different each time but just as emphatic. "Stop working on the case otherwise you will regret it," was the message. But it simply made me decide that I had to take on the case. Justice had to prevail.'

*   *   *

In May 1990, Raul Montecinos misled the press in the aftermath of Jonathan's death. While admitting to *The Independent* in London that Iraq had 'expressed an interest' in Cardoen's converted Bell helicopters, he still insisted that it was a civilian project.

'We are a prestigious company and we would not risk our reputation by doing something so blatantly illegal,' Montecinos said.

A few days after this, Chilean TV cameraman Riccardo Correo Poblete was working for Britain's Channel Four when he called Raul Montecinos to arrange an interview with him and Carlos Cardoen.

'He told me he met Moyle at the air force reception on the Friday night,' recalled Correo. 'I even asked him a second time because I was so surprised.

'Then he told me about them sharing a Pisco Sour which was just as surprising since the pathologist had claimed there was no alcohol in Moyle's body.'

Correo's conversation was witnessed by two journalists in his office because he had used the speakerphone facility.

The following day, Cardoen went missing and Montecinos refused to meet Correo or the Channel Four team.

Journalists from London's Channel Four News have confirmed Correo's account of what happened with Montecinos.

And their report, which aired on 14 May 1990, probably did more to prompt closer media investigation of the case than anything else up to this point.

Reporter Ian Williams's 7.00pm news segment from Santiago concluded that the British Embassy had deliberately encouraged the media to believe that Jonathan had committed suicide. Williams ended by telling viewers, 'Six weeks after Jonathan Moyle's death, the case raises many uncomfortable questions which have yet to be answered.'

Meanwhile, British broadsheet newspapers continued to probe the case. Journalists Tim Kelsey and Maureen Meehan of *The Independent* wrote a report headlined 'BRITON'S "KILLING" LINKED TO IRAQI ARMS SALE' which stated that it was likely Jonathan was 'the victim of his passionate, often indiscreet, enthusiasm for technical military reporting.' But while insisting that Jonathan's killers were the Iraqis, the paper could not uncover any conclusive evidence to back their claims.

A week later, the same writing team reported that blood had been found on Jonathan's sheets, which challenged police theories of suicide. But Kelsey and Meehan still conceded that the motive for the murder remained a mystery.

Three days later, *The Times* ran a long front-page article headlined 'MISSING DOCUMENTS ADD TO DOUBTS ON JOURNALIST'S SUICIDE'. The paper informed its readers about the wallet, briefcase and two files which OS7 had established were missing from Jonathan's hotel room.

* * *

In Chile, at the Fifth Precinct HQ, in the Palacio de Tribunales, there was a bitter battle of wills going on between Judge Solis and the Brigada de Homicidio detectives originally assigned to the case. They would not concede that they might have been wrong to pronounce it a suicide so quickly.

In desperation, the judge then turned his attentions to the pathologist, Dr Belleti, who reluctantly agreed to re-examine some elements of the case. But, he told Judge Solis, he remained convinced that Jonathan had committed suicide.

When Raul Montecinos heard that Judge Solis was still determined to prove that Jonathan had been murdered, he approached Dr Belleti with some 'suggestions' about how and why Jonathan died. Dr Cardoen himself had grown increasingly angry about claims that he and his company were in some way linked to Jonathan's death. He demanded that his public relations department do everything in their power to persuade the authorities that this was not the case.

Montecinos located a highly specialised book, which highlighted details of sexual asphyxiation. Montecinos met with Dr Belleti and showed him the book. It told how death from unintentional suffocation can sometimes occur because of masochistic actions of the victims. This has been described as auto-erotic death or sexual asphyxiation. Usually, a man is found hanged and either naked, dressed in women's clothes, underwear or with his genitals exposed. A rope or strip of cloth hung from within his reach is attached to his neck. It is soft to avoid bruising and hides any evidence of the activity. He is not known to be depressed and his death surprises friends and family. Usually, he has not suffered from any psychological disorders. The cause of death is asphyxia, usually from neck compression but other forms can involve chest compression, airway blockage or lack of oxygen.

After reading it, Dr Belleti thanked Montecinos profusely and immediately took the book round to show Judge Solis what he believed was conclusive evidence that Jonathan had not been murdered.

Meanwhile, Montecinos started to do what he did best as a skilled public relations executive; he launched a campaign to spread the word about 'English pervert' Jonathan Moyle.

*   *   *

Around this time, journalist Pedro del Fierro received

another angry call from Montecinos, who was still furious because del Fierro had been telling mutual acquaintances that Montecinos told him he had met Jonathan shortly before he died.

'I want you to retract what you have been saying. It is causing me a lot of trouble,' said Montecinos.

'Why?' asked del Fierro.

'You know why,' came the reply.

'No, I don't Raul. You tell me,' added del Fierro, almost playfully.

'Look, Pedro. I've talked to my people in Iraq and they are very unhappy about things. Now do you understand?'

'Goodbye, Raul,' said del Fierro putting the phone down promptly. He never talked to Montecinos again.

The following week, del Fierro noticed a man parked outside his office in Santiago. At first he ignored him, but by the third day del Fierro marched across the street and confronted the man.

'What the fuck are you doing?' demanded del Fierro.

'Nothing.'

'Come on! You've been watching me for three days and I don't fucking like it.'

'I'm a reporter.'

'Bullshit! You're trying to lean on me.'

The man started his car up and drove away.

A few days later, del Fierro noticed the same man outside the house where he had entertained Jonathan and the other journalists three days before Jonathan's death.

This time, the well-built del Fierro stormed into his house, went straight to a desk in his bedroom and pulled out his pistol. He walked back downstairs and went outside to where the man was waiting in his car.

'You see this mother-fucker!' he screamed, waving his pistol.

The man refused to open his window and drove away once again. Del Fierro didn't even bother reporting the incidents to the police. He knew there was nothing they could do.

'Next day the man was back outside my home. I just decided to stay away from him. They were trying to intimidate me. They wanted me to know they knew,' del Fierro stated later.

> 'The only real diplomacy ever performed
> by a diplomat is in deceiving their own people
> after their dumbness
> has got them into war.'
>
> *Will Rogers*

The British Ambassador's residence in Santiago stands like a miniature version of Buckingham Palace amongst the apartment blocks on Gertrudis Echenique, in the lush middle-class residential area of Golf. In many ways, it is a cliché in concrete, complete with iron gates, high railings and a gravel driveway. The front entrance features vast double doors opening into a circular reception area with a cloakroom just off it. Then there is a long hallway that runs the entire length of the building. The marble floor downstairs is in stark contrast to the plush carpets on the staircase and in the private quarters.

On one wall of the hallway was a large portrait of Lord Cochrane, which 39-year-old journalist Malcolm Coad never forgot because he was in the middle of writing a novel featuring Cochrane at the time of Jonathan Moyle's death. He also happened to be the *Guardian*'s South America correspondent.

Coad walked into a large reception room where a cocktail party for the visiting Archbishop of Canterbury, Dr Robert Runcie, was being held, at 7.30pm on 31 May 1990. At least 100 people had already arrived and some were wandering through the French doors into the Ambassador's garden. A huge striped canopy over the terrace made this very English scene complete.

Coad accepted a glass of wine from one of the waiters and headed towards a waitress with a silver tray of canapés. Then he moved to a group of people he recognised, including the editor of one of Santiago's daily newspapers and a tall blonde woman called Catherine Royle of the embassy staff.

After a few minutes of polite conversation, Coad turned around and headed off for another canapé. Just then, a small, bald-headed middle-aged Englishman called Bill Campbell caught Coad's eye.

Campbell clearly had something to tell Coad and purposefully moved towards him. After a few words of greeting, Campbell got to the point.

'What do you think about this Jonathan Moyle case?'

'This murder theory should be taken seriously,' replied Coad.

Campbell seemed perplexed.

'No, no, no. It's obvious what's happened here. He was mucking about with himself.' He hesitated. 'Getting off on it, you know.'

Coad was taken aback. Campbell sensed the hesitation in his response and continued, 'It's very common. Far more common than you think. It's called auto-eroticism.'

Campbell then launched into detail on his theories about Jonathan's death.

Coad was astounded but tried to remain low key. 'How interesting.'

'He seemed so well briefed. It was as if he deliberately sought me out,' says Coad.

Moments later, Coad turned round to get a drink and when he looked back, Campbell had gone.

Says Coad, 'He'd done his bit. He wanted to find out what I knew and he planted an outrageous story in my lap.'

Coad then turned back to the other guests he had been standing with before and said, 'Oh, I've just heard the latest theory about Jonathan Moyle.'

*　　　　　*　　　　　*

By day, the building always managed to appear virtually deserted. Dirty ground-floor windows; the underground car park sealed by a rigid steel barrier. Above it, 20 storeys of net curtains that hid the faces of some of Britain's most sensitive employees. This Cold War relic, known as Century House, sat sullen and unadorned behind Waterloo Station.

At night, in odd corners and on different floors, a handful of neon lights illuminated some of the rooms and corridors of power. Studious men and women living, and sometimes even dying, in the name of secret-keeping.

As the Cold War drew to a close, the world suddenly became more, rather than less, dangerous. Little wars were multiplying across the globe. Little gangs grew big. Crime went multinational on an unprecedented scale. And British intelligence could only watch from the sidelines, hampered by old laws and old thinking.

There has always been a close liaison between the British security forces and journalists. The connections sprang from a patriotic desire during the Second World War to help the Allies and give no inadvertent comfort to the enemy. The links, however, survived the change of conditions: an unspoken assumption of a common interest and a greater good has underpinned dealings between the security forces and some journalists ever since. The egregious example is David Astor, the liberal-minded editor of the *Observer*, who was persuaded to offer cover to double-agent Kim Philby when he was a journalist in Beruit. (Neither Astor or the Secret Intelligence Service then knew that Philby was working for the KGB.)

A whole section of the security services — known as the BAQ department — has been given over to cultivating these contacts, and another to giving regular off-the-record briefings to correspondents close to the front line. The ethics of these briefings have always been unclear. The journalists are free to discount what they are told, but they rarely do. But the pressure on journalists has always been intense.

So it was that in Whitehall, on the same day as diplomat Bill Campbell was 'leaking' the sex scandal story about Jonathan Moyle's death to Malcolm Coad, British intelligence officials offered the same information in a briefing to *Sunday Times* journalists in London.

The most important question was: Why should the British authorities bother to spread this kind of story or to speculate relatively openly, at least to third parties, about such a possibility? Pathologist Belleti had only just started to look into a possible link with sexual asphyxia so conveniently suggested by Raul Montecinos. Yet it was being leaked everywhere.

And it was a slur which travelled. It even reached some of Jonathan's old friends as far afield as Hong Kong.

On 1 June, Tony Moyle received a call from a *Guardian* journalist in London asking for a response to the allegations. Tony was aghast and immediately demanded to know who was spreading the rumours. He became even more irate when the reporter refused to identify the source.

The following day, Malcolm Coad's story about the attempt to smear Jonathan's name appeared in the *Guardian* ahead of what was expected to be a much more tawdry tale in the following day's *Sunday Times*, which had been sourced by the MoD in London.

Tony Moyle denounced the episode as '... foul, what on earth possessed somebody to say this?'

The *Guardian* story which appeared on 2 June 1990, read as follows:

DEAD JOURNALIST SEX SMEAR 'FOUL'

British officials in Chile are claiming that the dead defence journalist Jonathan Moyle was a sexual deviant who hanged himself while attempting to obtain pleasure. It is understood that members of MI5 have made the same assertion in London.

Last night Mr Moyle's father, Anthony Moyle, rejected the claim: "Nothing could be further from the truth. My son, my wife and myself were very close. This is just foul. What on earth possessed somebody to say this?"

No evidence has been provided to support the claims, which will smear Jonathan Moyle's reputation as investigators in Chile are casting doubt on the police assertion, immediately after his death, that he committed suicide.

Mr Moyle, aged 28 of Devon, was found hanged in the wardrobe of his room in the Carrera Hotel in Santiago on March 31.

He worked for the magazine *Defence Helicopter World* and was in Chile for the biennial Air and Space Fair put on by the Chilean Air Force.

He was interested in a Bell helicopter that the Chilean company Industrias Cardoen is converting to multi-purpose use, especially for Third World conditions and economies. He was then due to travel to Bolivia to write about military efforts there to combat drugs.

His interest in the helicopter — and suggestions that Iraq was trying to acquire it — plus the investigation into drugs have given rise to suggestions that he was the victim of skulduggery by international arms dealers or drug traffickers.

His family and friends in Britain were incredulous at the suicide explanation for his death. They pointed out that he had no history of depression and was about to get married.

According to colleagues, immediately before his death Mr Moyle was in excellent spirits, full of work projects and happy about his forthcoming marriage. It is understood that letters were found on him in which he wrote fondly of his honeymoon plans, trees he was planting in his garden, and a forthcoming visit to his prospective in-laws in Germany.

Mr Moyle believes his son's death was connected with his interest in the Cardoen helicopter.

"Before he died, he talked to Mr [Carlos] Cardoen himself," he said. "The judge [investigating the death] has detailed drawings of weapons which the Cardoen people were going to fit on to the helicopter and export to Iraq. My son would probably have printed that this would have made it potentially an attack helicopter."

However, the helicopter conversion has been well known for some time, and Mr Cardoen's dealings with the Iraqi regime are also well known. He said recently that Iraq would certainly be a potential customer.

On the morning of publication in London, Malcolm Coad received an angry call from Catherine Royle at the British Embassy in Santiago.

'What the hell have you been doing, Malcolm? Why did you file that article?'

Coad was surprised that Royle had been contacted so rapidly from London, and it was clear to him that her chief concern was that she might be blamed by her superiors for leaking the Moyle 'sex slur' story.

'The embassy are blaming me for what happened

because they saw me talking to you,' she continued. 'I'm very disappointed in you. I thought you were a serious journalist.'

Royle desperately tried to get Coad to tell her who had 'leaked' the story, although the embassy already knew who it might be because he had been spotted talking to Coad. They just wanted to be sure.

'It's nothing to do with you,' Coad told Royle. 'I'm not prepared to say who it was.'

Royle later told Coad that for two days 'a dark cloud hung over me' until the embassy realised that she hadn't been responsible. *But she never admitted to Coad she'd actually been at Aberwystwyth with Jonathan Moyle seven years earlier.*

'I was surprised when I later found out they'd been there together,' says Coad now. 'I suppose she was worried that if she'd said anything at the time, it would have been interpreted as being terribly significant.'

But the reverberations from the sex allegations story did not end there. In the House of Commons, Labour MP Ken Livingstone demanded to know if the Prime Minister had been briefed on the Moyle murder.

'If so, what is your response to the Chilean judge charged with investigating the murder, who stated that his investigation was obstructed by the unwillingness of British officials to co-operate?'

The Prime Minister accused Livingstone of making a series of 'unsubstantiated comments to which you know I will have no intention whatsoever of replying.'

Guardian journalist Malcolm Coad was then denounced in the House of Commons by Foreign Minister Tim Sainsbury, who described his report as irresponsible journalism.

The story had one important knock-on effect as far as Malcolm Coad was concerned. It made him doubly convinced that Jonathan Moyle was murdered.

Meanwhile, the British Embassy was becoming

increasingly adept at issuing denials. It denied that its military attachés Finnigan and Hall ever met Jonathan. It denied that any embassy official was the source of the cruel sex slur story. The embassy was actually back-pedalling like mad to try to cover its tracks.

Tony and Diana Moyle were so horrified by the sexual asphyxia rumours that Tony wrote to the Foreign Office demanding that they name the source of this apparent slur. He even threatened to make his own inquiries and publish the name himself if he didn't get an explanation.

On 25 June 1990, Junior Minister Timothy Sainsbury telephoned Tony at the family home in Branscombe, Devon.

Tony recalls, 'He said that the slur had caused him a lot of concern and he was very unhappy about it.'

Tony then lashed out angrily at Sainsbury over the British Embassy's 'negative' attitude.

'I'm afraid we can't interfere with the Chilean justice system, Mr Moyle,' came Sainsbury's reply.

'I'm not asking you to interfere with Chilean justice. All I'm asking is that you show a positive attitude rather than being so negative. I thought your job was to protect British lives, or at least British reputations.'

*   *   *

Jonathan Moyle's aunt Pat went, in her own words, 'ballistic' when informed about the sexual deviancy allegations against her nephew.

Guardian correspondent Malcolm Coad told her over the phone about the exact circumstances surrounding the 'leak' at the British Embassy in Santiago. He also let slip that William Campbell was back in London, living in an area called Berrylands, just five minutes drive from Pat Moyle's home in Kingston, Surrey.

She immediately tracked down Campbell's name and address in her local telephone directory. Not even Pat's deeply-held Christian beliefs and life-long membership of the Salvation Army could stop her from going round to Campbell's house one warm June evening.

'I was spitting blood. I wanted revenge,' says Pat today. 'I was capable of anything.'

Luckily for Bill Campbell, he wasn't in, but his wife took the full brunt of Pat Moyle's onslaught.

'You tell him to call me,' Pat told the woman.

'But my husband isn't even a representative of the British Government ...'

'Oh yes he is,' retorted Pat. She could see no difference between a commercial attaché and an embassy official. She scribbled out her phone number and demanded that Campbell call her when he got back that evening.

Two hours later, Campbell telephoned Pat from his home.

'I'm sorry I missed you,' began Campbell.

'Don't be, Mr Campbell,' Pat replied. 'You're a lucky man. I would have slaughtered you if you'd been in.'

Campbell insisted that the meeting at the British Embassy which had sparked the whole affair was just 'an innocent conversation'.

'Nonsense,' replied Pat. 'I have eye-witness accounts of what happened. You were going up to people.'

The line went dead for a few seconds as Campbell tried to recover his composure.

'I can assure you that was not the case,' he insisted.

As Pat recalled, 'Then he started blustering and back-tracking. It was pathetic.'

At that time, Pat was so consumed with rage about her nephew's death that she actually believed herself capable of killing the person — or persons — responsible.

Bill Campbell himself was put under immense pressure by the Foreign Office to make a personal apology to the Moyle family and this was the letter that arrived at their home in Branscombe on 3 July 1990:

Dear Mr Moyle,

I had wished to make personal contact with you earlier than this, but as you know, the FCO decided to discuss the matter with you before advising me to go ahead.

I am Bill Campbell, British Counsel Representative in Chile, and it seems that it was I who inadvertently gave an opportunity to the Press to cause you further distress. I would like to offer my sincere apologies for this. As I expect you will have been told, my conversation with the Guardian's correspondent was not in any way prompted by any 'official' wish to propagate any possible explanation of your son's death — on the contrary, I took the opportunity of our chance meeting, in order to ask him his own opinion of certain aspects of the case. I have, like the rest of the British community in Santiago, been very concerned that the truth should be established. It has therefore distressed me very much that the aim of the conversation should have been so distorted, and I realise that it was unfortunately unwise of me to have asked the correspondent's opinion.

I do hope that this explanation will help you to accept that neither I nor the FCO were trying to advance any theory, in contradiction to the official investigations which I understand are continuing — I have been away from Chile on my usual home leave since June 10. Please also accept my deepest sympathy in your tragic loss,

Yours sincerely

W Campbell

No real evidence was ever produced to back up the death-by-sexual-asphyxia claims, and it was clearly an attempt to smear Jonathan's reputation just as investigators in Chile were starting to cast doubt on the earlier suicide theory.

Tony Moyle remains convinced to this day that Campbell's letter was dictated for him by his superiors.

Tony explained to one journalist, 'Where he says, "I do hope that this explanation will help you to accept that neither I nor the FCO were trying to advance any theory in contradiction to the official investigations which I understand are continuing ..." Well I didn't know it had been suggested that he was putting forward an FCO idea or theory. I thought he was merely passing on either something that he'd heard or, as he says, just discussing the matter.

'I have a nasty feeling at the back of my mind that there was more to it than an inadvertent opportunity for the press to cause further distress. I tend to feel that there's a lot of questions that still need to be answered about their conduct down there.'

He was living in the hope that justice might one day prevail.

'Justice will not condemn
even the Devil himself wrongfully.'

Thomas Fuller, MD, Gnomologia (1732)

Ten weeks after the body of Jonathan Moyle was found in a closet in Santiago, a strange package turned up in the mailbox at the front of journalist Frank Colucci's modest, single-storey detached home off a busy intersection in Colonia, New Jersey.

As a curious Colucci walked back up his pathway, he ripped open the buff-coloured envelope and found drawings for the single-seat Cardoen converted Bell 206 helicopter. There was a hand-written note attached which simply read: '*For Jonathan.*'

As Colucci recalled, 'It was weird. There was no text other than the note. Just structural drawings like an engineering framework.'

The report was clearly marked 'SECRET' and all the names in the paperwork had been carefully erased.

'Somebody who worked on the Bell conversion felt very bad at this point and felt obliged to send the material to me. They probably thought it would be of use to the investigation.'

Colucci believes to this day that it was sent by someone either from Global Helicopters or Cardoen Industrias.

'That note saying "For Jonathan" meant that it was specially for him. They wanted to help us solve his murder.'

Within minutes of getting the package, Colucci telephoned the offices of *DHW* publishers, Shephard Press.

'I thought that, one way or another, they would be able to make use of the documents, so I agreed to send the envelope over to them immediately,' recalled Colucci.

But the package never reached London. Colucci believes his phones were almost definitely being tapped at the time and that the material was intercepted.

'It was probably taken from my mail box. For some stupid reason, I didn't make a photocopy. I didn't even keep the original envelope for the postmark. I guess I screwed up. In retrospect, that package was incredibly significant.'

Dan Pettus, then Vice-President of Global Helicopters, admits that the drawings sent to Colucci's home 'could only have come from Cardoen, the FAA or Global'.

Frank Colucci believes the package was to have been an admission of someone's guilt.

*   *   *

On 19 July 1990, Judge Solis began lengthy interrogations of witnesses involved with the case. He was particularly concerned because the medical examiner was insisting he had found no traces of alcohol in Jonathan's body, yet he had definitely been drinking the night before he died and alcohol should remain in the bloodstream for up to 48 hours after death.

Another judge, Lucia Baganay, who had been assisting Judge Solis with the case, interviewed a British intelligence agent in Santiago. But the details of this were never made public. And to this day not even the Chileans will talk about what happened during that meeting.

'The British were desperate for us not to publicise the meeting. But I can tell you the agent effectively refused to help our investigation,' a source inside Judge Solis's office confirmed.

Judge Solis himself admitted that 'only a very great turnabout' would lead him to the truth. He was convinced that Jonathan had been murdered but feared that proving it might be impossible. OS7 had uncovered many clues, including hotel staff who saw Jonathan out walking near the Carrera just hours before he died, but OS7 told the judge that they had exhausted all leads for the time being.

Jorge Trivino, the recently-appointed Moyle family lawyer, was still receiving threatening phonecalls, but refused to be intimidated. He armed himself and considered hiring a personal bodyguard if the threats continued much longer.

Trivino had already re-interviewed many of the witnesses including the chambermaid, Silvia Cabrera. All their testimony was more detailed than that which they had given to the police shortly after Jonathan's death. But none of them could categorically support the murder theory.

*   *   *

In Hurst, Texas, the death of Jonathan Moyle provoked a ripple of interest, but Global Helicopters fully intended to continue test flying converted Bell 206Ls complete with the single-pilot cockpit. Cardoen was especially anxious to press on with the controversial project.

Privately, Cardoen was still seething about all the publicity concerning Jonathan's death because it was threatening to expose the truth behind his beloved helicopter project. But he was doggedly determined to continue with his plans.

The confident Chilean even agreed to be interviewed on the NBC nightly news broadcast across America, on 19 July 1990. He intended to reassure the US authorities that his converted helicopters were entirely legitimate. Most of what was seen by millions of Americans would have meant little to them. But in a transcript of the full, unedited version of the interview, Cardoen made some revealing comments.

At one stage, Cardoen was accused of creating the entire Bell helicopter conversion scheme as a loophole through which he intended to manufacture hundreds of military helicopters while still insisting they were 'primarily' for civilian use.

Cardoen did admit to acquiring a majority share in Global Helicopters in order to manufacture the aircraft in the USA. He was also accused of going to Bell in 1988 to get them to help him develop the helicopter. They refused, but immediately referred him to Clem Bailey at Global. Cardoen was thrown by the ferocity of the questioning and insisted that he had not violated any arms embargo rules.

It was even suggested that Cardoen could sell the helicopter to Iraq as soon as he gained a US airworthiness certification. Cardoen denied this, but admitted that once he had it certified he could do whatever he pleased with the helicopter.

During the same TV appearance, Cardoen talked in some depth of his respect for Saddam Hussein. He said, 'I have a great deal of respect for President Hussein, although I'm not responsible for his opinions or his doings. I regret to see Iraq today losing a certain position that they enjoyed in the past.'

After the camera had been switched off, Cardoen claimed that Saddam Hussein was a classic example of 'the good guy becomes the bad guy overnight. Just like that. A switch. On and off ...'

But he knew he had to distance himself from the brutal dictator.

'The state is the servant of the citizen,
and not his master.'

John F Kennedy

It was a baking July day, but David Harvey was feeling so nervous he would have been sweating anyway. Just a few hours earlier he had received a mysterious phone call from a man who said he worked for the FBI and that two agents wished to meet Harvey as a matter of great urgency.

British-born Harvey — a freelance defence journalist based in Washington, DC — found himself the target for Bureau inquiries after telling a friend in the military that he was preparing an article on the death of Jonathan Moyle for a highly-specialised US forces magazine. Security services on both sides of the Atlantic had long been aware of Harvey's involvement with the former editor of *Defence Helicopter World*, Paul Beaver, who had been working with Jonathan Moyle on the Cardoen Bell conversion investigation for almost a year before Jonathan's death.

Harvey had called his contact for advice on how to get an official response to the death of the young magazine editor for the article he was writing.

Harvey's source — a weapons expert in the US navy — seemed sympathetic. But less than an hour later, the FBI called him. The agent said that two of his colleagues were planning to drive down from New York.

Soon, Harvey was heading ten miles north-west of DC on Highway 355 towards the small town of Bethesda, where he was instructed to find the Bob's Big Boy diner and wait for the agents to appear.

Harvey knew the moment he saw the dark-blue Ford Taurus turn into the parking lot next to the diner it was them. The two Feds, in their mid-30s, were dressed like city brokers. Both were wearing shades, naturally.

'They were two very clever guys. They gave nothing away. I didn't even know if they knew anything about the Moyle case but they wanted to know what I knew.'

Often their eyes would snap around the nondescript restaurant to check out the other customers. At one stage, a diplomatic car went by and one of the Bureau men checked it out in a book of diplomatic licence plates he had.

'They were classic watchers,' explained David Harvey. 'Saddam was about to invade Kuwait and it was a very tense environment.'

'What d'you know about Cardoen?' asked one of the agents.

Harvey then explained everything he knew about the Chilean; how he had been looking into Cardoen's activities ever since Paul Beaver contacted him more than a year earlier; how he was convinced Cardoen was using Global to license the helicopters which would then be used for military purposes.

Then Harvey decided to ask a question about Jonathan Moyle.

'Who did it?' he asked the two agents.

There was a moment of silence. Then: 'We can't tell you, David.'

The two FBI men then proceeded to debrief Harvey of every possible detail he had of the Moyle killing and Carlos Cardoen's known activities in the United States, especially concerning his involvement with Global Helicopters.

Harvey knew that Clem Bailey had set up Global as a 'skunkworks', as it was known in the defence industry. 'In other words, a group of employees left Bell and set up an entirely new company with Bell's approval.'

Cardoen's plans for converting the Bells were not considered legitimate enough for Bell to be directly involved, so Global had stepped in.

When Harvey's article was eventually published in the January 1991 issue of *Armed Forces Journal*, it provoked an intriguing response from one caller who rang up the journalist and told him, 'Jonathan's father will be very glad you did that. Thank you.'

Harvey tried to get the name of the caller who had refused to reveal his identity, stating only that he was speaking from England.

Harvey's *AFJ* article made the following conclusion:

> 'This story is being taken as a serious cautionary tale by many who know the problems associated with the international arms trade and its unpredictable directions. In the final analysis, say arms transfer experts, the Moyle story has at least brought attention to a situation which could have implications under US law, or at the very least, bears further investigation.'

In Chile, Dr Carlos Cardoen was about to find himself on the receiving end of some very heavy pressure.

'Jonathan was a true patriot.'

Brian Passey, Jonathan Moyle's close friend

Brian Passey drove his white rented saloon south on the International Parkway out of Dallas Fort Worth International Airport before turning right on the airport freeway and then heading south across the Texas flatlands on Highway 360.

Outside the comfort of his air-conditioned car, the temperature nudged towards 100 degrees. It was humid, windless and very uncomfortable. But it was all familiar territory for ex-fighter pilot and advertising director for Shephard Press Passey.

Passey drove into the Arlington Municipal Airfield and parked his car in preparation for a visit to one of Shephard Press's most loyal advertisers, the Helidyme Group.

Just 30 yards away, however, Clem Bailey, debonair ex-Bell helicopter test pilot and President of Global Helicopters, immediately noticed Passey from his third-floor office in a block overlooking the car park.

Passey began walking towards Helidyme, whose offices were just opposite the Global headquarters which he had regularly visited over the previous few years. As Passey moved across the car park, he noticed Clem Bailey rushing towards him. He was clearly anxious.

'Brian, great to see you. Come in ...'

Passey was completely thrown. He hadn't come to see Global yet Clem Bailey had him by the arm and was guiding him towards the entrance of the Global offices.

'Er, I'm not actually here to see you, Clem ...'

Bailey looked surprised.

Passey explained and promised to drop in for a cup of tea and a chat after his appointment. But Bailey's approach made him suspicious because it was clear that the Global President had something important he wished to discuss.

Fifty-five minutes later, Brian Passey entered the Global Helicopter offices. It was quiet and empty. He remembered that when he'd been at Global a few months earlier the place had been buzzing. Today, it was dead.

A handful of people at the rear of the open-plan space did not even look up when Passey appeared so he headed straight for Clem Bailey's office. It was unlocked. He sat in front of Bailey's desk and waited. He spotted a newspaper folded in the wastebasket. He took it out. The *Dallas Morning News*: IRAQ INVADES KUWAIT.

This was bad news. Passey had been travelling so much he had become virtually oblivious to the news of the decade. He snorted derisively. He believed the West had lost its guts. Why didn't we move straight in and get that bastard Saddam?

Passey turned some pages — there was a quarter page on Global boss Clem Bailey. The story centred around the company's connections to Carlos Cardoen and the Bell helicopter conversion kits.

He tore out the page and folded it just as Bailey walked into the room.

'We didn't have anything to do with it, Brian,' stated a cold-sounding Clem Bailey as he moved to his seat.

Passey was perplexed, 'I didn't know anyone was suggesting you did.'

'I know it looks bad, but there is no way we were involved with Jonathan Moyle's murder,' said Bailey, who'd obviously presumed when he saw Passey in the car park that he was calling on Global to discuss Jonathan's death.

Passey was so shaken by his encounter with Clem Bailey at Global that, as soon as he checked into a local motel for the night, he called Alexander Shephard in London to tell him what had happened. Both men decided that Passey should never go back there. 'Shephard was very twitchy,' recalled Passey.

That night, the local television news was running the Global story as their lead story. Global were in the final stages of getting airworthiness certification when Saddam Hussein invaded Kuwait.

Shortly afterwards, the US Government confiscated the only working Bell prototype on the grounds that it was intended for eventual military use and the Bell conversion scheme collapsed.

Global managed to raise the capital to buy back all 51% of the shares they sold to Carlos Cardoen shortly after Passey's visit to their offices. They knew it was imperative to distance themselves from Cardoen as quickly as possible. Cardoen lost millions of dollars in the process because Global's value had collapsed following the federal government raids.

Vice-President Dan Pettus never forgot how worried he and Clem Bailey had been. 'We both expressed fears about whether Cardoen had been involved in the death of Jonathan Moyle. We wondered if we'd misjudged him.'

Shortly after Jonathan's death, there was so much gossip flying around about Global and Cardoen that Pettus actually confronted Clem Bailey and another senior colleague.

'Gentlemen, if there are any ghosts in this closet, let's lay 'em out now.'

Both men insisted they had nothing to hide.

However, Pettus made Bailey agree not to talk to Cardoen except through Pettus, whose position inside the company had became far more powerful following the buy-back of shares from Cardoen.

'Clem never really communicated his personal problems to us here at Global and he certainly got it wrong when this whole thing blew up. Clem walked into problems. Clem was not the type of person who checked very thoroughly before he leapt into an opportunity. His personality was one that would have allowed him to get into something before he realised he shouldn't have.'

In some ways, Clem Bailey and Jonathan Moyle sounded one and the same.

Dan Pettus bravely confronted Carlos Cardoen about Jonathan's death some months after his body was discovered.

'Carlos, is it possible that somebody in your organisation, thinking he was going to protect your backside for some reason, would do that? Have you got anybody you can think of?'

Cardoen squinted in Pettus's direction, then looked him straight in the eye.

'Absolutely not ...'

Pettus never brought up the subject again.

But he has developed some intriguing theories over the past six years.

'Cardoen's power in the land made me think someone might have done it on his behalf. It wasn't beyond my imagination that he could have a person loyal to him who would do something stupid like that.'

*   *   *

By the middle of August 1990, the pressure was really taking its toll on Dr Carlos Cardoen: seven of his employees working at cluster bomb factories he established in Baghdad for Saddam Hussein had been put under house arrest following the invasion of Kuwait; he was being publicly linked with the death of Jonathan Moyle in newspapers and television reports across the world; and the CIA had launched an offensive against Cardoen to try to end his arms sales to his biggest customer, Iraq, once and for all. Federal agents were probing all his business interests.

In Santiago, Judge Solis was still carefully investigating the circumstances behind Jonathan Moyle's death. Silvia Cabrera was questioned again on 7 August. But, as she later explained, 'I told the judge everything I knew, but I was still very scared for my life. Cardoen is a powerful man and I believed he was quite capable of silencing me.'

Other staff at the hotel were just as fearful and many of them insisted on complete anonymity when summoned by Judge Solis.

British commercial attaché William Campbell, who mentioned the sex scandal story, was also interviewed on 9 August. The judge seemed determined to continue trying to solve Jonathan's murder. He even located the two hostesses at the Club Emmanuell who met a Spaniard who boasted about being an arms dealing spy. Solis was so concerned about his role in Jonathan's death that he made a formal request to Interpol to track down the Spaniard in Madrid.

He undoubtedly met Jonathan in the Hotel Carrera and he was well known to Raul Montecinos. Judge Solis started to wonder if there was a connection between the Spaniard and Cardoen's PR chief.

It also seemed relevant that the Spaniard was actually staying in the room next to Jonathan at the time of his death. Silvia Cabrera's claim that she heard movement between the two rooms shortly after Jonathan's death further raised the judge's suspicions.

When he was tracked down in Spain, he knew all about the alleged sex scandal and tried to use it as an excuse for his innocence. He sounded like someone who had been clumsily drilled on how to respond to questioning.

He told detectives from Interpol that Jonathan was just 'some fucking British pervert'. He even added, 'Many people in Britain are perverts.'

Frustratingly, Judge Solis was told he would need much more evidence of his involvement before it would be possible to seek the extradition of the Spaniard to Chile. For the moment, he would have to turn his inquiries to other characters, like Carlos Cardoen and Raul Montecinos, who were strangely quiet about the Spaniard.

When the judge dared to call the Chilean arms entrepreneur into his scruffy office in the Palacio de Tribunales, he knew that he was courting trouble. Cardoen was outraged that the judge should even suggest he might have been involved in Jonathan's murder. He answered all the judge's questions firmly but very briefly, and conceded nothing.

On 29 August 1990, Cardoen called a press conference in Santiago specifically to deny any involvement in Jonathan's death. The following day, his company faxed Shephard Press requesting a brochure on the advertising rates for *Defence Helicopter World*. Staff at Shephard were horrified and did not reply.

Twenty-four hours later, Raul Montecinos visited Judge Solis's chambers and made a declaration insisting he was not involved either. Montecinos claimed he was at Cardoen's FIDAE stand at 7.00pm on the night before Jonathan died. But he did admit to seeing Jonathan at the stand earlier in the week. He even mentioned to the judge that Jonathan had showed particular interest in the mock-up of the converted Bell. Then he was shown a photograph of Moyle and claimed he had confused him with another journalist. 'With Moyle's photo plastered all over the newspapers for months, how could he make such an error?' asked Jonathan's friend and fellow journalist Pedro del Fierro.

*   *   *

Jorge Trivino, the Moyle family lawyer in Santiago, found himself under severe pressure from the Cardoen camp shortly after the arms magnate was interviewed by Judge Solis.

Cardoen's own legal team launched proceedings against Trivino claiming that a wholly unfair campaign had been mounted deliberately against Cardoen to link him with Jonathan Moyle's death. Trivino knew perfectly well that Cardoen could not prove his case, but the young lawyer was worried for the safety of witnesses like Silvia Cabrera and other staff at the hotel.

He knew that Cardoen's well-publicised threat to sue him would effectively scare off anyone else involved in the Moyle case.

Trivino signed a written agreement not to link Cardoen publicly with the killing of Jonathan Moyle. Trivino did it to get Cardoen off his back so he could get on with the job of identifying the murderer.

Back in England, Tony Moyle was disappointed but completely understood Trivino's reasons for backing down. 'Basically, he had no choice,' he explained. 'I would have done the same thing in the circumstances.'

In any case, there was no proof linking Cardoen directly to Jonathan Moyle's death. Tony Moyle still believed that the intelligence services played a role in the murder of his son.

Carlos Cardoen was so determined to make sure his innocence was well publicised that he published Trivino's agreement not to link Cardoen with the case in the Santiago daily newspapers. Despite this, Trivino continued his investigations on behalf of the Moyle family.

Judge Solis himself decided to announce that, in his opinion, Jonathan Moyle was murdered in a 'simulated suicide'. He felt sure that this was the case, and he knew by making such an announcement this would increase the pressure on the guilty parties — whoever they might be. It was becoming increasingly clear, however, that the judge, Jorge Trivino and others in Santiago would have to be *very* careful.

29

Cologne, Germany

'Why is betrayal the only truth that sticks?'

Arthur Miller, After the Fall

It was an incredibly lucky break which found Adel Darwish, an Egyptian based in London and an expert in Arab affairs, on a Lufthansa flight to Germany one crisp autumn day in September 1990. He had been phoned by a contact telling him that an Iraqi defector was prepared to be interviewed for a book that Darwish was preparing on Saddam Hussein called *Unholy Babylon*.

Ironically, Darwish himself had almost been killed two years earlier when he exposed how Iraq was using trainer aircraft supplied by the British for military purposes. Darwish received a stream of threatening letters, and was even given Special Branch protection for three months after the SB were tipped off that Darwish might be a possible target for Iraqi government agents.

But Darwish survived and continued carrying out investigations into the Iraqis. This was how he came to be told by his contacts in 1990 that the Iraqi defector wanted to talk. Darwish was told to meet him in a Chinese restaurant in Bonn after first booking into a specific hotel in nearby Cologne.

A few hours later, just as Darwish was about to leave the hotel, there was a knock at his door. It was the Iraqi and two burly German police minders. He said he had come directly to the hotel because he did not have much time.

Darwish agreed to go with the Iraqi to a café of his own choice. They waited for a taxi at the hotel entrance.

'I've changed my mind. Let's go to a restaurant here ...'

Within minutes, they were sitting at two tables in an empty corner of the hotel restaurant.

The Iraqi introduced himself as 'Mr Ahmed', a former liaison officer with the feared Iraqi secret police, the Mukhabarat. His job under Saddam Hussein had been to 'keep an eye' on the dozens of German and Iraqi scientists who were working in Baghdad, and to carry out background checks. 'Ahmed' insisted on searching Darwish twice to make sure he was not secretly recording the conversation. Nearby, their plain-clothed escorts kept a close eye on them. Mr Ahmed's defection to Germany three months earlier had been a major coup for the Germans and they had no intention of losing their prize catch. Ahmed had been in Europe working with the Iraqi external intelligence at the time. He had even been involved in organising the security of a number of Iraqi/European fronted companies, set up to export technology and sophisticated weaponry to Baghdad.

Ahmed was a handsome, well-built man with a thick moustache, which made him look every inch an Arab intelligence officer. But he was very scared and only agreed to speak to Darwish if he could continually check the writer's notebook.

Darwish's initial intention had been to interview Ahmed about his knowledge of Saddam Hussein's atrocities against the Kurds, his long-planned scheme to invade Kuwait and the top-secret efforts to build nuclear weapons.

After talking about various arms deals, the name of Carlos Cardoen came up:

AHMED: The cannons from South Africa, they were assembled by Cardoen; shells, missiles, marine mines and radar systems from Britain and Spain, also the helicopter Bell which come from America, but Cardoen adds missiles [arms] into them to go to Iraq.

DARWISH: You mean the Bell 206?

AHMED: That is the one.

DARWISH: What use is it for the Iraqis?

AHMED: Gunships.

DARWISH: Did Cardoen arm them with missiles?

AHMED: Yes, it came separately from an American company.

DARWISH: Did the missiles come from America?

AHMED: Yes, but from England and Sweden, but mostly America, because of the radar to direct them.

DARWISH: Is that why Jonathan Moyle was killed?

AHMED: I am not sure why he was killed.

DARWISH: I understood he was investigating the helicopter and the missile and radar guidance system. You know they are banned from exporting to Iraq, and Chile?

AHMED: Everything is banned, that is why

	the Mukhabarat regard Cardoen as a big asset.
DARWISH:	Big assets must be protected?
AHMED:	Of course.
DARWISH:	Is that why the Mukhabarat killed Moyle?
AHMED:	Who told you that the Mukhabarat killed Moyle?
DARWISH:	Nobody. But Mukhabarat is the prime suspect. What do you know?
AHMED:	Cardoen and his people do their own protection. Mukhabarat do not deal with other agents.
DARWISH:	You don't mean that Moyle was an agent?
AHMED:	No. No. No. I do not know the man.
DARWISH:	So who killed him?
AHMED:	I tell you not Mukhabarat.
DARWISH:	Then who? I must know.
AHMED:	Why? Was he your friend, like Bazoft? Bazoft was stupid, crazy. [He was a London-based *Iraqi Observer* journalist shot on the orders of Saddam Hussein in 1988.]
DARWISH:	I want to know about Moyle. Why did the Mukhabarat kill him?
AHMED:	Listen, Mukhabarat did not kill him. I have seen the file.
DARWISH:	What did you see, and why was there a file on him if Mukhabarat did not kill him?
AHMED:	Journalists like Moyle. We follow

	their work. There is a file on you.
DARWISH:	Because I went to Iraq?
AHMED:	Don't be stupid, you know why, they will never forgive you for missiles secrets you published.
DARWISH:	They were no secrets.
AHMED:	The public did not know.
DARWISH:	Moyle did not write for a newspaper read by many people and did not write on missiles. Why was there a file on him?
AHMED:	There was no specific file on him, but his name came up on one of the security files on Cardoen. He was nosing around too much in Cardoen business. Cardoen business is Iraq's business.
DARWISH:	That is why people think Mukhabarat killed him.
AHMED:	Why should Mukhabarat kill him in Chile and have problems there? Cardoen people know what they are doing.
DARWISH:	Are you saying that Cardoen people killed him?
AHMED:	No. No. Cardoen people told him to go home and stop poking his nose.
DARWISH:	How do you know what they told him? Did you go to Chile?
AHMED:	I have seen the file. It was all there, they told him he could stay and enjoy himself, but if he was to keep snooping, then he will be sorry.
DARWISH:	Who told him that?

AHMED:	Big man in Cardoen company, the man knew him, they had dinner, he is the man of the public relations.
DARWISH:	Was he Raul Montecinos?
AHMED:	This is the man, the one who contacts businessmen and reporters.
DARWISH:	Are you saying that Moyle did not listen to the advice?
AHMED:	Obviously he didn't.
DARWISH:	So who killed him?
AHMED:	I don't know.
DARWISH:	What did the file say?
AHMED:	The file did not say what happened after the meeting between Moyle and the man from Cardoen.
DARWISH:	Is the file in Europe?
AHMED:	No. No. In Baghdad. I saw it in Baghdad.
DARWISH:	Were you presented with the file?
AHMED:	Oh no, it was outside my brief. I only saw it because it was in the same office. I was dealing with other arms imports from Europe.
DARWISH:	So who do you think would have killed him? Or who would be upset if Moyle was to discover the secret of the helicopters and the missiles?
AHMED:	Why are you interested in the helicopter?
DARWISH:	I am doing a book, on armament and the Mukhabarat.
AHMED:	I know that, you told me. But ...

	listen, what I mean is, Cardoen was dealing with many weapons not just the helicopters. There are other countries and other firms, any of them could have been watching your friend. Why you journalists say it is Mukhabarat?
DARWISH:	Who then?
AHMED:	I don't know.

At this point, Darwish began asking about other matters as 'Mr Ahmed' was becoming impatient and suspected that Darwish might have been working specifically on the Moyle case.

To this day Adel Darwish remains convinced that 'Mr Ahmed' knew who and why Jonathan Moyle was killed. He has also offered to sign an affidavit swearing that every word of his interview was true. All his notes were taken within minutes of 'Mr Ahmed' leaving the hotel.

'I did not tell him who Moyle was. He knew all about him. He had seen his name on that file. He tried to push me away from the Iraqis having done the killing and he kept ducking the question of who actually ordered the killing.

'But the risk of losing a deal for Cardoen and arms for Saddam is a good enough reason.'

Back in Chile, Judge Solis tried to request an interview with 'Mr Ahmed', but when he contacted the German authorities he was told Ahmed was considered too important 'regarding other matters' to be allowed to risk a trip to Chile. He was never interviewed by investigators on the Moyle case.

*   *   *

Raul Montecinos left his public relations job with Cardoen Industrias in September 1990 still insisting to journalists that he'd never met Jonathan apart from during his visit to Cardoen's stand at FIDAE. 'I know nothing about him,' he informed one reporter, despite what he had told at least three associates in the days following Jonathan's death.

Just before that, Montecinos's journalist friend, Gilles Boudain, travelled back to his home in France for three weeks. On his return, he called Raul Montecinos to find out why he'd left Cardoen Industrias.

'Raul, what happened?' asked the Frenchman when Montecinos answered his home phone.

'Who is this speaking? The French journalist or the friend?'

'Your friend, of course,' replied Boudain.

'I went because I was tired of lying to everybody. I'd had enough.'

A few weeks later Boudain and Montecinos had lunch together in Santiago. The veteran journalist/public relations executive poured out his true feelings about Cardoen. There was clearly little love lost between the two men. Privately, Montecinos felt let down by Cardoen.

'I showed great loyalty to Cardoen but I feel that he has not backed me when I needed it,' explained Montecinos to Boudain.

Towards the end of the meal, Boudain couldn't resist bringing up the subject of Jonathan Moyle.

'Well, Raul, what about the death of Jonathan Moyle?'

Montecinos looked up, took a long breath and scratched his chin thoughtfully.

'No, I never saw him. I never knew him.'

Boudain noticed Montecino's hands shaking. He was also starting to sweat.

'But surely you don't believe all this sex stuff, do you?' asked Boudain.

'You know, in Germany each year 187 people die like this. In England each year, 200 people. It is very common. It is not so surprising.'

Boudain was surprised that Montecinos seemed to know the statistics off by heart. 'It was almost as if he'd been rehearsing them,' the Frenchman later recalled. He didn't realise it was Montecinos who had told pathologist Dr Belleti about sexual asphyxia.

Montecinos would always remain obsessed with publicly denying that he and his boss Carlos Cardoen had ever properly met Jonathan.

'Montecinos lied because he genuinely believed he was protecting himself and Cardoen,' explained Pedro del Fierro. 'Even after leaving the company he knew he had to keep his mouth shut.'

*　　　　　*　　　　　*

In Spain, the Spaniard's sinister role as a suspect in the killing of Jonathan Moyle crumbled when Judge Solis began examining his background more closely. He was nothing more than a poorly paid advertising salesman for a military magazine that had a stand at that year's FIDAE. His story about being an arms dealing spy was simply a lie told to impress the $200-a-night hookers at the sleazy Club Emmanuell.

He was a classic red herring. He summed it up later by eloquently stating, 'Those fucking whores got me into trouble.'

The Spaniard believed that the two women from the club were angry that he would not pay the high rates they demanded for sex and drugs. 'They were trying to get their own back on me. I was stupid. I wish I'd never met them. I just want to forget all about what happened.'

Back in London, Jonathan's former boss inside the secretive MoD research unit, Sir Michael Armitage, categorically denied off camera that Jonathan had worked for him when Britain's Channel Four television news confronted him about Jonathan Moyle's 11-month employment within his specialist unit at the MoD.

Armitage's only comment was to describe Jonathan as a 'pervert'.

30
London

'Those who expect to reap
the blessings of freedom must, like men,
undergo the fatigue of supporting it.'

Thomas Paine

Chris Espin-Jones was a typical stiff-upper-lip, nose-in-the-air naval officer except that he would never dream of actually pulling rank on anyone. By most accounts, Espin-Jones was an old-fashioned sort of fellow with the common touch. And that was why, in October 1990, he found himself in the downstairs bar of a hotel in Kensington High Street, West London, just opposite the Princess of Wales' home at Kensington Palace, waiting to meet two intelligence officers from MI6.

Espin-Jones had been a family friend of the Moyles for more than 15 years when he got a call from Tony Moyle a few days earlier, asking him to try to help and establish what had happened to his son in Chile.

Espin-Jones was Director of Aircraft Policy for the Royal Navy in Whitehall, and at that time was in the middle of a long-standing inter-services dispute over who should command the helicopter squadrons — the navy or the air force.

Tony Moyle asked Espin-Jones to help him find out who murdered his son. Espin-Jones was extremely reluctant to help.

Tony was very disappointed at his old friend's attitude, but tried Espin-Jones again the following day. Espin-Jones, meanwhile, had heard rumours about Jonathan's connections with the security services and realised that Tony might be correct in believing that his son had been deliberately killed.

'There was no way Jonathan would string himself up, so I promised Tony I'd talk to some people about his son,' Espin-Jones later explained.

He phoned a friend in the security services and was immediately instructed to meet with two intelligence agents.

The two men who met Espin-Jones in that bar in Kensington were a naval Captain, and another man who was never formally introduced. Espin-Jones ordered a half of bitter but neither of the two agents drank alcohol.

Espin-Jones was dressed in civilian clothes for the meeting while both the other men were in raincoats. 'Talk about looking like they'd just walked off the set of James Bond! It was ridiculous,' recalled Espin-Jones.

All three chatted for about an hour and Espin-Jones told them everything he knew 'which wasn't much'. They were particularly anxious to find out what Tony Moyle had been told by his son. There were real fears inside the security services that Jonathan might have been rather open about his involvement with them.

'I realised from that moment that Jonathan Moyle must have been connected to the intelligence services,' says Espin-Jones today. 'But they were very careful not to tell me anything about Jonathan.'

It looked like a clear case of guilt by association.

A few days later, Espin-Jones decided to find out how the MoD press office were handling the case and was appalled by the department's negative attitude.

Espin-Jones tried to put the record straight to a senior MoD press officer. 'I was doing nothing more than suggesting Jonathan's death might have had something to do with intelligence gathering.' He immediately noticed a change of atmosphere.

One MoD official even admitted to Espin-Jones that 'other people' wanted to know what was happening on the case. It had even been given its own special code so that all developments were passed on to the security services.

There was also an instant clamp-down on information, which made Espin-Jones even more suspicious about the circumstances which led to Jonathan's death.

Everybody at the MoD became very sensitive about the case after Espin-Jones started asking awkward questions. He got the definite impression that the MoD wanted to cover it all up.

'People were really twitchy. It was a clear-cut case which had become not so clear cut. Jonathan Moyle was into something he should not have been,' he says now.

The briefing paper on the Moyle case that was circulating the MoD featured an explanation of what had been reported in the newspapers and on television, as well as precise instructions on how to react to any press inquiries.

The file also referred to how Jonathan had worked in the MoD under Sir Michael Armitage, something which Armitage continued to deny.

The briefing paper at the MoD also mentioned Moyle's work for the Special Branch at Aberystwyth, but all references to Operation Valkyrie were deliberately omitted.

There were even lists of typical press questions and how they should be answered. For example, if the Press asked: 'Was Jonathan Moyle in the secret service?' the MoD answer would be: 'It is not MoD policy to divulge such information.'

Espin-Jones says, 'The MoD was told not to acknowledge any connection. But with certain questions you had to be careful how you were answering because you were speaking on behalf of ministers.

'You would never say no. You would say it is not MoD policy to disclose such a fact.'

In Jonathan's six-page file there was even a small bracket telling whoever read it about any 'sensitive subjects'.

Espin-Jones explains, 'The MoD press office was told only to respond if pressed hard.'

He added, 'I knew there was more to the case because the briefing file was much thicker than it should have been. Normally, they were about five lines not six pages ...'

Another friend inside the MoD told Espin-Jones, 'We just want to put the whole case to bed once and for all.'

But when Espin-Jones tried digging further into the file, he was heavily reprimanded and told to keep his nose out of the Moyle affair. It seemed that many people had a lot to lose if the truth about Jonathan's life and death was ever revealed.

31
Santiago

'To deny all is to confess all.'

Spanish proverb

Chambermaid Silvia Cabrera couldn't help noticing the two men parked in a black Ford as she left work at the Hotel Carrera one afternoon in September 1990. They were in Bombera Salas, the busy side-street by the staff entrance to the hotel. As she crossed the cobbled street, the car's engine started up and it slowly pulled out. She increased her pace and heard the soft purr of the vehicle 30 yards behind her. Silvia feared the men were connected to the *Caso de Moyle*.

The car remained behind her as she walked down Santa Augustinas towards the narrow streets of the downtown quarter in the direction of her tiny first-floor apartment. The building lay on Victoria Subarcaseu beneath the shadow of Santa Lucia Hill and its blessed statue of Christ at its peak. She could still hear the soft hum of the Ford's engine.

By this time, Silvia was virtually running in order to get home as quickly as possible. She darted in between the crowds on the pavement and lost sight of the car.

Relieved, she slipped between two parked cars to cross the busy street. The road seemed clear so she walked out — just at that moment, the black Ford reappeared from a parking space only 20 yards behind her. She heard the car accelerate. They were heading straight for her. 'All I remember was that they were wearing matching sunglasses and big smiles,' she later recalled.

Silvia just managed to get across the street without being hit. She stopped to recover her composure and saw the back of the Ford turn sharply into a side-street. She had no doubts that she had been warned. But there was worse to come.

*   *   *

After two hours of familiarly tormented sleep, which involved twisting and thrashing amid images of black-suited men driving black Fords emerging from every side-street, Silvia Cabrera got up for work the following day. She walked out into the cool spring morning to find a man hanging around outside the entrance to her apartment block.

Silvia looked at the man nervously and walked on, fully expecting him to follow. He actually went in the opposite direction, but she had noticed the same man there every day for the previous two weeks and she believed it was another sign to keep quiet about the death of Jonathan Moyle.

A few weeks later, Silvia's 18-year-old daughter was accosted in the street outside their apartment. Then Silvia began receiving phonecalls from a man who simply stated, 'Watch yourself.'

Often, when Silvia walked out of her home and headed towards the Hotel Carrera, she was certain she was being followed. She told the Moyle family lawyer in Santiago,

Jorge Trivino, that she was scared. 'It was a very dangerous situation,' says Trivino. 'They were trying to intimidate her. She became very nervous.'

Silvia really wished she'd never set eyes on Jonathan Moyle.

32

Northumberland Avenue, Whitehall

'He that would make his own liberty secure
must guard even his enemy from opression;
for if he violates this duty, he establishes
a precedent that will reach to himself.'

Thomas Paine

It was dusk. Outside, the weather was worsening.
Commander Mike Taylor knocked at his boss's door
and walked in just as the green-shaded desk-lamp was
switched on. The centre of the room became a warm
yellow pool in which the leather top of the desk glowed
blood-red.

Taylor was about to be briefed on a very sensitive job
that required him going out into the field, something that
Taylor was not at all keen on doing. The Royal Navy's
Technical Intelligence Unit at the MoD were very
concerned that Jonathan Moyle might have told his father
some significant information about the supply of arms to
Iraq.

'We're not concerned about all these murder stories,'
Taylor's commanding officer told him. 'We want to know

what Moyle told his father. I'd like you to go down and talk to him.'

As Taylor later insisted, 'We wanted to know if equipment was ending up in the wrong hands. The conspiracy to kill Jonathan Moyle had damn all to do with us. That was the bane of MI-whatever. I am not being callous. It was just a question of what was relevant.'

After leaving his chief's office that day in October 1990, Taylor requested the security services file on the Moyle case and examined it closely. While it did not conclude that Jonathan had been murdered, the file contained highly classified information that clearly indicated Jonathan's involvement with the security services.

As Taylor explained, 'My impression from Moyle's file was that others in the security services had already looked at the case closely. Going to Devon was a fishing exercise. We needed to know if there was anything new in it.' He refused to elaborate on exactly what was in the file.

Taylor was, in many ways, an unlikely person to be a senior member of British Naval Intelligence. He was a friendly, duffel-coated character, rather like someone out of one of those jolly, patriotic British battleship B-movies from the 1950s, rather than the suave James Bond-type of the 1960s. His official title was Deputy Head of the Naval Technical Intelligence Unit at the MoD.

In the autumn of 1990, the atmosphere at the Naval Intelligence offices in Whitehall was far from relaxed. Saddam Hussein's decision to invade Kuwait had sparked a witch-hunt inside all three services, in an effort to discover who had been feeding the Iraqi leader with arms.

And the Moyle case was considered to be sufficiently important to be handled at a high level within the intelligence services.

Taylor's eventual visit to the Moyle home in Branscombe yielded little new information. Once again, the security services' paranoia about Jonathan Moyle giving away their secrets seemed to override any genuine attempt to find out by whom and why he was murdered.

When Taylor returned to London, he made out a four-page report on his findings — it is still in a top-secret Whitehall file to this day.

Taylor admits, 'I did not draw any conclusion. I presented facts. I gave my own personal impression based on what Mr Moyle told me. The impression I noted was to do with the likelihood that the story was true. I thought it seemed inevitable that someone had killed him as opposed to him doing it to himself.'

That report by Taylor went to his immediate superiors at Naval Intelligence and then higher up the chain to Military Defence Intelligence. After that, it was passed on to the relevant personnel at MI5 and MI6.

Taylor knows for certain that his report was discussed at meetings of the heads of the other agencies but he has no idea if his recommendations were ever acted upon. 'That is outside my sphere.'

To this day he refuses to reveal the exact contents of that four-page report on the Moyle case.

Taylor always categorically denied that the meeting with Tony Moyle ever took place.

But by May 1996, Taylor had retired and reluctantly agreed to talk about why he was investigating the Moyle case so thoroughly.

He was, like many others, appalled at the way that Jonathan's killers seemed to have got away with murder.

'His death was undoubtedly a travesty of justice,' says Taylor today. 'I'm just sorry that my inquiries did not uncover any concrete evidence.'

*   *   *

Tony Moyle was rapidly concluding that his son's death threatened to embarrass a great deal of people. And the negative attitude of the British authorities simply spurred him on in his efforts to find his son's killer.

Tony told one reporter at the time, 'I will go on and on until at least I get some of the truth. There are people who know exactly what happened to Jonathan, who know exactly who did it. Somewhere, somebody doesn't want the truth to come out.'

Even more tragically, Jonathan's death continued to have a devastating effect on his mother Diana.

At times, it seemed as if her whole character had changed. She had once been an active, gregarious, extrovert woman.

'She's fought hard, but she's a broken person. She was very close to Jonathan; this has shattered her whole life,' said Tony at the time.

On occasions, even Tony struggled to maintain his composure and resolve to offset the heartbreak, and the strain was clearly showing.

'The fact that I'm having to fight keeps me going. But one can't help but feel the strain on top of the grief that's already there. Yes, it's devastating,' he admitted.

During this period, defence journalist Terry Gander who had extensive contact with Jonathan in Chile, had his house broken into twice. 'They never took anything,' says Gander. 'Just moved a few things around. It was as if they were saying, "We're keeping an eye on you."'

He has never found out if these incidents were connected to Jonathan's death.

*   *   *

In October 1990, Florida-based Lebanese arms broker Nasser Mustafa Beydoun filed a lawsuit against Carlos Cardoen, alleging that the Chilean had deprived him of more than $5m as his commission for introducing Cardoen to Saddam Hussein.

Beydoun — a fast-talking character with a penchant for pastel-coloured linen suits and pretty young girls — even claimed that one of Cardoen's top executives had convinced Iraqi air force officials to ensure that Beydoun was banned from Iraq so Cardoen could sell direct to Saddam Hussein.

Beydoun insisted that Carlos Cardoen was a man who would stop at nothing in his pursuit of power and money. Back in 1983, Cardoen had even been briefly arrested by the Americans for trying to smuggle highly sensitive night-vision goggles into Chile, breaking the US-imposed arms sanctions. There were rumours that Cardoen was told to help the Americans monitor the sale of arms in the Middle East or face prosecution. Naturally, he took the former option.

But it is clear that Cardoen only provided the Americans with the minimum of details. He knew if he could keep them off his back, then he could set up a vastly lucrative worldwide arms-selling network.

'Cardoen was playing a little game with the Americans. He didn't want them hassling him, so he thought he would feed them titbits of information to keep them off his back,' explained one former Cardoen employee.

Meanwhile, Nasser Beydoun found himself locked in an expensive legal battle with Cardoen that would take years to settle.

Beydoun, a resident of the millionaire's resort of Coral Springs, near Miami, claimed that Cardoen stopped paying him after the first sales deal with Iraq went through in 1983.

In his lawsuit, Beydoun said that Cardoen referred to him as his company's 'Golden Key' to Iraq.

'When I opened the market, he crossed the bridge and he burned it, leaving me behind,' Beydoun told one journalist in Florida at the time.

Beydoun even claimed that he had tried to settle the dispute with Cardoen amicably just weeks before Iraq invaded Kuwait. But Cardoen's lawyers rejected the claim.

Beydoun's suit was fascinating because Cardoen had always claimed back home in Chile that his relationship with Saddam was based purely on good luck. 'I bought a ticket, took a plane and offered what I had,' he told one reporter proudly.

Beydoun also said that Cardoen — by the summer of 1990 — had sold at least $467m worth of arms to Iraq, making him the fifth-richest arms dealer in the world.

Eventually, in desperation, Beydoun went to the US customs service and offered to inform on Cardoen's illicit dealings through his American-based companies. In a remarkable move, they agreed to pay him a total of $750,000 for his evidence. The Americans considered it a small price to pay for hooking Dr Carlos Cardoen.

Beydoun was so pleased to be paid such a huge amount by the US Government that he, his brother Nader and nephew Mustafa, posed for photos at Beydoun's extravagant Florida home with the cash payment piled up in front of them. When those photos were released to the Press, they soon reached Carlos Cardoen. He was incensed.

It was a brave move by Beydoun. It was also the first bit of bad luck Carlos Cardoen had ever suffered. The US Government were now determined not to let Cardoen slip through their grasp. Their aim was to strike a blow at Saddam's war machine as effectively as possible — and that meant stopping people like Cardoen, whatever the price.

33

Santiago

'No notice is taken of a little evil,
but when it increases it strikes the eye.'

Aristotle

On the wall of Carlos Cardoen's office were the photos of the two men who had helped shape his career. One was despised. The other deposed. The former was Iraqi President Saddam Hussein, arguably the most dangerous man in the world, the 'mad dog' of the Middle East. The latter was General Augusto Pinochet, the brutal Chilean dictator. But neither of them could help Cardoen as he watched a video tape on the 20-inch television set in his spacious office overlooking the River Mapocha.

The video was a copy of the lead item on the NBC nightly news bulletin presented by anchor man Tom Brokaw. Cardoen's career as one of the world's biggest arms suppliers was beginning to go seriously awry following Saddam Hussein's invasion of Kuwait.

'If ... If the United States goes to war with Iraq, it will face a $50bn war machine loaded with Western-made weapons,' Brokaw announced dramatically.

'Tonight, NBC's Pentagon correspondent, Fred Francis, looks at one arms dealer with close ties to Iraq ... a man who tried to manipulate US government agencies in the process.'

NBC correspondent Fred Francis then took up the story as tens of millions of Americans watched.

'Earlier this year, in the skies above Dallas, a modified Bell helicopter was being put through its paces by the Federal Aviation Administration. The tests were routine. The helicopter, its owner told the FAA, was for agricultural purposes.

'But that was only part of the story, according to US intelligence sources. The helicopter, launched last year with much fanfare by Carlos Cardoen, a Chilean entrepreneur and sometime Miami resident, was destined for Iraq and was not only going to be spraying pesticides.'

Fred Francis continued: 'This is the sales brochure Cardoen showed Iraqi Air Force officers last year in Baghdad. It describes an attack helicopter capable of firing 50-calibre cannon or anti-tank missiles.

'When NBC News told the FAA about this brochure, it was within hours of certifying the helicopter as airworthy ... the final step needed before Cardoen could sell 50 of them to Iraq.'

NBC pointed out that just weeks before Iraq's invasion of Kuwait, Cardoen insisted to one journalist, 'I have never, ever sold any product to an enemy of the US. Never.'

NBC News effectively pulled the rug from under the feet of Carlos Cardoen.

What few realised was that the item on NBC News had been supplied and approved by the CIA. They wanted to put the maximum pressure on Cardoen and hit him where it really hurt.

Watching that TV news item in his Santiago office,

Cardoen's face turned to stone and he thumped his desk with anger. Things might have been so different if Jonathan Moyle had not died.

* * *

In October 1990, the inquest into Jonathan Moyle's death was reopened again in Exeter. Annette Kissenbeck attended the hearing, which was told that a British post mortem inquiry had been inconclusive because vital organs including the brain, kidneys and stomach — necessary for poison tests — were missing.

Tony Moyle told the inquest that many officials in Chile now believed his son to have been murdered. But with so few details available, the coroner had little choice but to adjourn the proceedings.

A month later, Home Office pathologist Dr Albert Hunt presented a new post mortem report on Jonathan's death, which was to be sent to Chile to help investigators led by judge Alejandro Solis.

However Hunt concluded ominously that the autopsy could not be 'scientifically complete, nor conclusive'.

Once again, the coroner adjourned the proceedings.

Tony Moyle was still angry that no one would pass comment on the mark seen on his son's shin, which clearly indicated he had been given some kind of injection. 'They seemed afraid to draw any conclusions. It was not satisfactory,' he recalled later.

* * *

In Santiago, the detectives who initially handled the Moyle case continued to try to justify their claims that he died from sexual asphyxia.

Detective José Torres claimed that he had 'pieces of information' that clearly implied that Jonathan had some sort of record as a sexual deviant. It was all totally untrue but the Chilean Investigaciones were desperately trying to prove to Judge Solis that they had been right about Jonathan's death from the start.

The judge's staff, however, had long since concluded that the sex death story had been deliberately leaked 'to distract us from the direction our investigation is taking.'

On Friday, 23 November 1990, *La Tercera* newspaper in Santiago ran a story claiming that Jonathan was murdered because he had access to confidential information about arms deals. The Iraqis were clearly linked to his death.

Meanwhile, the Iraqis themselves were trying to back their way out of their supposed involvement. At their embassy in Buenos Aires, Argentina (they did not have one in Chile) a diplomat issued a statement to the Press insisting on their innocence. But their move had been precipitated by Saddam Hussein's worldwide policy of trying to convince the world that he was not a duplicitous war-monger.

In both cases, it seemed a little late in the day to turn the clock back.

34

The White House

'The weakness of the many
make the leader possible.'

Elbert Hubbard

The inconspicuous green sedan car drew up quietly at the diplomatic entrance to the President's residence beyond the view of any insomniac reporter who might be afoot at that unseemly hour. It was 6.34am on a grey December day in 1990.

A neatly-dressed civil servant nodded to the armed guard beside him, slipped out of the car with a thick, black leather case in his hand, and flashed his plastic ID to the Secret Service detail, and quietly made his way through empty public rooms to the kitchen of the family wing where the President's breakfast was being prepared.

When the presidential silver, crested porcelain, damask napkin, orange juice, scrambled eggs, toast and coffee were ready, he extracted from his black case a sealed eight-and-a-half-by-eleven manila envelope and placed it on the left side of the tray. He then watched through the open door as the tray was delivered to President George Bush. Then, assured his mission had been accomplished with security, he vanished as quietly as he came.

This ritual — performed daily at the White House or wherever the President may be — is known as 'The President's Brief', eight pages of double-spaced typing on fine bond paper, the most expensive eight sheets of rag paper to be found in the world. The annual cost of producing these pages, which are word-processed between 4.00-5.00am in the rambling building in Langley, Virginia, the home of the CIA, has been estimated at $30bn, give or take a few hundred million.

On this particular December morning, the President's Brief included intelligence gathered by the CIA from its worldwide network of permanent stations and operatives in preparation for Bush's impending trip to Chile.

It also drew on the daily intercepts of the National Security Agency, the electronics monitor that had a capability so sensitive and satellites so pervasive that it had, in the past, boasted of picking up the conversation of one Soviet leader as he drove through the streets of Moscow in his bullet-proof limousine, talking with a companion about the young women with whom they had spent the night.

The brief contained three paragraphs on the death of Jonathan Moyle, the case's continuing link to Dr Carlos Cardoen and Cardoen's close ties with Saddam Hussein who had rocked the West by invading Kuwait. It mentioned Cardoen's Bell conversion project as part of the long-standing Operation Exodus, a Customs Service enforcement programme targeted at stopping the transfer of high-tech equipment and illegal weapons. The programme had produced 1,300 arrests and $1bn in weapons seizures since 1981. The brief also mentioned that Cardoen's Bell conversion was on a list of projects, all of which had just had their FAA certification process cancelled.

It also pointed out that Cardoen was supposed to have been informing the CIA about relevant arms movements but had supplied so little data that he was not deemed worthy of their protection.

Within the brief was a newspaper cutting from a recent issue of the prestigious *Wall Street Journal* which was headlined 'INVESTIGATORS SAY CHILEAN DEALER SMUGGLED U.S. WEAPONS TO IRAQ'.

The piece revealed that Cardoen had been watched by the CIA for years. As early as 1984 the CIA believed that Cardoen 'was the primary supplier of cluster bombs for the Iraqi government' and an 'important supplier' of other munitions throughout the Middle East.

The Americans' concern over the Moyle case was fuelled by their understandable obsession with cutting off all arms supplies to Saddam. Agents were reporting that Cardoen was being paid tens of millions of dollars by Iraq each year for various weapons. But when news of Jonathan's death and its possible link to the development of the Bell conversion kits became apparent, the CIA went into overdrive.

The agency was desperate to prove it could still provide effective, preventative cover since it was severely embarrassed when people like General Norman Schwarzkopf complained bitterly about the poor intelligence provided in advance of Iraq's invasion of Kuwait.

The Americans were becoming obsessed with tracking down and punishing anyone responsible for providing arms to Iraq.

President Bush made his two-day visit to Chile in mid-December and Carlos Cardoen's name was very high on his agenda. He wanted the Chileans to help construct an airtight case against Cardoen for illegal arms exporting. But Cardoen had friends in high places, including President

Aylwin himself. Perhaps not so surprisingly, news of the American's plans reached him swiftly at his headquarters in Santiago. The message from his friends inside the Chilean Government was loud and clear; drop all your arms dealing and keep an extremely low profile.

At first, Cardoen was reluctant to quit such a lucrative business, but after George Bush's visit to Santiago, it was made clear that the alternative was to hand him over to the Americans.

They were incensed by Cardoen's cavalier attitude and stepped up their campaign to prosecute him. Carol Hallett, Commissioner of the US Customs Service, called him a 'black widow' spider with a web of companies and bank accounts that 'circled the entire globe'. She also described him as 'one of the world's most notorious merchants of death'.

Hallett's federal agents had been gathering evidence against Cardoen for almost two years so her conclusions were very significant.

Cardoen even admitted to colleagues that if Jonathan Moyle hadn't been killed, then none of these 'problems would exist'.

'He had been perfectly happy selling vast quantities of arms to the military across the world and couldn't understand why anyone was sticking their noses in his business,' explained one former Cardoen Industrias employee.

Carlos Cardoen was used to always getting his own way.

35

Fort Lauderdale, Florida

'In our complex world, there cannot be
fruitful initiative without government,
but unfortunately there can be government
without initiative.'

Bertrand Russell

The view from special agent Bob Schoonmaker's
Department of Commerce export enforcement office
was east, past the white buildings and palm trees to
the edge of the Atlantic Ocean. But the view meant little to
him as he tried to build a formidable prosecution case
against Dr Carlos Cardoen.

Schoonmaker's agency wanted to bring Cardoen, who
owned businesses and a home in Florida, to justice, but he
remained untouchable as long as he stayed in Chile. Cardoen
knew that the moment he set foot outside South America he
would be arrested. Cardoen had openly admitted to certain
colleagues that he could not afford to take the risk.

Bob Schoonmaker had spent more than ten years at the
DoC. He liked it in southern Florida; he liked the motionless
heat pressing through the sun-bleached streets; he even

rather liked the mass of high rises that had sprouted up on the sea-front. They were clean, reconstructed among the recent flat decay of the area with all the charm of Disney World.

On 18 January 1991, as Iraqi missiles were hitting Tel Aviv during the Gulf War, federal agents led by Bob Schoonmaker raided the headquarters of a Miami real estate and management group, Swissco, which they believed was a front for Cardoen's business, obtaining sensitive technology for Iraq.

The agents even allowed a TV camera crew to join the raid so that the message to Saddam Hussein and Carlos Cardoen was made crystal clear.

In the raid, initiated by the Pentagon, agents seized filing cabinets and boxes full of documents as they searched for evidence of stolen and smuggled American technology.

The raid in Miami was part of the worldwide US-inspired investigation into Cardoen and the hundreds of millions of dollars worth of arms he had sold to Iraq over the previous ten years.

Cardoen continued to insist that all his dealings were completely above board and that he had always kept the US authorities fully informed of his transactions. The Americans denied this emphatically.

Allied bombing raids on Baghdad targeted the two Cardoen factories which had been specifically built near the Iraqi capital to arm Saddam Hussein's war machine.

US prosecutors eventually filed a civil suit against Carlos Cardoen, accusing him of money laundering and of illegally exporting 100 tonnes of zirconium, a material used in the manufacture of cluster bombs.

Cardoen's defence was (and still is) that he kept the US fully informed of all his arms trading from as far back as 1984. But he refused to leave Chile to face US prosecutors.

It all seemed like a classic game of bluff and counter-bluff. As long as Cardoen remained in his homeland, he was untouchable.

*   *   *

About a year after Jonathan's death, Cardoen's office contacted Santiago-based British journalist Malcolm Coad and asked if he would like to interview the Chilean arms entrepreneur. He was told that Cardoen had a story of major importance to tell the journalist. Coad was instructed to be at Cardoen's mansion in a quiet Santiago suburb at 10.00am the next day.

'Actually, all he wanted to do was give his side of what was happening with the Americans and their efforts to indict him,' recalls Coad.

But Coad couldn't resist throwing in a question about the Moyle case. Cardoen's facial expression immediately changed and he categorically denied any involvement in Jonathan's death.

'I never even met the guy,' said Cardoen.

'He was very convincing at first,' recalls Coad.

Then Coad noticed that Cardoen's mood became much darker. He started snapping out replies, then shortly after that, he got up and walked out of the interview.

*   *   *

In the House of Commons, the Government was coming under more pressure to provide some answers about the Moyle case.

Secretary of State for Foreign and Commonwealth Affairs Mark Lennox-Boyd, told the House that the British Ambassador in Santiago had called on the Director General of Political Relations at the Chilean Ministry of Foreign Affairs to ask what steps could be taken to identify and bring to justice those responsible for the murder of Jonathan Moyle.

This was a very significant concession by the British

Government because they were actually stating that Jonathan had been murdered.

In November 1991, British Foreign Office Under-Secretary Sir John Coles visited Chile. He admitted to journalists that his government was 'very worried' about Jonathan Moyle's murder.

But Coles refused to be drawn further on the subject and told reporters that 'it is not very polite to talk about that.'

In fact, a week before Coles's visit, an 'advance party' of British intelligence officers slipped quietly into Santiago under diplomatic cover. Their mission was to investigate the Moyle case further, because of fears within the Government that British companies could be involved in either Jonathan's death or with Carlos Cardoen.

The British officers also suspected that a drug known by the nickname of 'Andrea' could have been used to kill Jonathan. The poison produces instant death but its effects disappear within minutes leaving no traces whatsoever. If 'Andrea' had been used on Jonathan, it would explain the injection mark on his shin and the fact that his body was hidden in the cupboard to ensure it would not be discovered for the maximum length of time.

When British minister Lennox-Boyd was once again pressed about the Moyle case, he admitted to the House of Commons that 'those responsible for Mr Moyle's death should be brought to justice.'

But the investigation in Britain and Chile was clearly running out of steam.

Lennox-Boyd eventually did a complete about-turn and would only refer in the House to 'Moyle's tragic death'. He insisted that the British Embassy in Santiago was still keeping in touch with the Chileans about their investigation.

But it was clear the British just wanted the case to fade into oblivion.

36

London

'The First World War was meant to be the war to
end all wars, but we just don't seem to learn.'

*Jim Allan, an El Alamein veteran summing up the
mood of the day at Remembrance Day Sunday,
8 November 1991*

Ninety-one years into this battered and bloody
century, thousands of people gathered at the
Cenotaph in London on 8 November 1991, to
salute comrades, friends and family who had fallen in the
cause of a promised better world.

For all the solemn rituals of remembrance and the
pealing of the bells of Westminster Abbey, it was
impossible to forget that the world continued to be torn
apart by new conflicts.

While former warriors marched proudly past the
memorial, badges and medals glinting under the grey
November skies, guns still rumbled across the globe. It
had been 74 years since Passchendale, 49 years since El
Alamein and 9 years since the Falklands. Yet the British
were once again under fire in the Balkans.

Three royal women stood on the Foreign Office balcony that day: the Queen Mother, the Princess Royal and the Princess of Wales.

Detachments from the Royal Marines, the Royal Navy, the Royal Air Force, the Grenadier Guards and the Royal Horse Artillery flanked the Cenotaph as massed bands launched into 'Rule Britannia' and 'Men of Harlech'. As the veterans assembled, John Major, Neil Kinnock, Paddy Ashdown, Douglas Hurd and three former Prime Ministers, Sir Edward Heath, Lord Callaghan and Baroness Thatcher, took their positions.

In Whitehall, crowds six-deep applauded as the old soldiers, sailors and airmen filed past the Cenotaph to the sound of military bands.

At 11.00am, Big Ben and a field gun in Horse Guards Parade signalled the start of the two-minute silence. The Queen stepped forward to lay the first wreath of red poppies, followed by Prince Philip, the Duke of Kent and Prince Michael of Kent.

Among the remembrance wreaths around the Cenotaph lay a simple dozen red roses. There was a card, inscribed:

> *'Jonathan Moyle,*
> *murdered for, covered up and betrayed by his country.*
> *A K'*

Annette Kissenbeck left the card as evidence of her bitterness and bewilderment at the complete lack of progress into the death of her fiancé.

'Jonathan believed so much in his country and yet they turned round and abandoned him, even in death. He felt so strongly about Britain but his loyalty was wasted,' she says today. 'He thought he could live forever but the gods were not on his side.'

*   *   *

The chiming clock echoing through Highcliff House woke Diana Moyle one cold and windy night about 18 months after the death of her son. That noise reminded Diana of Jonathan and provoked a flood of tears.

Then, as she quietly tried to sob herself back to sleep, she heard the dogs barking furiously in the back yard next to the open fields.

'Tony! Tony!'

Tony Moyle woke in an instant, sat bolt upright and listened. The dogs became silent. He thought he heard something, but it could have been the breeze rustling in the trees.

As he switched on the bedside light, the dogs started up again.

'There's someone out there,' whispered Tony.

He slowly lowered his hand underneath the bed and pulled out the 12-bore shotgun he'd kept in their bedroom ever since Jonathan had died.

Just then, the dogs stopped again. Tony sat in virtual suspended animation waiting for one more sound before he went down to investigate. Next to him, Diana looked petrified.

For ten minutes he waited, but the dogs were quiet and there were no more noises. Tony and Diana didn't sleep a wink more that night.

At daylight, Tony strolled over towards the field where the dogs had been barking. A set of freshly-made car tracks had sliced through the foot long grass. Someone had been watching them. On the way back to the house he noticed that a tub by the kitchen door had been smashed.

That incident made the Moyles feel even more lonely and vulnerable in their large three-storey house. They even decided to move up to the top-floor attic bedroom because it had a trap door which could be sealed.

'We felt safer up there,' Tony later explained. 'We just wanted to hide away. The attic became like a self-contained wooden box. I even put a bolt on the trap door to make us feel safer.'

The circumstances behind Jonathan Moyle's death had fuelled his parents' fears. They no longer felt safe.

On one occasion, Diana Moyle found herself alone in the house when Tony was in London trying to whip up support for a fresh investigation into their son's death.

She said, 'It was so windy the trees were almost bending double and the barn door was banging. As I walked across the yard, I could see the valley below and the church where Jonathan was.

'I kept looking right down into the valley as I walked along the drive. It felt like something out of *Dracula*. The misery within me, the sheer loneliness and fear. It felt like some ghastly horror story except our nightmare was real. I remember getting a chill up my spine as I thought about the empty ten acres of fields around us. Anybody could have been there.'

37

Chile

'Justice is like a train
that's nearly always late.'

Yevgeny Yevtushenko,
A Precocious Autobiography (1963)

Judge Alejandro Solis was sitting alone in his office at the Palacio de Tribunales. He was staring at the crime scene photos, specifically the suspended body of Jonathan Moyle.

'This man was murdered,' he told himself repeatedly. Moyle was tortured and killed by someone. What he was looking at was an abomination. He examined each photo in order, over and over again, faster and faster until the scene virtually came alive in his mind like animation.

Moyle's death had to be solved. Justice must be done.

'I have absolutely no doubt that Jonathan Moyle was murdered,' Alejandro Solis told his colleagues. 'The problem is finding out who did it.'

The *Caso de Moyle* was chipping away at the judge's belief in justice always prevailing. However hard he tried, he could not crack open the investigation and establish the concrete facts needed to track down Jonathan's killers.

Even Chilean Defence Minister Patricio Rojas said the Chilean Government was 'very irritated by the crime', and insisted that the police would continue to follow up all possible leads. They appeared to be keen to encourage the judge to continue his investigation.

In the summer of 1992, Judge Solis officially reopened the case and reiterated the cause of Jonathan Moyle's death as murder. He hoped that fresh publicity about the case might persuade new witnesses to come forward.

These were Judge Solis's main problems:

1. The amount of tranquillizer found in Jonathan's body was enough to knock him out. Where did it come from?
2. No one who had met Jonathan before, during and on the way back from his Punta Arenas trip was directly interviewed by Judge Solis. They were all seen by a military judge who issued an order prohibiting Judge Solis from seeing them. 'It is not necessary,' he was told. He was powerless to argue. So he never had an opportunity to ask them any important questions.
3. The way that the sexual asphyxia story was leaked simultaneously in London and Santiago made him even more suspicious that certain forces wanted to ensure that it did not appear that Jonathan had been murdered. 'It was far too coincidental,' said Judge Solis.
4. The original police inquiries were sloppily executed. The judge said, 'They had to keep to their first version of the events or admit they had made a mistake. They couldn't bring themselves to do that.'

Judge Solis was convinced that Jonathan had been drugged,

suffocated with a pillow, injected in the shin with a lethal substance and then strung up in the closet. But he was still baffled by the most important question of all: why was he killed?

Until that question was answered satisfactorily, Judge Solis knew that there was little chance of actually solving one of the most significant murder mysteries in Chilean history.

*   *   *

In Devon, Tony Moyle continued to try to lobby support for a proper explanation of his son's involvement with the British security services. But it was proving to be an uphill battle.

In London, the Foreign Office continued to try to control any information about the Moyle case. Tony Moyle had what he later described as a very unsatisfactory meeting with Foreign Office minister Mark Lennox Boyd on December 12 1992.

When the *Mail on Sunday* newspaper began an investigation in the middle of 1992, reporter Richard Holliday was summoned to the Foreign Office by a press officer.

'They were at pains to stress that their consul in Santiago had been to see investigating magistrate Solis on at least 40 occasions,' explained Holliday.

Intriguingly, the FO also tried to take credit for the Chileans continuing their investigations. 'They even claimed it was their insistence that Moyle was a "sound man who came from a good family and had everything to live for" that the current investigation was launched,' added Holliday.

Faced with little in the way of new information on the case, Holliday and the *Mail on Sunday* dropped their plans for a major investigation into the case.

38

Chile

'Although the world has changed, it remains a
deeply turbulent and dangerous place.'

*Douglas Hurd, British Foreign Secretary,
speaking in the House of Commons,
22 February 1994.*

British Foreign Secretary Douglas Hurd sat back in his
very comfortable first-class seat on British Airways
flight 245 from London to Santiago, and began
examining the file on Jonathan Moyle. He was particularly
concerned by Malcolm Coad's article in the *Guardian*
which implied that the sexual asphyxia claims were
deliberately leaked to put a smoke screen around the case.

Hurd knew full well that on arrival in Santiago for his
official two-day visit on 10 January 1993, he would be
expected to field dozens of questions about Jonathan
Moyle's death. Yet he and his colleagues at the FO were
actually more interested in issues such as boosting trade
between Chile and the UK. There was particular concern
that Chile was levying a 78% duty on Scotch whisky
imports.

Hurd had been bombarded in London with letters from Tony Moyle's Chilean attorney Jorge Trivino asking for more British involvement in the case. In addition, Hurd had already been warned that Trivino was expecting a meeting with him on arrival in Santiago.

'We're going to have to see this guy, otherwise we'll have all hell to pay when we get back. Let's fit him in. We can't lose anything by giving him 15 minutes,' Hurd told one of his civil servants on the BA flight.

When they did meet, Hurd disappointed Trivino by insisting that it was up to the Chilean authorities to investigate Jonathan's death. He later told a packed Press conference at the British Embassy, 'I have no information which confirms stories which have been circulating for two years now.'

Guardian correspondent Coad was surprised by how well informed Hurd was about the case.

As Coad was leaving the Press conference in Santiago, he walked out of the embassy at the same time as Hurd and asked the Foreign Secretary if he really knew any more details about the Moyle case.

Hurd hesitated for a split-second, then told Coad, 'The British Government has no information which could help the Moyle investigation. The Ambassador has told the investigating judge that we will give any help we can. But I have no information at all which could confirm some of the stories which have been circulating for two years now ... this is a matter for Chile.'

When asked directly to deny rumoured links between Jonathan and British intelligence, Hurd said: 'Obviously, we have made inquiries into all the stories which have reached us, but we have found no collateral, no confirmation.'

Hurd did discuss the case with Chilean Foreign Minister Enrique Silva Cimma during his two-day visit.

*   *   *

In early 1993, the British Government's controversial 'Inquiry into exports of defence equipment and dual-use goods to Iraq', headed by the Right Honourable Lord Justice Scott, sent an important letter to Jonathan Moyle's father Tony.

In it, the Secretary to the Inquiry, Mr CPJ Muttukumaru, admitted that Scott and his team were *not* interested in Jonathan's death, despite its links with 'Merchant of Death' Carlos Cardoen.

'Your son's tragic death is not a matter which Lord Justice Scott proposes to investigate for its own sake,' Muttukumaru wrote.

Tony Moyle was bitterly disappointed but not surprised.

When Chilean investigating judge Alejandro Solis asked the Scott Inquiry to pass on any information connecting Jonathan's death with Chilean and British arms supplies to Iraq before the Gulf War he did not even get a response.

It seemed increasingly that the Foreign Office was well aware of the role played by British firms in supplying components for Saddam Hussein's military build-up.

What was certain is that Iraq owed huge sums of money to British companies and had no intention of paying up following the Gulf War. In 1992, the Department of Trade and Industry even supported the granting of a £340m line of credit to Iraq so they could pay off those debts. A lot was riding on maintaining good relations with the Iraqis at the time.

*   *   *

Meanwhile the US Department of Justice continued to place Cardoen at the head of their Most Wanted list. They had discovered that Iraq had paid Cardoen by sending oil to South Africa where it was turned into cash and then transferred to Cardoen's Florida operation.

In June 1993, Cardoen mounted a public relations offensive and told the BBC that he had been willing to give evidence to the Scott Inquiry into illegal arms sales to Iraq, but said that he was worried about travelling outside Chile in case he was kidnapped by the US authorities.

The BBC interviewer then completely threw Cardoen's PR plans off course by asking him:

'They call you a dealer in death. What do you think about that, Señor Cardoen?'

Carlos Cardoen looked up, smiled briefly and answered, 'This is an expression from people who do not understand how this country makes business. We are respected because we produce guns.' It was the same reply he'd given to journalists across the world to defend the questionable morals of his business.

During the BBC television interview, Cardoen continued to deny ever having met Jonathan Moyle. One former Cardoen employee said, 'He didn't care to discuss it with anyone.' Insisting that he had never met Jonathan was Cardoen's easiest riposte.

It seemed hard to believe that only a few years earlier, Cardoen had enjoyed regular contact with US intelligence officials. At that time he'd brilliantly played everyone off against each other — his own wallet was the only winner.

But that was the past. Carlos Cardoen's double dealing was finally catching up with him.

39
Santiago

'Cowards die many times before their deaths;
The valiant never taste of death but once.'

William Shakespeare, Julius Caesar

A s Carlos Cardoen's PR chief Raul Montecinos
neared the doorway to the Palacio de Tribunales,
close to the downtown fish market, he met an old
acquaintance coming the other way. It was one of the
reporters with whom he had once worked on a Santiago
daily newspaper, though they seldom saw each other
now. The journalist smiled, obviously wanting a few
words for his paper, and although Montecinos's mind was
preoccupied with other things, he stopped momentarily.
Then, as the other man held out his hand, Montecinos
remembered an argument they had had years earlier.

'I can't talk to you now,' said Montecinos.

'Come on, Raul, we've known each other how long?'

'Too long ...' came the snappy reply.

Then Montecinos saw a crowd of other reporters,
photographers and television camera crews moving

towards him from the police station opposite. His nightmare was far from over.

Raul Montecinos was finally appearing before an identity parade in front of chambermaid Silvia Cabrera in January 1993, almost three years after Jonathan Moyle was killed. Montecinos's appearance was the culmination of an extraordinary 32-month cat-and-mouse game with Judge Alejandro Solis.

It all started in August 1990 when Judge Solis had summoned Montecinos to be interviewed at the downtown Santiago courthouse. Montecinos was furious about being linked with Jonathan's death and refuted all claims that he had met with Jonathan the night before he died.

With the financial backing of Cardoen's lawyers, Montecinos even tried to get the Chilean courts to declare that the judge had no right to interview him about the Moyle case. At that stage, Montecinos was still claiming he'd never even met Jonathan (a statement he later retracted).

Those legal arguments raged for more than a year as Montecinos' s lawyers tried to attack the judge's powers in favour of their client.

Moyle family lawyer Jorge Trivino also demanded that Montecinos should make a full declaration of his conversation with Jonathan the night before he died. Montecinos denied that the meeting with Jonathan had taken place, despite his admissions to Pedro del Fierro, Gilles Boudain and Ricardo Correo to the contrary.

On 22 October 1991, Montecinos was ordered to attend the first series of identity parades designed to establish his presence at the Hotel Carrera on the night before Jonathan's death. He never appeared.

The judge adjourned the inquiry until January 1992. Having waited hours, a nervous Silvia Cabrera fled pursued by television cameramen.

Defence journalist Pedro del Fierro pointed out the

obvious. 'Montecinos was afraid the chambermaid would identify him.'

In a declaration made shortly afterwards, Montecinos insisted, 'Just because I met Moyle does not mean I was involved in his death.' Montecinos seemed to be backtracking; now he was admitting to having met Jonathan.

On 21 November 1991, Judge Solis ordered that Raul Montecinos be arrested for failing to turn up for that identity parade on 22 October. But he was never actually detained after his lawyers appealed against the decision.

On 21 January 1992, judges threw out another appeal by Montecinos not to appear in the identity parade.

On 27 January 1992, Montecinos failed to show up again for an identity parade and another order for his arrest was made.

On 7 February 1992, the Chilean Supreme Court refused to rubber stamp the arrest order for Montecinos for failing to turn up for yet another identity parade.

On 28 February 1992, Montecinos once again failed to appear.

A new date was set, rather appropriately for 1 April 1992. This time, no arrest warrant was issued for Montecinos as Judge Solis accepted he would simply order his lawyers to overturn it. Montecinos immediately claimed he was being wrongly accused of involvement with the Moyle case and succeeded in having the date postponed.

By July 1992, Montecinos was still appealing to avoid attending the identity parade. In August, his appeal was thrown out by High Court judges.

On 7 September 1992, Montecinos applied for a court order banning any public reference to him being involved in Jonathan's death. He also tried to get further legal backing to avoid the identity parade that Judge Solis was planning. The judge refused the request, but was effectively prevented from calling an identity parade until these legal arguments were settled.

By this time Silvia Cabrera's nerves were understandably shot to pieces. She had become a virtual recluse in her apartment, only ever venturing out to her job at the Hotel Carrera. To make matters worse, every time she showed up at the courthouse for an identity parade, it was cancelled. She was convinced that people like Raul Montecinos and Carlos Cardoen had more power than the Chilean judicial system.

On 11 November 1992, another identity parade was finally ordered by Judge Solis. Once again, Montecinos failed to turn up and this time the judge finally went public and accused Montecinos of 'deliberately trying to avoid the identity parade.'

On 16 November 1992, an arrest order was made for Montecinos because of his continual failure to appear.

A furious Judge Solis arranged for an immediate date of 10 December for a parade. Montecinos made it clear he had no intention of turning up for that one either.

So, early on the morning of 10 December, Montecinos was arrested at his home on Avenido Pedro de Valdivia. This time Judge Solis was determined to get him to the parade. It was going to happen. But Silvia Cabrera had other ideas. She locked herself in her apartment and refused to come out, saying she could no longer stand the strain of preparing for identity parades that never happened. She had to be given medication to calm her down. Montecinos was released later that day and the judge adjourned the parade until a month later. Silvia Cabrera later admitted that a man had approached her in the street outside her apartment that very morning and warned her to 'be careful'.

On the morning of 5 January 1993, the identity parade was held at 11.00am inside the crumbling, red-brick 5th Precinct building. Seven other similar-looking men were called to stand alongside Montecinos. They all had been recruited from the Carmel Publica — the city jail — across the street.

Silvia Cabrera, shaking and pale, walked up and down examining each man closely. Montecinos looked infuriated. His eyes were locked on Silvia Cabrera. She walked past him to the end of the line-up and then hesitatingly asked to look at each of the men again. At no time was she offered an opportunity to look at the men through a screen which would have been much less intimidating.

Silvia then told Judge Solis that none of them was the man she had seen outside Jonathan's room on the Wednesday evening before his death, although she did concede that she'd only seen the back of the man's head.

'He did not have grey hair. He was a younger man ... smaller ... thinner,' she told the judge nervously. It was the exact opposite of the description she gave to Judge Solis just a few months earlier. She left the court that day in tears. The judge later recalled, 'It was disappointing, but she was very scared.'

Afterwards, Montecinos explained to waiting reporters why he had been so reluctant to take part in the identity parades.

'I did not want to go with other criminals. It was a bad situation. To participate where there are other people I have never known and maybe she would say she saw me, but I was not there.'

But as *Guardian* correspondent Malcom Coad says, 'The key question is: why did Montecinos keep trying to avoid the identity parade? This really bothers many people.'

40

Anaheim, California

'Each of us when he appears before his fellows
is clothed in a certain dignity. But every man
knows what unconfessable things pass within the
secrecy of his own heart.'

Luigi Pirandello,
Six Characters in Search of an Author *(1921)*

In early 1993, Global Helicopter's President Clem
Bailey was staying at the Anaheim Hilton for an
airshow, when he bumped into Washington-based
defence journalist David Harvey, who'd found himself
earlier embroiled in the Moyle affair after being
approached by the FBI.

'I need to talk to you, Clem,' said Harvey.

'I'm real busy.'

'Clem, I got to talk to you about this Moyle thing.'

Bailey looked startled but Harvey persuaded him to
join him in the hotel café.

'I heard stories about you taking bags of money to
Switzerland for Carlos Cardoen, Clem. What's really
happened?'

Harvey was trying to shake Bailey down in the hope

of getting to the bottom of what really happened to Jonathan Moyle.

Bailey stalled on every question. He told Harvey he couldn't explain anything because he didn't know what was going on.

Then he suddenly broke down and started sobbing.

'There isn't a night that goes by when I don't think about what happened to Jonathan. I'm haunted by it.'

This wasn't the smooth talking, debonair Clem Bailey of a just a few years earlier.

'He was a broken man ... older, tired, worn out ... on the verge of giving up the battle,' Harvey later explained.

But Harvey wouldn't give up. He pressed Bailey further.

'Do you know who killed Jonathan Moyle?'

Bailey hesitated. Then he replied, 'I've asked myself this question a million times. I wish I knew the answer. I really do ...'

But Bailey did admit to Harvey, 'Anybody in the entire frigging world who wanted their own helicopter gunship could have one thanks to this kit and they didn't have to go through a military procurement system. This was Cardoen's biggest bucks exercise of all time.'

With an estimated 4,000 Bell helicopters in use across the world, the ability to make vast sums of money out of the conversions had seemed endless back in 1990.

Clem Bailey walked out of Global in mid-1993, leaving his colleagues to pick up the pieces. His conscience was so blurred by what happened to Jonathan that he returned to being a working pilot, flying for the United Nations. It made him feel better to be helping people.

But the shadow of Cardoen and Jonathan Moyle's fate were never far away.

Today, David Harvey remains utterly convinced that Clem Bailey was involved in a money laundering operation that involved Cardoen and the vast payments he was getting from Saddam Hussein up until mid-1990.

Harvey insists, 'I used to think that Clem was a straight guy who got caught up in something out of his depth. But now I'm not so sure ...'

New Global President Dan Pettus also says that Clem Bailey was involved in a number of deals with Carlos Cardoen that he was not privy to.

'A lot of people at Bell did not like Clem. Clem was not a good businessman. He was a very nice and capable test pilot but I didn't always know what he was up to. He had much more to do with Cardoen than I did.'

Clem Bailey died of a heart-attack in July 1994. Pettus remains convinced to this day that two events wrecked what might have been a very lucrative working relationship with Carlos Cardoen. 'If the Gulf War hadn't happened and Jonathan Moyle hadn't got killed, no one would have gone after Cardoen.'

However, Pettus did admit for the first time the real truth behind Carlos Cardoen's plans for his converted Bell helicopters.

'The kit was designed as a primarily agricultural surveillance aircraft, with limited changeability for a defence or anti-drug operation. Cardoen admitted the dual role to us from the beginning. Never any question in our minds about that. We discussed it at great length.'

But Pettus refused to say why Global hadn't insisted Cardoen went public about his real intentions for the converted Bell helicopters.

In fact, Cardoen told Pettus that he had a handshake deal to sell 800 converted Bells at $3m each. 'They'd probably discount them at $2.5m,' admits Pettus today. This meant Cardoen stood to make $2bn, which would have made him one of the world's richest individuals.

Jonathan Moyle had heard rumours about this 'handshake deal' through his journalistic colleague Paul Beaver.

But was that a deal worth killing for?

Pettus hesitated when asked this question. Then he drew a long breath.

'Who knows? ...'

Then he added, 'Cardoen could have been President of Chile in a heartbeat. But he may also be the devil in disguise ...'

*   *   *

In Santiago, there was a dangerous backlash against journalists still trying to uncover the truth about what really happened to Jonathan Moyle.

They were threatened with violence if they persisted with their inquiries and a number of reporters were actually offered bribes to halt their activities.

'When I contacted Cardoen Industrias I was firmly "advised" not to continue my investigations as it could be seriously damaging to my health,' recalled one Chilean reporter.

In London, the CIA passed on important data to the British security services which showed that Iraq's arms purchases worldwide were being co-ordinated from Britain through the offices of Cardoen International Marketing SA (CIMSA) a company controlled by Carlos Cardoen.

This clearly indicated that not only was Cardoen manufacturing arms for Iraq, but he was also helping Saddam scour the world for other weapons and spares for his vast arsenal.

CIMSA — which also traded under the name of Cardoen International Ltd (CIL) from an office at 23 College Hill, near Cannon Street station in the City of London — had also attracted the attention of the British security services.

CIMSA and CIL were part of a web of Cardoen companies set up in Britain and the Channel Islands, that had branches in Washington, Geneva, Miami, Athens and Santander, Spain.

The Americans officially requested that Interpol should arrest Cardoen if he ever set foot in Europe. There was a price on his head.

But Cardoen proved just how powerful a figure he was in Chile when the Chilean Supreme Court blocked attempts by a US grand jury in Florida to question him and examine documents in Chile linked to Cardoen's activities. Cardoen's friendship with many of Chile's most powerful politicians had paid off handsomely. He was still very much in control of his own destiny.

*   *   *

Highcliff House looked as good as new, just finished, the last coat of paint applied perhaps no more than a week before. But that did nothing to stop reminding Tony and Diana Moyle of Jonathan. The couple were still so frightened that they spent each night huddled together in the attic bedroom following those earlier incidents.

Tony and Diana undertook the painstaking process of finishing off the improvements to the house because they wanted to sell it as it reminded them so much of Jonathan. The Moyles hoped it might help to alleviate the deep sense of guilt and loss over Jonathan's death. The guilt remained because they believed they should have stopped him from going to Chile. But how could they possibly have known what was going to happen?

After more than a year of trying, the Moyles finally managed to sell Highcliff to a couple who insisted they would change the name as soon as the purchase was complete, because it was known in the area as a cursed house.

Just a few days before moving into a smaller, 'safer' house in the centre of Devon, the Moyle's found themselves facing up to the realities of life. The front room of Highcliff House was full of packing cases and plastic sacks containing letters and documents relating to their desperate battle for justice. Lying on the floor was a family photo album still open at the page showing Jonathan as a little boy. Diana had collapsed in tears the previous evening when she tried to look through the album.

The emotional turmoil and the endless battle for justice had taken an awful toll.

Tony and Diana felt as if they just couldn't take it anymore. They wondered if anyone would ever find their son's killers. Diana could not even face seeing her son's memorial stone in the graveyard of St Winifred's Church, Branscombe. She kept wondering what it would have been like if Jonathan had been shot down in a plane in the middle of nowhere. Then she wouldn't even have known how he died.

Diana kept thinking she should have had the perfect life; a lovely house, a fine family, nice dogs. But now one of the people who was vital to the success of that vision was gone.

She tried to block Jonathan out of her mind but that was impossible. She was tired of the feeling of injustice. She was tired of the self-pity. None of it was going to bring him back.

*   *   *

The Jonathan Moyle investigation was closed by Judge Solis on 8 June 1993. He said he had run out of evidence. He had no doubt that Moyle had been murdered, but he could not discover by whom or why.

On 18 October 1993, Judge Solis reopened the case on the basis of a statement by ex-hotel security man José Salvadore Vilagra's testimony. He made a sworn statement to the judge saying that he had been working at the hotel that night between 12.10-2.00am and then between 4.00-7.00am on the Saturday morning.

Vilagra said he saw two suspects coming out of Jonathan's room that morning and heard strange movements in the early hours of the morning of Jonathan's death including a thud which could have been caused by someone falling. He said it sounded like a piece of wood breaking. He claimed the two men he then saw leaving Jonathan's room had blond hair, and one of them looked very nervous.

Vilagra said he did not tell anyone about this before because the head of hotel security had told all the staff not to say anything.

Vilagra left his job at the hotel shortly after Jonathan's death.

On 18 April 1994, Judge Solis was promoted to the Chilean Supreme Court. The case was closed yet again. Judge Solis handed it to Judge Juan Carlos Urrutia Padilla Juez, who has dragged his feet on the inquiry ever since.

On 5 September 1994, lawyer Jorge Trivino tried to reopen the case but the new judge simply declared the case closed.

It seemed as if the hunt for Jonathan Moyle's killer had finally ground to a halt.

In late 1994, builders dismantled room 1406 at the Hotel Carrera and integrated it with the room next door so that it no longer existed ...

'Revenge proves its own executioner.'

John Ford (1633)

Nasser Beydoun was nervous. He'd spent years trying to force the hand of Dr Carlos Cardoen to get the $5m worth of commission he believed was his due for introducing Cardoen to Saddam Hussein. He'd even given the US authorities key evidence to help them indict Cardoen in exchange for $750,000 in cash. But Cardoen continued living freely in Chile and now everything had gone quiet.

Nasser Beydoun was one of the few people in the world who knew the real events surrounding Jonathan Moyle's death, but he was never approached by Chilean investigators. Beydoun himself believed that his inside knowledge was the key to his own survival. It was his secret trump card.

But when no one returned Beydoun's calls in early

1995, he began to become seriously worried. Even the FBI didn't seem to want to know the 53-year-old, Lebanese-born US citizen. They'd used him and now he was on his own.

Beydoun had been holed up for many months in his 14-room apartment overlooking Copacabana Beach, enjoying a constant supply of cocaine, porn videos and teenage call-girls. To say he was uneasy would be an understatement. This was a man who never walked a block down the street without checking to see if he was being followed.

When Beydoun decided to hold a small party at the apartment in June 1995, he deposited a large bag of white powder on his glass coffee table and told his three resident schoolgirl hookers to put on their skimpiest dresses and highest heels. A bottle of Moët Chandon was opened and within an hour they were all coked up to the point of speechlessness.

When the front door entry-phone buzzed, Beydoun's two on duty servants dared not disturb their master to ask if he was expecting more guests. They pressed the button allowing the caller free access to the well-guarded apartment block. The rest was easy.

The front door burst open just as Beydoun started fondling a 17-year-old blonde called Bianca and a 16-year-old brunette called Sanny on the sofa. The three men were wearing grey Ninja warrior masks with sleek double-breasted linen suits. Beydoun knew why they were there.

'Everyone lie on the floor, hands above your heads,' shouted the leader of the three men, a Latin-sounding character in low-slung Gucci loafers with white socks.

There followed a strange moment of calm — some would call it expectancy.

The leader grabbed Beydoun by the scruff of his neck and pulled him to his feet.

Then two of them marched Beydoun into the nearest bedroom while a third man casually waved his gun at the other house guests before herding them into a marble-lined bathroom.

Back in the bedroom few words were spoken between Beydoun and his assailants. He was forced face-down down on the bed. Then one of them grabbed a pillow and held it over the back of Beydoun's head. He had already given up the struggle.

Beydoun had a fraction of a second before the muzzle of a gun pressed against the soft pillow and exploded. The force of the bullet shook Beydoun's body for a few seconds. Goose feathers fluttered around as his shoulder jerked. A second bullet ensured he would never move again.

They heard the pop and a thud in the bathroom. One of the hookers wet herself but everyone remained glued to the cold marble floor as the three assassins left the apartment almost as quickly as they had entered.

They took $1,000 in cash and seven Rolex watches, but ignored tens of thousands of dollars' worth of foreign currency, jewellery and electrical equipment.

Investigating Rio police detective Aledio Americo dos Santos said, 'Beydoun used to say he was afraid of dying, but he liked to live dangerously.'

The assassination of Nasser Beydoun lifted the lid on his extraordinary role as a Cardoen associate-turned-US government-informer.

Beydoun had been running a very unhealthy loan-sharking business on the side while living in Rio. In the garage of his apartment block were Porsches and Hondas he had confiscated from people who'd failed to pay back loans.

He had also been trying to set up a huge arms sale to Ecuador to help them in their war against Peru. In the apartment, police found videos on bombs and tanks, brochures of guns that could be attached to planes and helicopters, nine telephone lines, numerous video cameras and telephone bugging equipment. On his expensive mahogany desk was a framed photograph of Beydoun with his brother and nephew standing in front of the $750,000 cash he was paid by the US Government. It was a photo which would have irritated Carlos Cardoen.

There was even a copy of a book called *The Secret History of How The White House Illegally Armed Iraq* by respected journalist Alan Friedman. Beydoun was quoted extensively in the book, something which further infuriated his enemies.

Beydoun was a born predator and Carlos Cardoen's biggest threat until he was shot dead. Before his entirely predictable murder, Beydoun informed one associate that he'd been told Jonathan Moyle was killed after hearing from someone inside the Cardoen organisation that Iraq was intending to invade Kuwait.

'He was a spy. He got what he deserved,' was Beydoun's cold-blooded assessment of the Moyle case.

*   *   *

Only three months before those two bullets ended his life, Beydoun had testified about his relationship with Carlos Cardoen at the Miami trial of two employees of Cardoen's Teledyne Industries Inc in Albany, Oregon.

Beydoun had introduced Cardoen to Saddam Hussein in 1982, at the height of the Iran–Iraq conflict. He effectively opened up a veritable goldmine for the Chilean. Conservative estimates put Cardoen's income from arms sales to Iraq at $500m. It was probably much more.

Over the previous five years, Beydoun had waged his brave, some would say foolhardy, campaign to force Cardoen to pay him the $5m in commission he reckoned he was owed for setting up all those lucrative arms deals with Saddam Hussein.

When Nasser Beydoun was murdered, it sent a shiver down the spine of US Department of Commerce special agent Bob Schoonmaker because he knew that Beydoun had been killed by hitmen and he had a good idea who was behind his assassination. Beydoun's death also provoked the Americans into re-examining the Moyle case to see if it provided further evidence.

Schoonmaker explained, 'We had heard that the Iraqis had volunteered to take care of someone else, but Cardoen said it was not necessary. Whether the Iraqis murdered Jonathan Moyle I don't know, but I will say that someone interfering with the business relationship could have provoked them.'

The Americans have sworn that 'if Cardoen steps on to any allied country or US soil he will be grabbed. We want him.'

Schoonmaker confirmed that the CIA had a 'still active' file on Jonathan's death, but it was so highly classified that he would not discuss its contents.

Schoonmaker even called up Jonathan's father to see if he had any other clues that might help them.

'It always bothered us because Moyle was a decent guy and this happened to him. After Beydoun was murdered, we started thinking about it again.'

The CIA carried out a low-key investigation into both Beydoun's and Jonathan's deaths through agents on the ground in Santiago and Rio.

Schoonmaker made contact with the British embassy in Santiago during his investigations and was very disappointed by their attitude. 'They didn't seem interested in helping us.'

Schoonmaker's partner, George Norwicki, a recently retired special agent for the US Treasury Department, was more forthcoming about one of the most salient points in the entire Moyle investigation.

'I can categorically assure you that Raul Montecinos met with Jonathan Moyle on the last night of his life. We verified that through our people in Santiago.

'The thing that always mystified us was why the British Government did not pursue the case with more vigour.'

By the end of 1995, it seemed as if the murder of Jonathan Moyle would never be solved. Then another tragic event occurred which finally brought the truth to the surface.

42

Santiago, Chile
January 1996

'Guilt always hurries
towards its complement, punishment:
only there does its satisfaction lie.'

Lawrence Durrell

The bone-dry wind swept dust and grit from the gravel pathways that ran between the carefully manicured lawns of El Parque del Requirdo, Santiago's finest cemetery. Slowly, the funeral procession passed through the vast, grey metal entrance gates led by a cumbersome, gleaming black Cadillac hearse. The gravel crunched beneath its huge tyres.

A few minutes later, Raul Montecinos's oak casket was lowered into the red earth as a small group of family and friends looked on. Only two people spoke briefly about their friend. That was the way he wanted it to be.

Twenty yards away, a tall man in a black suit, white shirt and black tie stood and watched impassively. Earlier, he'd introduced himself as a representative of Dr Carlos Cardoen, but the reaction had been so muted that he pulled back and watched the proceedings from a tactful distance. He was just near enough for them all to be aware of him.

His family and friends all knew that Raul Montecinos would have been infuriated to have such a man at his funeral. His relationship with Cardoen had been tense. Many of Montecinos's family privately felt that Montecinos's health problems had been brought on by his unhappiness since Jonathan Moyle had died in 1990. None of them knew why Raul Montecinos had been so incredibly anxious all the time, but he'd begun an inescapable downward spiral from the moment Jonathan Moyle had died.

*   *   *

Raul Montecinos was a broken man. His career had sapped him of enthusiasm and happiness; his guilty conscience was a constant reminder of his sins; his heavy smoking provided yet more evidence; and his failing health seemed a fitting epitaph. Perhaps it was what he deserved.

It was almost six years since Jonathan Moyle's death, yet — as he lay dying in the last few weeks of his life — there wasn't an hour when he didn't think about what had happened to the young magazine editor.

Riddled with cancer, barely surviving with hits of oxygen from a mask that lay permanently by his side, Montecinos became convinced that God was punishing him. He'd bottled up the truth for so long.

His Italian-born wife Elza always knew that something was driving him ever closer to death, but Montecinos did not want to burden her with his problems. It wouldn't change the past, or the future for that matter.

Montecinos had confessed all his sins to a priest, but that wasn't enough. He needed to tell someone who would understand, someone who knew just how significant that evil deed had really been.

But Raul Montecinos did not have any really close friends. In any case, he didn't want to shatter people's illusions about him. So he chose a man inside the arms business whom he felt could cope with the terrible secret burden that Montecinos had bottled up for all those years. They had known each other for many years and formed a bond of trust that had remained unbroken. Most importantly, Montecinos's friend was not Chilean, so he could not be accused of any direct involvement.

The man was summoned to Montecinos's bedside just after Christmas 1995. They talked about colleagues. They talked about his health. Then Raul Montecinos laid his soul bare.

'Iraq threatened to pull out of the helicopter contract if we didn't do something about Moyle. I got so angry with him. I tried to warn him, but he was so arrogant, so sure of himself. He couldn't understand that his life was in danger.'

Montecinos took another gasp and weakly held the oxygen mask to his face. As it filled his lungs, his chest expanded hesitantly.

He continued, 'So I took the decision myself. I didn't tell Cardoen. I felt under so much pressure. If Moyle quoted me by name I would be finished. I talked to the Iraqis. They told me who to get to do it, but said I had to organise it myself. I had no choice.'

Montecinos's deep regret about his actions manifested itself when cancer was first diagnosed in 1994. Montecinos was convinced that the strain of bottling up the truth for all those years had encouraged the illness to spread through his body. Yet, even after cancer was discovered, Montecinos remained too afraid to tell anyone his dreadful secret. He never even told his boss Cardoen what had happened.

Montecinos was philosphical at the end. 'I did it to protect myself and everyone around me. Now I've got what I deserve.'

After Montecinos's bedside confession and subsequent death, this author encountered the man to whom Montecinos told his deepest, darkest secret at FIDAE in Santiago in March 1996. That informant remained terrified of retribution if he openly revealed the truth.

'My life would be in danger if anyone knew Raul had told me what happened. You have to understand, Raul Montecinos was the worst type of employee. He never stopped worrying about his job. It was his life.'

Within days of Montecinos's death, his widow Elza destroyed the huge file on Jonathan Moyle which Montecinos kept locked in a cabinet in his office at home. She never questioned her husband's motives in insisting she should do this as soon as he died.

The only remaining evidence of Montecinos's collusion in the murder of Jonathan Moyle is an obscure medical textbook which sits in the bookcase of the sitting-room at his home. In it is a marker on a page which describes the act of asphyxia for sexual enjoyment.

So ends the riddle of room 1406 — the bizarre death of young adventurer Jonathan Moyle on a dangerous assignment in South America.

Final Words

JONATHAN NICHOLAS
MOYLE
1961 – 1990
NOR SHALL DEATH BRAG
THOU WAND'REST IN HIS SHADE

GIUSEPPE TOTA PORRO
28·2·1914 – 8·12·1979
FRANCESCA COLASUONNO GISSI
2·2·1920 – 12·5·1990
SADI RAUL MONTECINOS ROSAS
20·9·1927 – 22·1·1996

A TRIBUTE TO
JONATHAN

Jonathan Moyle, editor of Defence Helicopter World, died in March while covering the FIDAE '90 airshow in Chile.

Jonathan's body was found hanging in the wardrobe of his hotel bedroom and initially the Chilean police treated the matter as suicide. However, his family friends and colleagues were convinced that this was inconceivable.

Determined to prove that his son did not kill himself, Tony Moyle mounted a campaign to interest the media in the case. They responded magnificently. Channel 4 News sent a film crew to Chile to cover the story and their report sparked off interest among the British national press. The Independent on Sunday also sent an investigative team to Santiago and The Times published a leader article on the affair.

As a result of new facts and information being exposed by all this coverage, and with questions being asked in the British Parliament, pressure has been put on the Chilean authorities for a full and thorough enquiry.

The circumstances surrounding Jonathan's death are still under scrutiny. But thanks to the courage of the investigating magistrate, Judge Alejandro Solis, who has overruled the suicide theory of the local police and called on Chile's top criminal investigation squad to take over the case, it is hoped that the true facts about this tragedy might soon come to light.

Meanwhile, the entire team at the Shephard Press, together with Jonathan's many friends in the helicopter industry and the armed forces, extend their sincerest condolences to his parents and his fiancée.

Alexander Shephard
Publisher

In peace sons bury their fathers,
but in war fathers bury their sons.

King Croesus (550BC)

Afterword

Raul Montecinos's deathbed confession was not so much an ending as a final turning point in this complex story. The horrible events set in motion by Montecinos left indelible marks upon so many people:

TONY AND DIANA MOYLE live in a smaller house in Devon where they lead a quiet existence, rarely going out or entertaining friends. Diana Moyle has only just started talking openly about her son after almost seven years of anguish.

ANNETTE KISSENBECK has attained everything she could ever want professionally, but her heart continues to bleed for Jonathan Moyle. She still wears the antique, single-diamond engagement ring he gave to her. 'My life has been lonely, desolate and empty. For the first 18 months I just felt numb. I didn't know who to turn to. My world had fallen apart.'

PAT MOYLE still lives in the same house in Kingston, Surrey, that her family have owned for 50 years. She recently retired from her job as a matron at a nearby hospital. She says there isn't a day when she doesn't think about her nephew.

SILVIA CABRERA remains a very frightened woman. At her tiny apartment just ten minutes' walk from the Hotel Carrera, she said she felt sorry about the death of Raul Montecinos 'but he went to his grave knowing the whole truth about what happened to Moyle.' Silvia still works as a chambermaid at the hotel.

DR CARLOS CARDOEN continues to be a 'prisoner' in his homeland of Chile. He has stopped manufacturing and selling arms and switched his interests to producing jeans, fruit and vegetables. His home is a vast mansion in the city of his birth, Santa Cruz. Cardoen is currently trying to buy 100 acres of land on remote Easter Island because he wants 'to get away from all these problems and lead the rest of my life in peace and solitude'. The Chilean government have so far refused all Cardoen's approaches for permission to build on the island, long considered a sacred nature reserve. But his former brother-in-law is no longer President. On Cardoen's last attempt, he offered $50m for a patch of land. His power and influence has certainly diminished, although his personal wealth is still estimated to be in the region of $300m.

At ABERYSTWYTH UNIVERSITY, a version of Jonathan Moyle's thesis, *Soviet Conventional Air Attack against the UK*, remains a restricted document classified by the British Government. It is locked in a cupboard at the University's Hugh Owen Library.

JUDGE ALEJANDRO SOLIS's brave attempt to solve the murder of Jonathan Moyle won him promotion to Chile's Supreme Court, and he has personally fuelled the continuing investigation into Moyle's death.

PEDRO DEL FIERRO — the man threatened by Cardoen PR man Raul Montecinos after saying publicly that Montecinos had admitted to meeting Jonathan the night before he died — was the victim of an armed robbery recently. Two men broke into his house and searched through every part of the property before taking 300,000 pesos but ignored ten times that amount in a closet drawer. The robbers tied up two maids and del Fierro's sister during the raid. They were eventually arrested and it emerged that were freelance criminals who had been expressly hired to rob the del Fierro house. But they refused to say who had hired them.

GLOBAL HELICOPTERS have thrived since breaking away from Cardoen's vice-like grip. New President Dan Pettus says that the Bell conversion scheme was part of their past and they are now building for the future.

BELL HELICOPTERS remain sensitive about the role they played in introducing Cardoen to Clem Bailey at Global. They refused to answer many questions about the Moyle case and denied ever having any involvement with Cardoen — either official or unofficial.

JONATHAN MOYLE — his pursuit of the truth led only to his premature death. Perhaps only now can we understand why.

OPERATION VALKYRIE continues to run from within the security services. Much of the information recently gathered has been invaluable in estimating the military capabilities of dictators such as Saddam Hussein.

In November 1997, the Santiago Appeals
Court decided to reopen investigations into
Moyle's murder — following information
from the author to the Chilean authorities.

In February 1998, the inquest
into Moyle's death was also reopened
by the South Devon Coroner's Office.

Postnote

I owe many individuals, who have helped to make this book possible, my deepest thanks. But without Tony and Diana Moyle, this book would never have been written.

Also, my heartfelt gratitude to everyone in the warm and welcoming country of Chile, whose help and guidance while investigating Jonathan Moyle's death was unswerving. Top of the list was my loyal and informative associate Patricio Vargas, who fearlessly pursued many angles and leads on my behalf. Others in Santiago include: Carola Karlovak, Roberto Campusano, Paul Pryor, Geraldo Moro, Gilles Boudain, Jorge Trivino, Dr José Beletti, Pedro del Fierro, Javier Montero, Detectives Arellano and Torres, Judge Alejandro Solis, Malcolm Coad, Michael Ryan.

In Brazil: Ruth de Aquino, Deborah Cohen and Denis Wright.

In England the list is endless, but includes Tony and Diana Moyle, Pat Moyle, Ian Maun, Mark Brewer, Stan McKay, Professor John Garnett, Professor John Baylis, Colin

McInnes, Annette Kissenbeck, Steve Weatherley, Steve Airey, Nick Lappos, Peter Donaldson, Paul Beaver, Martin Pace, Patrick Allen, Mike Gething, Rhoda Parry, Adrian English, Terry Gander, Ian Parker, Brian Passey, Adel Darwish, Chris Espin-Jones, Mike Taylor, Richard Holliday, Jon Ryan, Peter Wilson, Graeme Gourlay, Ex-Detective-Superintendent Jim Hutchinson.

In the USA: Frank Colucci, Dan Pettus, Owen Day, Mike Robbins, David Harvey, Bob Schoonmaker.

There are dozens of others who have asked that their identities remain secret.

THE MURDER OF RACHEL NICKELL
The truth about the tragic murder on Wimbledon Common
Mike Fielder

VIGILANTE!
One man's war against major crime on Britain's streets
Ron Farebrother with Martin Short

CAGED HEAT
An astonishing picture of what really goes on behind the walls of women's prisons
Wensley Clarkson

SUNDAY BLOODY SUNDAY
A chilling collection of tales from the *News of the World*'s Sunday Magazine
Drew Mackenzie

BROTHERS IN BLOOD
The horrific story of the two brothers who murdered their parents
Tim Brown and Paul Cheston

ONE BLOODY AFTERNOON
What happened during the Hungerford Massacre
Jeremy Josephs

KILLER WOMEN
A heart-stopping selection of tales about women who kill
Wensley Clarkson

SISTERS IN BLOOD
True stories of the most extreme and bloody crimes committed by women.
Wensley Clarkson

TO KILL AND KILL AGAIN
The chilling confessions of a jewellery thief and serial killer.
Roy Archibald Hall